ACCOUNTING
history

An Analysis of the Development and Nature of Accounting Principles in Japan

Yukio Fujita

GARLAND PUBLISHING, INC.
New York / London
1991

Library of Congress Cataloging-in-Publication Data

Fujita, Yukio.
An analysis of the development and nature of accounting principles in Japan /
Yukio Fujita.
    p. cm. — (New works in accounting history)
Thesis (doctoral)—University of Illinois, 1968.
Includes bibliographical references (p.   ).
ISBN 0-8153-0005-0 (alk. paper)
1. Accounting—Standards—Japan—History. 2. International business enter-
prises—Accounting—Standards—History. I. Title. II. Series.
HF5616.J3F85 1991
657'.0952—dc20   90-21627

Manufactured in the United States of America

Printed on acid-free 250-year-life paper

INTRODUCTION

More than twenty years have passed since the original text of this thesis was completed in 1968. During this period many events, some quite unexpected, have occurred in the field of accounting principles at both national and international levels. In this new introduction to my thesis, these developments are briefly summarized by focusing on the international harmonization of accounting principles.

The Development of Accounting Principles in Japan

Chapter VI focused on two issues. First, the revision of the *Commercial Code* in 1962 and the enactment of the *Regulation for Corporate Balance Sheets and Income Statements* marked a turning point in the development of accounting principles in Japan. Second, *A Statement of Business Accounting Principles* (hereafter the *Statement of Principles*) lost its autonomy and changed its character from the "autogenous" type of accounting principles to the "compulsory". This change was endorsed by the revisions of the *Statement of Principles* in 1974 and 1982, following the revisions of the *Commercial Code* in 1974 and 1981.

When it was revised in 1974, the *Commercial Code* introduced a new provision: "fair accounting conventions shall be taken into account for proper interpretation of accounting provisions on the preparation of financial statements." Concerning this new provision, the Business Accounting Deliberation Council, the accounting standard setting body in Japan, declared that the *Statement of Principles* was a summary of fair accounting conventions and therefore it would serve as a guideline for the interpretation or application of accounting provisions in the *Commercial Code*. For a quarter of a century since 1949, the *Statement of Principles* had played a very important role in the improvement of the financial reporting system in Japan by maintaining a position independent of the *Commercial Code*. Upon revision in 1974, however, the *Statement of Principles* subordinated itself to the *Commercial Code*.

In addition, in 1974 the *Commercial Code* introduced a new system of auditing for large-sized stock corporations. *A Special Law for Auditing of Stock Corporations* was enacted which required all the large-sized stock corporations, including unlisted ones, with more than 500 million yen of total equity capital or more than 20 billion yen of total liabilities, to be audited by certified public accountants or audit corporations. A system of auditing by independent certified public accountants was first introduced into Japan by the enactment of the *Securities Exchange Act* and the *Certified Public Accountants Law*. The *Statement of Principles* was originally formulated in 1949 for the effective implementation of these two laws and its preface stated that it was a set of standards which should be observed by certified public accountants when they audit financial statements based upon the *Securities Exchange Act* and the *Certified Public Accountants Law*. But, upon the revision of the *Statement of Principles* in 1974, the *Business Accounting Deliberation Council* declared that this document would serve as a set of standards for effective auditing based upon the *Commercial Code*. Thus, the *Statement of Principles* strengthened its ties with the *Commercial Code* not only in accounting but also in auditing.

In 1982, the *Statement of Principles* was revised for the third time, again after the revision of the *Commercial Code*. For the past eight years, no revisions in either have appeared.

Given the double-track system of financial reporting and auditing based upon the *Commercial Code* and the *Securities Exchange Act*, a reconciliation or unification of the *Statement of Business Accounting Principles* with the *Commercial Code* might be necessary. But the greater legal force of the *Commercial Code* in relation to the *Statement of Principles* became an impediment to the sound development and international harmonization of accounting principles. Compared with the "autogenous" type, the "compulsory" type of accounting principles is rather inflexible. Economic activities of business enterprises, which are objects of accounting recognition, are always changing and developing at both national and international levels. Therefore, accounting principles should be flexible and dynamic so that they can be revised and improved in a timely fashion in response to changes in economic events like diversification and internationalization.

The trend of development of accounting principles in Japan towards the "compulsory" type has caused some difficulties in coping with such economic changes, and also with the movement toward the international harmonization of accounting principles that was initiated by the International Accounting Standards Committee in 1973. To avoid these difficulties, the Business Accounting Deliberation Council tried to formulate accounting standards for particular issues with which the *Commercial Code* is not concerned, notably, *Principles for Consolidated Financial Statements* in 1975, *Accounting Standards for Foreign Currency Transactions* in 1979, and *Standards for Disclosing Financial Information by Segment* in 1988.

These three standards were formulated to meet the information needs of international investors. The application of these standards is limited only to those listed stock corporations which must file their financial statements with the Securities Bureau of the Ministry of Finance based upon the *Securities Exchange Act.* The function of the Securities Bureau is similar to that of the Securities and Exchange Commission in the United States. The separate publication of these standards implies that the Business Accounting Deliberation Council was forced to change from a comprehensive to a piecemeal approach in accounting standard setting, and that the whole structure of generally accepted accounting principles in Japan was also changed from a single comprehensive set of principles to more pluralistic sets. By changing its approach, the Business Accounting Deliberation Council has tried to find a new way to develop the international harmonization of accounting principles. This welcome change was acceptable to the Bureau of Securities of Ministry of Finance, which is a member of the International Organization of Securities Commissions.

The Development of Accounting Principles at the International Level

The ultimate objective of international accounting is to develop and communicate accounting data which provide reliable information on which to base decisions, regardless of national origin. To realize this objective the information should be developed and communicated using "generally accepted" international accounting principles. Audits, too, should be based on international auditing standards.

Since the early 1970s, many international organizations such as the International Accounting Standards Committee, the International Federation of Accountants, the United Nations, the Organization for Economic Cooperation and Development, and the European Economic Community have made an effort to achieve this objective. These efforts reflect a growing awareness of increasing global economic interdependence.

International Accounting Standards Committee.

The International Accounting Standards Committee has played an important role in harmonizing international accounting standards by publishing thirty separate standards and a *Framework for the Preparation and Presentation of Financial Statements*. The Committee is now trying to revise a series of standards based upon the 1989 Exposure Draft 32, *Comparability of Financial Statements,* which tries to eliminate most of the alternative accounting treatments currently permitted under existing International Accounting Standards. However, the Committee faces difficulties because it was founded in 1973 by an agreement among professional accountancy bodies in nine countries and has no real power to enforce the International Accounting Standards.

Since 1973, the business of the International Accounting Standards Committee has been conducted by the Board, the Steering Committees, and a full-time Secretariat, and membership in the Committee has been mainly limited to practicing accountants from member bodies. But by recognizing the need to be fully reprsentative, the Committee has made several important changes in its operating structure. The first change was the establishment of the Consultative Group in 1981. International organizations representing many of the principal users and preparers of financial statements are invited to the Consultative Group to meet regularly with the Board and to discuss matters of principles and policies arising from the work of the Committee.

The original members of the Consultative Group were Federation Internationale des Bourses de Valeurs, the International Association of Financial Executives Institute, the International Chamber of Commerce, the International Confederation of Free Trade Unions and World Confederation of Labor, and the World Bank. In addition, the Organization for Economic Cooperation and Development and the United Nations Center on Transnational Corporations are participating in the Consultative Group as observers. In 1987, the Consultative Group was expanded to include representatives from the Financial Accounting Standards Board, the International Banking Association, the International Bar Association and the International Organization of Securities Commissions.

The second change in its operating structure was the participation of the International Organization of Securities Commissions in the work of the Steering Committee in 1987. In 1977 the Board of the International Accounting Standards Committee adopted a policy to open the Steering Committee to non-Board members, including representatives of developing countries. In March, 1987, representatives from France, Japan, the Netherlands, South Africa, and the United States were appointed as members of the Steering Committee on Comparability of Financial Statements. In addition to these members, three representatives of the International Organization of Securities Commissions were invited to join the work of the Steering Committee as observers. This marked the first time the International Accounting Standards Committee accepted representatives from governmental organizations, although only as observers.

In addition to these changes the Committee took two steps to improve its standard setting procedures. The first was the development of a conceptual framework for financial statements. In May, 1988 the Committee published the *Exposure Draft of the Framework for the Preparation and Presentation of Financial Statements*, the final version appearing in July 1989. Its purpose was to assist the Board in both reviewing existing international accounting standards and developing future standards, and in promoting harmonization of regulation, accounting standards, and procedures relating to the presentation of financial statements by providing a basis for reducing the number of alternative accounting treatments permitted by International Accounting Standards.

When a piecemeal approach is adopted in developing accounting principles, a conceptual framework is indispensable. The development of accounting principles in the United States since the 1930s furnishes a valuable lesson. Although G. O. May intended to develop a comprehensive statement of accounting principles, the Committee on Accounting Procedures was forced to consider *specific* accounting topics of great urgency and often recommended one or more alternative procedures as being definitely superior to current practice. However, over a period of 20 years, the Committee on Accounting Procedures was unable to formuate a set of basic principles.

Accounting Research Study No. 1, *The Basic Postulates of Accounting* (1961) and Accounting Research Study No. 3, *A Tentative Set of Broad Accounting Principles for Business Enterprises* (1962) were originally published as a conceptual framework for the individual opinions published by the Accounting Principles Board (this had replaced the Committee on Accounting Principles Board, which had in turn replaced the Committee on Accounting Procedures in 1959). However, in 1962 the Board rejected both studies, stating that they were radically different from generally accepted accounting principles. The Board continued to issue is opinions without any conceptual framework until 1973.

The Financial Accounting Standards Board has been concerned with developing a conceptual framework since its inception in 1973, and has published a series of statements of financial accounting concepts that are used as models in developing similar types of framework at both the national and international levels. A number of countries, including Australia, Brazil, Canada, and the United Kingdom, have elaborated their own frameworks. The Intergovernmental Working Group of Experts on International Standards of Accounting and Reporting of the United Nations also published a report *Objectives and Concepts Underlying Financial Statements*, in 1989.

If a conceptual framework is to serve as a base for formulating a series of individual accounting principles, it should be developed as an ideal and systematic statement and in advance of the formulation of accounting principles. The relation between a conceptual framework and accounting principles may be equivalent to that between natural law and positive law. When the formulation of accounting principles is *followed* by the development of such a conceptual framework, as is presently the case, it is not easy to keep an organic relation between them.

The second step in the improvement process in international accounting standards was the publication of Exposure Draft 32, *Comparability of Financial Statements*. This project revises accounting treatments on twenty-nine issues involving thirteen international accounting standards to ensure a higher degree of comparability in financial statements. Free choices between alternative treatments were considered necessary in the past to gain wider acceptance of certain standards. On the other hand, such choices are impediments to the higher degree of comparability in financial statements. Therefore, the International Accounting Standards Committee had to solve the conflict between gaining a wider international acceptance of the International Accounting Standards while removing free choices of accounting treatments. To gain the strong political backing necessary to resolve the conflict the Committee asked the International Organization of Securities Commissions for assistance in drafting the Exposure Draft 32.

For the past several years, the International Organization of Securities Commissions has been concerned with the possibility of reciprocal recognition of prospectuses which would simplify the administrative procedure of supervisory authorities, reduce the cost for issuers, and speed the launching of market operations.

Reciprocal recognition of prospectuses requires common accounting standards. At its twelfth conference in 1987 this body recommended that regulatory authorities examine practical means of promoting the use of common accounting standards. The thirteenth conference in 1988 encouraged the International Accounting Standards Committee to act promptly to improve International Accounting Standards and to make them the common accounting standards in the world.

The United Nations

The Activities of the United Nations in the area of international harmonization of accounting and reporting goes back to Resolution 1721 (LIII) by the Economic and Social Council in 1972. The twenty-member group of Eminent Persons to Study the Impact of Multinational Corporations on Development and on International Relations established under this resolution submitted a report, *The Impact of Multinational Corporations on Development and on International Relations*, to the Economic and Social Council in 1974. Among other things, the report proposed establishing a center and a commission on transnational corporations, recommended that the commission convene a group of experts on international accounting and reporting standards (noting that there was a serious lack of financial and non-financial information in usable form on the activities of transnational corporations), and also called for an international system of standardized accounting and reporting for transnational corporations.

In 1974, the sixth special session of the General Assembly adopted the *Declaration on the Establishment of a New International Economic Order and the Programme of Action on the Establishment of a New International Economic Order*. One of the twenty principles for a new international economic order states that all efforts should be made to formulate, adopt, and implement an international code of conduct for transnational corporations. The problem of information disclosure has been down for discussion in parallel with the formulation of the code of conduct.

The Group of Experts on International Standards of Accounting and Reporting was appointed in 1976 by the Secretary General of the United Nations. After two sessions of discussion in 1976 and 1977, its report, *International Standards of Accounting and Reporting for Transnational Corporations,* was submitted to the Commission on Transnational Corporations. It was concerned less with accounting than reporting and with minimum requirements for the reporting of and non-financial information.

The Economic and Social Council decided in 1979 to establish an *Ad Hoc* Intergovernmental Working Group of Experts on International Standards of Accounting and Reporting to review the 1977 report of the Group of Experts and to gain an intergovernmental agreement on the international standards. The working group was composed of thirty-four members: nine from African states, seven from Asian states, six from Latin American states, nine from Western European and other states, and three members from Eastern European states. The report stressed that accounting and reporting by transnational corporations should take account of the information needs of users, particularly in home and host countries, and especially in developing countries, for their better understanding of the economic and social impact of transnational corporations. Comparability of information also was stressed as an important factor.

In 1982, the Economic and Social Council decided to create a new group, the Intergovernmental Working Group of Experts on International Standards of Accounting and Reporting. The objective of this new working group is to serve as an international body to consider accounting and reporting falling within the scope of the work of the Commission on Transnational Corporations that would improve the availability and comparability of information disclosed by transnational corporations. Since 1983, the new working group has met annually and tried to act as a catalyst in the development of international standards. It has also reviewed the work of the standard-setting bodies, particularly the work of the International Accounting Standards Committee, with a view to meeting the needs of home and host countries. Although the United Nations publishes the annual report of the Intergovernmental Working Group of Experts, with documents prepared by the Center on Transnational Corporations for the discussion by the group, this work is not well known. To give it wider circulation, the United Nations published in 1988 a booklet, *Conclusions on Accounting and Reporting by Transnational Corporations*, which contains the results of discussion and deliberations.

For more than seventeen years, the United Nations has made an effort to promote international harmonization in accounting and reporting, especially in information disclosure by transnational corporations, through the activities of the Group of Experts, the *Ad Hoc* Intergovernmental Working Group, and the Intergovernmental Working Group. Although one might criticize the activities of the United Nations because of conflicts of interest among member states, the Intergovernmental Working Group of the United Nations is expected to play at least two roles.

While the number of its members is now limited to thirty-four countries, the working group is the only international body to consider accounting and reporting issues with the participation of both western and eastern countries and developed and developing countries. In addition, intergovernmental organizations such as the European Economic Community and the Organization for Economic Cooperation and Development, and non-governmental international organizations such as the International Chamber of Commerce, International Confederation of Free Trade Unions, International Accounting Standards Committee, and International Federation of Accountants, are participating as observers. This exchange of views and experiences is of particular value for all countries, especially for developing countries.

Since its first session, the Intergovernmental Working Group has discussed items it has identified using materials provided by the International Accounting Standards Committee through the Center on Transnational Corporations. By agreeing on certain items, the group has endorsed the international accounting standards originally developed by the International Accounting Standards Committee. This role of international endorser of accounting standards is essential to the world-wide observance of those standards.

Towards International Harmonization of Accounting Principles

Two types of accounting principles, the Anglo-American or "autogenous" type and the Franco-German or "compulsory" type, have been identified. This distinction seems to exist because of the differences in national attitude towards social norms. But, even in a country such as the United States, where the "autogenous" type has been developed, would it have been possible for the accounting profession to develop principles with the high level of quality and comprehensive coverage without any legal backing by the Securities Act and the Securities Exchange Act? In the area of enforcement even the "autogenous" type of accounting principles needs strong support from the government.

The International Accounting Standards Committee was born in the private sector in 1973, but has gradually been receiving world-wide recognition and support from both governmental and non-governmental international bodies, representing preparers and users of financial statements. Exposure Draft 32 demonstrates the possibility of cooperation between the private and public sectors in developing accounting principles at the international level.

One of the most practical and efficient ways to promote international hamonization of accounting principles is to enforce international accounting standards through the mechanism of international financial markets. Closer cooperation between the International Accounting Standards Committee and the International Organization of Securities Commissions is essential to the free flow of capital. But in the long run, cooperation between the International Accounting Standards Committee and the United Nations also is essential to the orderly development of world economy through the international harmonization of accounting and reporting.

Since 1973, international accounting principles have been developed mainly by and for western countries. The recent drastic changes in international politics and economics may predict the end of an era in which international accounting principles were dominated by western countries. Cooperation between western and eastern countries, including lesser developed nations, will become essential. People around the globe are now seeking a peaceful and democratic world where everyone can live freely as a human being. Truly international accounting principles are those which make a great contribution to the realization of that new world. The movement towards international harmonization of accounting principles in this direction needs a new conceptual framework. One of the most basic or fundamental concepts for this framework is *justice*.

Yukio Fujita

An Analysis of the Development and Nature of Accounting Principles in Japan

ACKNOWLEDGMENT

The author is sincerely grateful to Professor Vernon K. Zimmerman, Director of the Center for International Education and Research in Accounting of the University of Illinois. His enthusiasm for accounting history and international accounting inspired this study, and his valued guidance and encouragement completed this work. The author also wishes to thank Professor Norton M. Bedford whose valuable suggestions made possible an application of a sociological framework for systematic analysis to this study. Further, the author is appreciative to Professor Clive F. Dunham who read this work carefully and offered comments.

The author could not have completed his doctoral study at the University of Illinois without the patient help of the faculty members of the School of Commerce, Waseda University in Tokyo from where he has been on leave of absence since 1964. The author is particularly indebted to Professor Kyojiro Someya of Waseda University who continuously encouraged him and assisted him in obtaining invaluable material for this study from Japan. Acknowledgment also extends to Professor Toshio Iino of Hitotsubashi University in Tokyo who gave the author many valuable suggestions during his serving as Visiting Professor at the University of Illinois, 1966-67.

Finally, deepest appreciation to K.F., Y.F., and E.F., the Author's "providential" partners in this as in all his ventures.

TABLE OF CONTENTS

CHAPTER I

THE JAPANESE SETTING

Need for the Study

This study is an exploration of the historical development of
accounting principles in Japan. The objective of the study is to
increase professional understanding and knowledge of the international
dimensions of accounting. A brief review of the growing recognition
of the importance of international accounting and a critical analysis
of the current status of research efforts in this area accent the
need for this study.

Recent Recognition of the Importance of International Accounting.
An increased awareness of the international aspects of accounting
seems to have developed since 1950.[1] Although efforts for international
co-operation began as early as 1904 when the First International
Congress of Accountants met in St. Louis, little in the nature of
concrete action resulted. Of the many efforts by accountants during
the 1950's to advance the concept of international accounting, such
as the establishment of the Union Européenne des Experts Comptables
Economiques et Financiers in 1951 and both the Sixth and Seventh
International Congresses of Accountants (1952, 1957), the speech by
Jacob Kraayenhof at the 1959 annual meeting of the American Institute
of Certified Public Accountants (AICPA) provided perhaps the greatest

---

[1]Gerhard G. Mueller, "Curriculum Aspects of International
Accounting Matters," Mimeographed copy of the paper presented at the
Second International Conference on Accounting Education in London,
August 31, 1967, p. 7.

impetus toward recognition of the unique role possible for accounting in the international dimension.[2] In his speech, Kraayenhof urged the American Institute to take the initiative in the movement toward international uniformity in accounting principles.

> In this light and considering your privileged position, I feel convinced that under the circumstances the international challenge for the profession should be made a "challenge for your Institute": to invite the establishment of standing committees in other countries and to offer permanent contacts in order to achieve greater uniformity in the field of accounting principles.[3]

Since then the importance of international accounting has been widely recognized by practicing accountants and accounting educators. Both of the recent International Congresses of Accountants held in New York and in Paris (1962, 1967) stressed greater international uniformity in accounting principles. The Committee on International Relations of the American Institute of Certified Public Accountants helped stimulate an increasing demand for improvement and greater uniformity in international accounting practices by publishing the first world-wide survey of accounting practices, principles, and related information under the title Professional Accounting in 25 Countries in 1964.[4]

---

[2]Vernon K. Zimmerman and Arthur R. Wyatt, "Recognizing a New Dimension." The Illinois CPA, Vol. XXV, No. 2, (Winter, 1962), p. 44.

[3]Jacob Kraayenhof, "International Challenge for Accounting," The Journal of Accountancy, Vol. 109, No. 1, (January, 1960), p. 38.

[4]AICPA Committee on International Relations, Professional Accounting in 25 Countries (New York: AICPA, 1964).

In the area of accounting education, the University of Illinois recognized the new area of international accounting by sponsoring the First International Conference on Accounting Education in 1962 and by establishing the Center for International Education and Research in Accounting in the same year.[5] The Second International Conference on Accounting Education was held in London in 1967. Meanwhile, the American Accounting Association established a Committee on International Accounting in 1964 to devote special attention to this new dimension of accounting. The Committee recommended in 1966 that a course or seminar on "International Accounting" be included in the accounting curricula of institutions of higher learning. A part of the function performed by the Committee was recently delegated to the newly established International Liaison Committee (1967). All these activities, and this is an incomplete enumeration of them, evidence the growing recognition of the importance of international accounting.

A significant part of the recent recognition of the importance of international accounting stems from problems in accounting practice. Some of these problems were recently identified by the Committee on International Accounting of the American Accounting Association.

1. Expansion of international business and investment activities along with the related demands for international financial reporting, auditing, and accounting and auditing standards;
2. Emergence of international corporations - companies owned and controlled in more than a single country;
3. Efforts toward regionalization and the consequent need for accounting developments transcending national boundaries;

---

[5]The Center for International Education and Research in Accounting, Proceedings - International Conference on Accounting Education (Urbana, Illinois: The Center for International Education and Research in Accounting, 1962).

4. Advancement of accounting thought on a multinational
   scale to foster better insight into conceptual matters
   and avoid unnecessary duplication of research efforts.[6]

In summary, the need for acquiring an understanding and knowledge of

the international dimensions of accounting is widely recognized.

Current Status of Research Efforts in International Accounting.

Despite general recognition of the importance of international accounting

and numerous efforts to further its developments, no systematic approach

to the problem has yet been developed. Even the term "international

accounting" does not have a universally accepted definition. An

attempt to provide such a definition was made by Gerhard G. Mueller,

as follows:

> International accounting is the producing, exchanging, using,
> and interpreting of accounting data across national borders.
> In an ideal state, international and domestic accounting
> would be indistinguishable, because under such a condition
> an international viewpoint would be applied to all accounting
> considerations. Until a transnational basis is achieved
> for accounting, international accounting will exist as an
> area of specialization in accounting in order to focus atten-
> tion on problems of an international nature and in order to
> interject the broadest possible perspective into the develop-
> ment and application of accounting thought.[7]

---

[6]The Committee on International Accounting, American Accounting
Association, International Dimensions of Accounting in the Curriculm,
A recommendation by the Committee on International Accounting (Leaflet),
AAA: (Spring, 1966). This identification of reasons for international
accounting seems to be derived from the earlier identification by
Gerhard G. Mueller:
1. Increasing international business and international investments.
2. Emergence of the international corporation.
3. Furthering accounting research and development.
4. Alignment with other disciplines.
(Gerhard G. Mueller, "Whys and Hows of International Accounting," The
Accounting Review, Vol. XL, No. 2, [April, 1965], pp. 387-90.)

[7]Gerhard G. Mueller, "Whys and Hows of International Accounting," p. 387.

Mueller, with a help of Irving L. Fantl,[8] recently proposed a new definition of the term "international accounting": "International accounting is (1) concerned with international implication of the various national accounting thoughts and practices, and (2) measuring and communicating, in financial terms, international business events and transactions."[9]

---

[8]"Letters to the Journal" (from Irving L. Fantl), The Journal of Accountancy, Vol. 120, No. 3, (September, 1965), p. 29. For better understanding of a newly proposed definition of international accounting by Mueller, the following quotation from Fantl's letter seems useful:

The first of these, and the one which a layman might first envision, is some sort of uniform system of accounting which could be adopted by all nations. This Esperanto of the ledgers could be a great step forward in international understanding and its blessings were extolled at the last International Congress of Accountants....

The second usage of the term "international accounting" refers to the complexities facing the practitioner who must consolidate foreign and domestic activities of a multinational or international organization....

The third interpretation of "international accounting" is purely descriptive. The publication of the AICPA committee on international relations, Professional Accounting in 25 Countries, is an excellent example of this approach. This accounting Baedeker conducts a tour of strange lands without suggesting how to reconcile or reform their differences....

[9]Mueller, "Curriculum Aspects of International Accounting Matters," p. 6.

The second definition, unfortunately, does not really improve the first one. It does convey, to some extent, a concrete notion about international accounting as contrasted with the first one. This, however, does not necessarily represent a desirable refinement of the definition. In fact, such a dual definition seems too explanatory in one sense and too restrictive in another. This definitional deficiency may be explained by noting that the validity of a definition should be based on the extent to which the definition clearly to separate objects belonging to the defined category from other or similar objects that do not belong to it.[10] That the mere enumeration of what has been done or is being done in a special field of accounting is not sufficient for a definition of "international accounting" follows logically.

Neither of Mueller's definitions of international accounting are a sine qua non for the field of international accounting. They do not establish a basis on which the development and communication of international accounting information could be founded. The first definition does not clearly separate international accounting from national accounting since producing, exchanging, using, and interpreting accounting data across national borders are all still possible, to some extent, within the present systems of accounting. The second definition is based upon the identification by Fantl of three aspects of international accounting. Mueller's second effort represents an attempt to synthesize the three aspects -- normative, practical, and descriptive features -- for definitional purpose. But Mueller neglects the normative aspect of international

---

[10]Richard Mattessich, Accounting and Analytical Methods, (Homewood, Illinois: Richard D. Irwin, Inc., 1964), pp. 18-19.

accounting in his synthesis since his inductive and pragmatic approach
leads to a conclusion that international accounting uniformity is not
a reasonable goal in view of the state of the art today -- both conceptually and practically.

At the present time no set of principles for developing international accounting information exists which is universally applicable and
apparently such a set of principles will require a long time to develop.
If the term "international accounting" is defined in terms of empirical
data describing the present status of international accounting practices,
as Mueller's definition does; it might be very difficult to describe such
a set of principles in the definition. This would indeed constitute a
serious definitional deficiency for no definition of international accounting seems to be workable without reference to a set of principles. Otherwise the definition would fail to describe the method by which international
accounting information could be developed and communicated.

The best definition of the phrase apparently would suggest what
ought to be done in the area of international accounting. Accordingly,
one of the most important final goals of international accounting is to
develop and communicate internationally understandable accounting information so that users of the information, regardless of the originating
country, can make informed judgments and decisions. To be internationally
understandable, accounting information should be developed and communicated
based upon a set of international accounting principles. In this sense,

---

[11]Gerhard G. Mueller, International Accounting (New York: The
Macmillan Company, 1967), p. 235. He states: "...a set of absolutely
uniform international accounting standards is as unrealistic as an attempt
to force the accounting concepts and practices of a single country upon
all the rest of the world." (p. 244)

the development of a set of international accounting principles would
occupy a central position in the field of international accounting.
From this analysis, the following tentative definition of international
accounting is proposed as useful for a systematic research of the field:

> International accounting is a discipline concerned with
> developing and communicating accounting information based
> upon a set of internationally applicable accounting principles.

According to this definition, the development and communication of
internationally understandable accounting information could not be
completed until a set of internationally applicable principles is established. This does not mean, however, that international accounting cannot exist until a set of internationally applicable principles is
established. Rather, the field cannot be fully developed until the
principles exist. That is, a set of internationally applicable accounting principles is an essential tool for achieving the final goal of
international accounting and its establishment in turn constitutes a
subgoal of international accounting. In the process of achieving the
final and subgoals, many individual problems peculiar to the field of
international accounting must be solved. The tentative definition of
international accounting should enable the study of all portions belonging to this field of study.

The preceding discussion of the definition of international accounting suggests a systematic approach to study in this field: all research
in the field of international accounting should be systematically
developed toward the goal of formulating a set of international accounting
principles. To facilitate that objective, the identification of three
aspects of international accounting will provide a better understanding

of various problems involved in international accounting. Each aspect
may constitute a special study area in international accounting. These
three aspects are normative, practical, and descriptive features. They
should not be isolated from one another. Rather they should be organ-
ically systematized for research purposes. For example, Norton M. Bedford
recently emphasized a need for a fundamental and comprehensive study of
accounting at the theory level to facilitate the development of an international discipline.[12] This type of study constitutes a fundamental part
of an organized approach to international accounting.

At least, two steps seem to be necessary for the establishment of
a set of international accounting principles. The first step involves
the useful arrangement and annotation of the mass of existing information
concerning accounting practices and principles presently accepted in
each country, together with other information on prevailing business
organizations and legal systems. Several research projects of this type,
including several doctoral dissertations, have been completed, but most
of them deal only with European and Latin American countries. One of the
most comprehensive works of this type is Professional Accounting in 25
Countries by the Committee on International Relations of the American
Institute of Certified Public Accountants. The second step in developing
international accounting principles involves the comparison and reconciliation of similarities and differences so that the possibility of formulating
a set of international accounting principles may be ascertained. According

---

[12]Norton M. Bedford, "The International Flow of Accounting Thought,"
The International Journal of Accounting Education and Research, Vol. 1,
No. 2, (Spring, 1966), pp. 1-7.

to Alvin R. Jennings, only by this comparison can steps be taken toward
formulating broad international standards of professional practices from
which no difference of opinion could really exist.[13] In fact, the mere
comparison of accumulated information concerning accounting principles
in each country might be a shortcut to the goal of formulating a set of
international accounting principles. More systematic research concerning
methods of information collection, however, would seem to be necessary
before the second step in the formulation of a set of international
accounting principles could be completed.

The mere identification and comparison of currently accepted accounting practices may reveal neither the true similarities nor differences
which should be recognized as a useful foundation for the formulation of
a set of international accounting principles. This is unfortunate for
it seems that most research works on international accounting have been
primarily concerned with descriptions of the technical aspects of accounting principles and practices. Nevertheless, there is no compelling
reason to believe that such descriptions provide the best base for
developing international accounting. In fact, it may induce reasoning
errors. For example, using only these descriptions practicing accountants
have tended to emphasize a close relationship between accounting principles and capital investment. Theodore L. Wilkinson states: "One
simple conclusion is that when the citizens of one country invest capital

---

[13]Alvin R. Jennings, "International Standards of Accounting and
Auditing," The Journal of Accountancy, Vol. 114, No. 3, (September, 1962),
p. 42.

in a second country, the accounting principles of the investor nation

will follow the capital."[14] But there is no reason why a second country,

which has an organized body of accounting principles, would accept

accounting principles of the first country without hesitation. One may

well ask whether the single force of capital investment can change the

accounting principles of the country in which the investment occurs.

The author believes a basic analysis of the social function of

accounting principles in each country could offer a more useful starting

point for the identification and acceptance of international accounting

principles. This means that an analysis of the social consequences of

accounting principles in each country is more important than a mere

comparison of the existing accounting principles and practices for the

study of international accounting. This type of analysis has not been

a part of the traditional study of accounting principles at tne national

level. The point is that accounting principles and practices as cultural

---

[14]Theodore L. Wilkinson, "Can Accounting Be an International
Language?" The Price Waterhouse Review, Vol. VIII, No. 2, (Summer, 1963),
p. 16. In another article, he refers to how accounting principles move
from one country to another as follows:
> The accounting principles of one country have never been
> "sold" to another country on the basis of convincing
> arguments in support of those principles. Accounting
> principles of one country have moved to another country
> when two conditions have existed:
> 1. The second country had no organized body of accounting
>   principles in the first place, and
> 2. Large amounts of capital from the first country were
>   invested in business in the second country, with the
>   consequent ability on the part of those investors to
>   impose their own accounting requirements on the businesses.
("United States Accounting as Viewed by Accountants of Other Countries."
The International Journal of Accounting Education and Research, Vol. 1,
No. 1, [Fall, 1965], pp. 11-12.)

institutions do not exist in a vacuum. They exist in a distinct cultural climate of each country. They also exist in a changing society with certain changing political, economic, and cultural environments, and these must be studied and understood before basic international accounting principles can be developed.

The primary motive which actuated this study, dealing with Japanese accounting principles, is the belief that the accounting principles and practices in Japan are not well understood by most American accountants. Two quotations from recent literature support this conclusion:

> Japan is evolving accounting practices specially along United States lines, also quite probably in consequences of economic relationship.[15]

> The accounting principles and practices in Japan do not differ materially from those in the United States.[16]

These two statements are not false but they are somewhat superficial and appear to have been derived from limited observation or comparison of currently accepted accounting principles and practices in both countries without noting certain fundamental background or conditions. The author believes that this type of descriptive statements cannot serve as a useful foundation for the formulation of international accounting principles. A historical analysis of the function of accounting principles in Japanese society should provide a more useful and quite different statement than the above-quoted statements. Since no historical study of the social

---

[15]Gerhard G. Mueller, "Some Thoughts about the International Congresses of Accountants," The Accounting Review, Vol. XXXVI, No. 4, (October, 1961), p. 550.

[16]AICPA Committee on International Relations, op. cit., p. 23-18.

function of Japanese accounting principles has been undertaken previously,
a significant part of this study will be directed to that objective.

Purpose and Scope of the Study

In relation to the historical development of accounting principles
throughout the world, two different types of principles may be distinguished:
(1) Anglo-American type -- "Autogenous" accounting principles and (2)
Franco-German type -- "compulsory" accounting principles.[17] According
to Asaba, the first "autogenous" type of accounting principles should be
understood as a historical development of the second "compulsory" type.
Therefore, this study will first consider two questions: (1) Are Japanese
accounting principles "autogenous" or "compulsory"? (2) Is there a
discernible pattern of development from the "compulsory" to the "autogenous"
type in the history of Japanese accounting principles?

One of the purposes of this study is to analyze historically the
social function of accounting principles in Japan using a sociological
framework to determine the nature of Japanese accounting principles which
have been developed in a unique social climate. The possible contribu-
tions of this study to the new area of international accounting are
(1) providing an accurate knowledge of the manner in which Japanese
accounting principles have been developed and functioned in Japanese
society, and (2) presenting a commonly applicable framework for analysis
and comparison of accounting principles in different countries. The
study assumes that a set of accounting principles exists and serves as

---

[17]Jiro Asaba, Kaikei Gensoku no Kiso Kozo (Basic Structure of
Accounting Principles) (Tokoyo, Japan: Yuhikaku, 1959), pp. 42-47.

a rule for social control. That these principles have been adopted or professed as a guide to accounting actions, that they are influenced by certain political, economic, and cultural structures of society, and that they change as these social structures evolve is also assumed.

The study will emphasize <u>Kigyo-Kaikei</u> <u>Gensoku</u> (A Statement of Business Accounting Principles) which was released by <u>Keizai</u> <u>Antei</u> <u>Honbu</u> <u>Kigyo-Kaikei</u> <u>Seido</u> <u>Taisaku</u> <u>Chosakai</u> (Investigation Committee on Business Accounting System of the Economic Stabilization Board of Japan) in 1949 and revised in 1954 and 1963. <u>A</u> <u>Statement</u> <u>of</u> <u>Business</u> <u>Accounting</u> <u>Principles</u> does not necessarily represent a summary of those procedures generally accepted as fair and proper in the practices of business accounting in Japan. Rather, under the special circumstances existing after World War II, the Committee was established to solve the urgent problems involved in the reconstruction of the Japanese economy.

This statement was the first written pronouncement of accounting principles in Japan although there had been several laws and rules regulating accounting practices such as <u>Shoho</u> (Commercial Code of Japan) which was originally promulgated in 1890 and amended several times before 1963, <u>Zaimushohyo</u> <u>Junsoku</u> (Working Rules for Financial Statements) by <u>Shokosho</u> (Ministry of Commerce and Industry) in 1934, and <u>Seizo-Kogyo</u> <u>Zaimushohyo</u> <u>Junsoku</u> <u>Soan</u> (Tentative Standards for Financial Statements of Manufacturing Companies) by <u>Kikakuin</u> <u>Zaimushohyo</u> <u>Toitsu</u> <u>Kyogikai</u> (Uniform Financial Statements Council of the Planning Board) in 1941.

The nature of <u>A</u> <u>Statement</u> <u>of</u> <u>Business</u> <u>Accounting</u> <u>Principles</u> is considerably different from these earlier laws and rules. As will be discussed in more detail later, <u>A</u> <u>Statement</u> <u>of</u> <u>Business</u> <u>Accounting</u>

Principles is primarily based upon Anglo-American accounting thought while the Commercial Code of Japan was based upon Franco-German legal thought. A Statement of Business Accounting Principles was the historical product of a series of movements directed to the improvement and unification of the financial statements used in Japan. This study, therefore, will examine the predecessor laws and rules to determine their influence on the formulation of A Statement of Business Accounting Principles.

In 1963 Homusho (Ministry of Justice) released Kabushiki-Kaisha no Taishaku-Taishohyo oyobi Soneki-Keisansho ni kansuru Kisoku (Regulation for Corporate Balance Sheets and Income Statements) which dealt with an amendment of the Commercial Code of Japan. The regulation prescribed procedures for preparing the financial statements required to be submitted at the general meeting of stockholders in accordance with Article 281 of the Commercial Code of Japan. Enactment of this regulation forced a change in the nature of A Statement of Business Accounting Principles since the former has priority in its legal effect. This study will include an analysis of the interrelationship between A Statement of Business Accounting Principles and the Regulation for Corporate Balance Sheets and Income Statements.

For analytical purposes the development of accounting principles in Japan can be best divided into three sections or time periods, each having significantly different characteristics:

1. The first stage: Groping for uniformity in financial reporting (1890 - 1947),
2. The second stage: Establishment and improvement of A Statement of Business Accounting Principles (1947 - 1962),
3. The third stage: Reconciliation of the Commercial Code of Japan and A Statement of Business Accounting Principles (1962 -   ).

A short history of Japanese accounting principles is given in Chapter II
to clarify the interrelationships among the subjects to be analyzed in
depth in Chapters III, IV, and V.

Basic Viewpoint of the Study

The assumption that a set of accounting principles constitutes a rule
for social control is derived from the commonly recognized viewpoint that
the business enterprise, for which accounting information is developed and
communicated, is a social institution.[18] It is a social institution to
the degree that management, shareholders, creditors, suppliers of goods

---

[18]In the literature of sociology, where the term "social control"
is primarily used, two interrelated but significantly distinguishable
meanings are expressed by the term "social control":
1. It denotes the fact that a person is conditioned and
   limited in his actions by the groups, community, and
   society of which he is a member; and that this limita-
   tion and conditioning of actions performs functions,
   latent or manifest, for the groups, community, and in
   so far as the person shares the goals and norms of the
   social units, for the person himself.
2. It denotes the fact that in all social interaction, in
   so far as the person limits or conditions the actions
   of others or has his actions limited and conditioned
   by others, by social groups, communities, or society of
   which he may or may not be a member, the mechanisms by
   which this limiting and conditioning occur are themselves social in character. The mechanisms are social
   in that they themselves in one way or another involve
   the actions of others: the use of sanctions, the process
   of socialization, internalization, the deliberate
   manipulation of symbols, etc.
The choice between the two usages of the term depends upon ideological
tradition of sociology; the first usage has been and is dominant in one
tradition of sociology, that stressing social unity and shared normative
systems and the second usage has been stressed in another tradition of
sociology, that stressing conflict, power, and control as related to the
divers and sometimes opposing interests, individuals, and groups in
society. (Julius Gauld and William L. Kolb [eds.] A Dictionary of the
Social Sciences [New York: The Free Press, 1964.] , pp. 650-51.)

and services, labor, customers, and government can be identified as
independent interest groups in the business enterprise. Robert Aaron
Gordon refers to various outside groups associated with a large corporation as "interest groups" in his discussion of the relationship between
interest groups and business leadership. He defines an "interest group"
as one whose economic welfare depends directly and to an important degree
on the activities of a given firm.[19] He also presents the following

---

The term "social control" has been seldom used in the accounting literature
and the term has not been defined clearly even in the case where it has
been used in a few, rather exceptional, literature such as:

1. DR Scott, "The Tentative Statement of Principles" The Accounting Review, Vol. XII, No. 3, (September, 1937), p. 296.
2. DR Scott, "Accounting Principles and Cost Accounting," The
   Journal of Accountancy, Vol. 67, No. 2, (February, 1939), p. 75.
3. The Committee to Prepare A Statement of Basic Accounting Theory,
   American Accounting Association, A Statement of Basic Accounting
   Theory (Evanston, Illinois: AAA, 1966), p. 4.

In this study the author follows the usage of the term by Talcott Parsons:

> The mechanisms of social control comprise aspects of the two classes
> of mechanisms of personality which have been called mechanisms of
> defense and of adjustment. They constitute, that is, defense and
> adjustment relative to tendencies to violate role-expectations....
> Of the two classes, however, for obvious reasons the mechanisms of
> personality adjustment are dynamically the more closely related to
> the mechanisms of social control. It is, after all, in the inter-
> relations with social objects that both the problems of adjustment
> of the personality and of control for the social systems, arise.
> On the other hand functionally, the mechanisms of social control
> are more closely analogous with the mechanisms of defense, since
> both are concerned with the process by which a system of action is
> internally integrated, and disruptive tendencies are held in check.
(Talcott Parsons, The Social System, [New York: The Free Press, 1951] , pp.
206-7.)

[19]Robert Aaron Gordon, Business Leadership in the Large Corporation
(Berkeley and Los Angeles: University of California Press, 1966), p. 147.

list as a possible classification of interest groups. In this classification each category represents an economic group which, to further its own
interests, may seek to influence the decisions, and thereby the activities,
of the corporation.

1. Owners (stockholders), whether ownership arises from
   investment of capital or watered stock.
2. Lenders of money funds, both short-term and long-term.
3. Suppliers of goods by sale or lease, for example,
   materials, equipment, land, and so on.
4. Customers.
5. Firms in the same or related industries affected
   through competitive relationships.
6. Labor.
7. The government, both as provider of certain services
   and collector of taxes and also as the representative
   of the public welfare (as this is conceived by those
   in political power).
8. Providers of organization services, chiefly financial,
   legal, and engineering.[20]

The notion of "interest group(s)," regardless of the specific use
of the term itself, has long been common in accounting literature
although authors have not been unanimous in their enumeration and
description of them.[21] Accounting literature, in fact, has not provided
sufficient discussion of the types and treatment of interest groups.

------

[20]Ibid., p. 148.

[21]Several studies in accounting literature, referring to the notion
of interest group(s), would be classified into the following three categories in terms of their treatment of interest groups:
1. Those which do not distinguish management groups from
   other groups: Thomas Henry Sanders, Henry Rand Hatfield,
   and Underhill Moore, A Statement of Accounting Principles
   (American Institute of Accountants, 1938. American
   Accounting Association, 1959 [reprint]), A Study Group
   at the University of Illinois, A Statement of Basic
   Accounting Postulates and Principles (Urbana, Illinois:
   The Center for International Education and Research in
   Accounting, 1964), and Dwight R. Ladd, Contemporary
   Corporate Accounting and the Public (Homewood, Illinois:
   Richard D. Irwin, Inc., 1963).

Sprouse and Moonitz, for example, merely state that the principles of
financial accounting developed in their study are designed to meet the
needs of all interested groups, although reference is made to management,
owners, government and others as having bona fide interests.[22] As
Leonard Spacek noted in his comments on the Sprouse and Moonitz study,
the subsequent discussion leading to the statement of principles does
not answer the question of how or why the so-called principles meet the
needs of all interested groups.[23] Clearly, this question cannot be
answered without an identification of the needs of all interest groups
and this would require an analysis of the nature of each group and the
interrelationship among the groups. The same criticism is also applied
to Dwight R. Ladd's study, which is called a sociological approach by
Eldon S. Hendriksen.[24]

---

2. Those which distinguish the management group from other
   groups:
   2.1 Those which emphasize the paramountcy of investors
       group over all groups other than management groups:
       American Accounting Association, Accounting and Report-
       ing Standards for Corporate Financial Statements
       Iowa City, Iowa: AAA, 1957 and Herman W. Bevis,
       Corporate Financial Reporting in a Competitive
       Economy (New York: The MacMillan Company, 1965).
   2.2 Those which treat equally all groups other than
       management groups: W. A. Paton and A. C. Littleton,
       An Introduction to Corporate Accounting Standards
       (American Accounting Association, 1940), Robert T.
       Sprouse and Maurice Moonitz, A Tentative Set of
       Broad Accounting Principles for Business Enterprises
       (AICPA Accounting Research Study No. 3) (New York:
       AICPA, 1962), and James W. Pattilo, The Foundation
       of Financial Accounting (Baton Rouge, Louisiana:
       Louisiana State University Press, 1965).

[22]Sprouse and Moonitz, op. cit., p. 1.

[23]Ibid., p. 77.

[24]Eldon S. Hendrikson, Accounting Theory (Homewood, Illinois:
Richard D. Irwin, Inc., 1965) p. 14.

To further this discussion of interest groups, the following two
statements are compared with Gordon's.

> All of the following discussions of accounting concepts and
> procedures are based on the foregoing definition of the
> corporation's responsibility, and it is assumed that this
> responsibility is owed to several constituencies -- stock-
> holders, management, workers, customers, suppliers, and the
> public.[25]

> The parties interest in the firm's operations are share-
> holders, managers, labor, creditors, customers, government,
> and general public. These society segments may be divided
> in reference to the enterprise into two groups of interest;
> managerial accounting is directed to the internal operational
> needs of managers, and financial accounting is externally
> directed to the other segments.[26]

Our first problem is concerned with the enumeration of interest
groups. Compared with Gordon's enumeration of interest groups Ladd's
list excludes lenders of capital (or creditors), government, firms in
competitive relationships, and providers of organization services but
adds the public as an interest group. Pattilo excludes suppliers of
goods (or suppliers), firms in competitive relationships, and providers
of organization services, while adding the general public as an interest
group. Of four interest groups, which are identified by Gordon but not
by Ladd, lenders of capital (or creditors) and government certainly seem
to have the characteristics of interest groups. Suppliers of goods (or
supplier), which are not identified as one of the interest groups by

[25]Ladd, op. cit., p. 13.

[26]Pattilo, op. cit., p. 43.

Pattilo, also appear to have the right to be described as an interest
group. On the other hand, it is believed that the public in Ladd's,
or the general public in Pattilo's study should not be identified as
an interest group for a reason to be explained later. That any enumeration of interest groups should not be arbitrary but ought to be derived
from a sound concept of an interest group is axiomatic. Both Ladd's
and Pattilo's studies fail to show the bases for their enumeration
although they start with some observations on the nature of modern
business enterprises. The author does not agree completely with Gordon's
enumeration in that his list contains both firms in competitive
relationships and providers of organization services.

What is interest group? According to Ralf Dahrendorf, "an interest
group shall mean any organized collectivity of individuals sharing
manifest interests."[27] To Dahrendorf, the separation of manifest
interests from latent interests is important since any collection of
individuals sharing positions with identical latent interests but without having organized themselves do not constitute a group in the strict
sense of the sociological term. Manifest interests means orientations
of behavior which are articulate and conscious to individuals, and which
oppose collectivities of individuals representing imperatively coor-
dinated association.[28] Judging from the sociologist's definition of

[27]Ralf Dahrendorf, Class and Class Conflict in Industrial Society
(Stanford, California: Stanford University Press, 1959), p. 238.

[28]Ibid.

interest group, Gordon's definition seems to be insufficient for at least two reasons: (1) it fails to take into consideration the required consciousness of individuals to their interest and roles, and (2) it neglects the mode of behavior of any group of individuals while it emphasizes economic welfare as a resultant of the activities of a given firm. In other words, there is no logical relationship between Gordon's definition of an interest group and its classification. In so far as we follow strictly his definition, each interest group is not distinguishable from one another.

For the purpose of this study, the term "interest group" is defined, with a slight modification of Dahrendorf's definition, as:

> any collectivity of individuals who perform, being conscious
> of the same type of interests and role-expectations, a part
> of the functions which are common within a group and essential
> for a given business enterprise to achieve its goals.

This definition contains two requirements for interest groups which may be used as criteria for identification and classification: (1) to be conscious of the same type of interests and role-expectations, and (2) to perform a part of the functions, which are common within a group, for a given business enterprise.

Identification of the public (or general public) as an interest group by Ladd and Pattilo would not be accepted since it constitutes, at best, that which Dahrendorf refers to as "recruiting field for groups." As a group, the public has no common mode of behavior which is a characteristic of interest group.[29] Firms in the same or related industries affected through competitive relationships, as Gordon emphasized, exert

---

[29]Ibid., pp. 180-82.

the greatest influences on business leadership and their economic welfare depends upon the activities of a given firm.[30] It is not enough, however, to regard an aggregate of firms in competitive relationships as an interest group since the interests of individual firms in competitive relationships are more in conflict with one another than in common and they do not perform a part of the functions essential for a given firm to achieve its goals. Although providers of organization services, such as lawyers, engineers, and accountants, who supply specialized technical services to the firm, exert unique, significant influence on business leaders, their interests and functions in a business enterprise do not differ fundamentally from that of either labor or the management group.[31] They may be classified as a subgroup of a larger labor group or as a subgroup of a larger management group.

Before making a list of interest groups based upon this concept of an interest group, brief reference should be made of the relationship between a business enterprise and its economic and political environments. The economic environment consists of four markets with which the business enterprise has various types of interactions. They are the capital funds market, the procurement market, the labor market, and the sales market. These four markets are represented by a variety of groups of individuals whose functions are essential for the business enterprise to achieve its goal of producing goods and services for others. The capital funds market is the environment in which the business enterprise

[30]Gordon, op. cit., p. 246.

[31]Ibid., pp. 258-67.

is concerned with the acquisition of money resources. Shareholders and
creditors are the interest groups in this market. The procurement
market is a pool of goods and services to be supplied to the business
enterprise for its use. Its interest group is composed of the suppliers
of goods and services. The labor group which represents the labor market
is concerned mainly with the utilization or recombination of acquired
service resources although it is generally concerned with all phases of
business activities from acquisition of money resources to disposition
of produced goods and services. The sales market is the environmental
field where the business enterprise disposes its newly produced goods
and services. Those individuals who buy goods and services for their
own use in the sales market are called customers, and they represents a
distinct interest group.

Each interest group attempts to achieve its own economic goal, that
is, to maximize its income or welfare by participating in a variety of
activities with the business enterprise in the market which it represents.
From the economic viewpoint of the business enterprise as an organization,
all necessary factors of production should be combined in the most effective and efficient way in order to achieve the goals of the enterprise.
Since man lives in a world of scarce means, this is also the viewpoint
of society as a whole.[32] The function of organizing and directing a
business enterprise, of making decisions which determine the course of
an enterprise's activities is usually performed by a professional group,
called management or top management, and it represents a distinct interest

---

[32]A Study Group at the University of Illinois, op. cit., p. 5.

group in our society.

The business enterprise is also surrounded by political environment, including a legal system. The business enterprise can neither exist nor continue to carry out its activities without having contact with its political environment. The term "government" is used in a very broad sense to represent all interests in the policital environment. The definition of interest group, coupled with the foregoing brief description of the relationships of a business enterprise with its environments, leads to the following list of interest groups in business enterprise: (1) management, (2) shareholders, (3) creditors, (4) suppliers of goods and services, (5) labor, (6) customers, and (7) government.

The economic treatment of the interest groups identified in the above list is another problem. An adequate determination of the rights of each interest group calls for a further discussion of the relationships between the business enterprise and each interest group. The relationships are shown concisely in the Figure 1 (page 26). It presents a diadic model of the economic actions of individuals. The large square represents a business enterprise located in its economic environment. Each side of the square constitutes a boundary between business enterprise and the four markets. The large square is divided into four triangles, each representing the four main functions of the enterprise:

Figure 1 Relationships between the Business Enterprise
           and Interest Groups

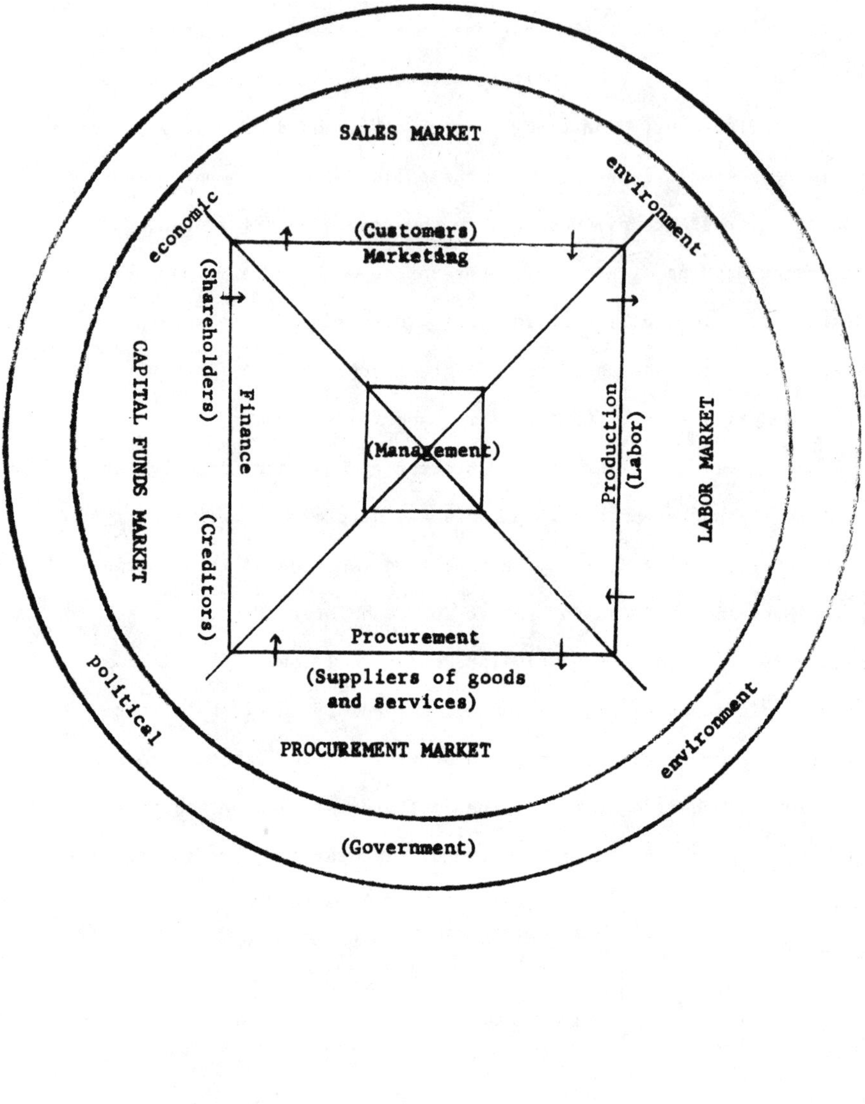

(1) finance, (2) procurement, (3) production, and (4) marketing, respectively. As mentioned earlier, the business enterprise performs these functions in order to achieve its final goal. That is, it produces goods and services for others by bringing together the requisite factors from a variety of sources and by cominging them under the right conditions and in the right proportions. It is evident that the business enterprise cannot perform its functions without having interactions with those who control the factors of production. The relationship between the business enterprise and the individuals in each interest group who control the different types of factors of production may well be regarded, in sociological terms, as a relationship between ego and alter with complementarity of expectations. In interaction ego and alter must, in some sense, both have need-dispositions which require one set of actions and attitudes by ego and another set by alter; and ego must require of himself what alter requires of him; conversely, alter must require of himself what ego requires of him.[33] Applied to a particular interaction situation of the business and interest groups, ego stands for the business enterprise and alter for individual in each interest group from the enterprise's standpoint; ego stands for individual in each group and alter for the business enterprise from the interest group's standpoint.

The business enterprise must acquire facilities in the most general form from the capital funds market in order to achieve its production goal. In this adaptive process the business enterprise as ego expects

---

[33]Talcott Parsons and Edward A. Shils, "Values, Motives, and Systems of Action," in Talcott Parsons and Edward A. Shils (eds.) Toward A General Theory of Action (New York: Harper & Row, Publishers, 1962), p. 115.

someone else in the capital fund market to transfer his money resources to the business enterprise. Individuals, controlling money resources and seeking the most favorable opportunity of their utilization, respond as alter to the expectation of the business enterprise. They in turn expect the business enterprise to reward them for their performance. In so far as the reward (interest), which is to be given to them by the business enterprise, gratifies their expectation, they would satisfy the expectation of the business enterprise by supplying it with the money resources. Thus, interaction of ego and alter, which is usually called exchange, takes place in a market. Although the general function of investors is to provide the business enterprise as a social unit of production with general facilities, namely, money resources, the separation of shareholders group from creditors group is important. The shareholders supply the enterprise with money resources which can be used by it for an indefinitely long time. This means that the function of shareholders is to guarantee the permanent existence of the business enterprise. The creditors, on the other hand, supply the business enterprise with much of its rather short-term money resources to guarantee its liquidity. Although the creditors often supply it with long-term money resources, the performance and expectation of shareholders to the business enterprise still differ from those of creditors in that the creditors normally have a definite date when funds are to be returned.

Another adaptive function of the business enterprise is to obtain goods and services, which are to be used for its production purpose, from the procurement market. In this market exchanges take place between the business enterprise and the suppliers of goods and services such as

machines, raw material, and utilities. The supplier of goods and services
provides the business enterprise with a special type of goods or services
as he responds to the expectation of the business enterprise. The amount
of contribution by the supplier depends upon his expectation of sanction
or reward from the business enterprise. Conversely, the amount of sanction
or reward, which is commonly expressed in terms of price, is a function
of the amount of contribution.[34]

The second functional imperative of a system of action is goal attainment and this function in a production system covers production, distribution (marketing), and sales in the conceptual scheme developed by Parsons
and Smelser.[35] The separation of production in a narrow sense from
marketing, however, seems to be useful for the discussion of at least
one interest group. By production is meant the process of combining
acquired goods and services and human services (labor) into a new product
or service which satisfies human wants.

Although the utilization of human services in the business enterprise is not limited to this stage of business activities, labor services
will be discussed in connection with the production function for the
purpose of clarity. In order to carry out the production function the
business enterprise needs human services which combine acquired goods
and services into a new form of goods or service for customers. These

---

[34]Talcott Parsons and Neil J. Smelser, Economy and Society (New
York: The Free Press, 1956), p. 10.

[35]Ibid., pp. 198-99.

human services are acquired in the labor market. The business enterprise expects the laborer to supply his services; the laborer offers his services to the business enterprise in exchange for money income (wages) which are to be used for the maintenance of welfare of his household. Since the typical occupational contract between the business enterprise and the laborer integrates three partially independent systems of action: (1) the organization in which ego is employed; (2) the household of which ego is a member, and (3) the personality of ego, the labor-supply decision by the laborer depends upon many non-economic factors such as the security of his family, his personal satisfaction with the job, and his pride in being a part of a "first-class" business enterprise.[36] This sociological view of a laborer's behavior, however, does not necessarily deny the importance of economic considerations in the labor market. Contractual settlement will be achieved by bargaining between the business enterprise and the laborer or the labor union as a group.

Another goal attainment function of the business enterprise is to distribute goods or services to customers in the sales market. As indicated in the diagram, the sales market is located on the side opposite the procurement market. The business enterprise provides a customer with newly produced goods or services to satisfy his wants. The customer rewards this performance by a payment of money. The price of goods or

[36]Ibid., p. 114.

services is the common expression of a sanction or reward by the customer for the performance by the business enterprise and it should originally be determined by the customer. Although there are several exceptions, a modern sales market (or market for customers' goods) is characterized by the one-price system which means the practice of standard pricing for a product; where the purchaser may accept or reject the price, but is not normally able to modify it.[37] Under these circumstances the customer is very much interested in the pricing process used by the business enterprise as well as in the quality of the product.

The foregoing discussion focused on the relationships between the business enterprise and the five interest groups without questioning whether the business enterprise as an organization can be *ego* or *alter* by itself. Organizations are defined as social units (or human groupings) deliberately constructed and reconstructed to seek specific goals and characterized by: (1) division of labor, power, and communication responsibilities, divisions which are not random or traditionally patterned, but deliberately planned to enhance the realization of specific goals; (2) the presence of one or more power centers which control the concerned efforts of the organization and direct them toward its goals; these power centers also must review continuously the organization's performance and re-pattern its structure, where

---

[37]Neil J. Smelser, *The Sociology of Economic Life* (Englewood Cliffs, New Jersey: Prentice-Hall, Inc., 1963), p. 92. See also Parsons and Smelser, *op. cit.*, pp. 157-59.

necessary, to increase its efficiency; (3) substitution of personnel,
i.e., unsatisfactory persons can be removed and others assigned their
tasks.[38] No organization can act as ego or alter and make its own
decisions without the presence of one or more power centers in it. The
role of this power center has been referred to as the executive role,
the top managerial role, or leadership. In this study the simple term
management is used to mean a person or a group of persons who perform an
integrative function with the power to control the organization activities.
In the foregoing discussion of the five interest groups only one interrelationship between the business enterprise and each interest group was
recognized. In the case of management this same type of interrelationship
exists between the business enterprise and the management since the latter
provides the business enterprise with a special type of human services.
This relationship is, however, not an ego-alter relationship in reality,
but an ego-ego relationship. The management that represents the business
enterprise has an ego-alter relationship between itself and each interest
group other than itself. Therefore, the relationship between the business
enterprise and each interest group in the foregoing discussion should
be replaced by a new relationship between the management of the business
enterprise and each interest group. It follows that the management,
though an interest group, should be treated differently than other interest
groups.

The government, viewed as an interest group in the business enterprise, is complex in its nature. the government sometimes acts as an
investor and sometimes as a customer. In these cases its relation-

---

[38]Amitai Etzioni, Modern Organizations (Englewood Cliffs, New Jersey: Prentice-Hall, Inc., 1964), p. 3.

ship to the business enterprise constitutes a more or less regular
performance-sanction type relationship. In the case where the government acts as a tax collector, however, it is difficult to find a
performance-sanction type relationship between the performance by the
government (the guarantee of legal existence in a political boundary)
and the sanction by the enterprise (the payment of tax). The business
enterprise, as a system of action, should perform a latent-pattern
maintenance function internally in order to maintain technical production or the flow of the production. The relevant technical roles in
this function are performed by a machine tender, foreman, plant engineer,
plant inspector, etc.[39] The government performs an external latent-
pattern maintenance function for the business enterprise by guaranteeing
its legal existence in a political boundary. In this sense the government's function to the business enterprise is not a direct one, but it
is essential for the business enterprise. Therefore, the government
has been located outside the economic environment. An outer big circle
in the figure shows the political environment.

In summary, co-operation among all interest groups, who control
the factors of production, is essential for the business enterprise to
achieve its production goal. The interests of these groups, however,
are not necessarily the same. They are often in conflict with one
another. These groups need specific accounting information, as well as
certain nonquantitative information, to optimize their decisions

---

[39]Parsons and Smelser, op. cit., p. 199.

concerning their relationships with the business enterprise. Under
these circumstances, accounting information should be developed and
communicated so that any conflict among interest groups can be reduced
or eliminated. This is an important part of the integrative functions
performed by the management. In other words, a concern for the fair
protection of the interests of all groups should be reflected in accounting information. Thus, it is necessary to establish a set of accounting
principles, to be called "generally accepted accounting principles" or
"socially accepted accounting principles," as a rule for social control
which guides the development and communication of appropriate accounting information by the management of the business enterprise to other
interest groups and serves as a conflict-minimizing mechanism.

The Framework of Analysis of the Study

The "autogenous" type of accounting principles is a general rule
adopted or professed as a guide to accounting actions by professional
societies of accountants. To those who have been and are responsible
for the development and recognition of the "autogenous" type of accounting principles, it would be a great misfortune if accounting principles
were to be prescribed by government.[40] Although the government agencies
have not fully exercised their statutory powers in countries such as
the United States, where the "autogenous" type of accounting principles
has been developed, there is always the possibility that accounting

[40]Marquis G. Eaton, "Financial Reporting in a Changing Society,"
The Journal of Accountancy, Vol. 104, No. 2, (August, 1957), p. 30. and
George R. Catlett, "Factors That Influence Accounting Principles," The
Journal of Accountancy, Vol. 110, No. 4, (October, 1960), p. 47.

principles may be incorporated into law or regulation. The "compulsory" type of accounting principles refers to a kind or a part of low or regulation. Regardless of its type, however, a set of accounting principles must be regarded as a rule for social control since its function in society is very similar to that of law. The following statements on the function of law by a sociologist and an accountant seem to support this conclusion:

> Let us suggest that in the larger social perspective the primary function of a legal system is integrative. It serves to mitigate potential elements of conflict and to oil the machinery of social intercourse. It is, indeed, only by adherence to a system of rules that systems of social interaction can function without breaking down into overt or chronic convert conflict.[41]

> Because man's experience is fragmentary; because conflicts do arise and their adjustment is a condition of cultural survival, law arises as a basis for the adjustment of conflicting interests and legal institutions arise as means of enforcing the group sanction.[42]

According to Talcott Parsons, there are four major problems that must be solved before a system of rules can operate determinately to regulate interaction: (1) legitimation, (2) interpretation, (3) sanctions, and (4) jurisdiction.[43] These four problems correspond to four independent

---

[41]Talcott Parsons, "The Law and Social Control" in William M. Evan (ed.) Law and Sociology (New York: The Free Press of Glencoe, 1962), p. 58.

[42]DR Scott, The Cultural Significance of Accounts (Reprint) (Columbia, Missouri: Lucas Brothers Publishers, n.d.,) p. 177. This book was originally published by Henry Holt and Company of New York in 1931.

[43]Parsons, "The Law and Social Control," pp. 58-59.

functional imperatives or "problems" which must be met adequately if
equilibrium and/or continuing existence of the system is to be maintained:
(1) adaptation, (2) goal gratification, (3) integration, and (4) latent-
pattern maintenance and tension management.[44] Brief comments concerning
the four concepts by the original writers are quoted to increase the
understanding of their application:

A. Adaptation. Successful adaptation involves (a) an
accommodation of the system to inflexible "reality
demands," and (b) an active transformation of the
situation external to the system. In both instances
there is a consequent emphasis on cognitive orienta-
tion. The eventual mastery of the external situation
through instrumental activity necessitates "realistic"
judgments in terms of generalized predictions concerning the behavior of objects.

G. Goal Gratification of Enjoyment of Goal-state. Goal
attainment involves intrinsically gratifying activity.
It is the culminating phase of a sequence of preparatory
activities. Any anterior instrumental-adaptive
activities were associated with an inhibition on ten-
dencies toward premature gratification, that is, were
pursued with an attitude of neutrality. Then, when
the culminating activities are about to be carried out,
the inhibition on gratification is suspended and
affectively suffuses the goal consumative activity.

I. Integration. Successful integration involves a deter-
minate set of relations among the member units of the
system such that it retains and reinforces its boundary-
maintaining character as a single entity.

L. Latency. To put the matter somewhat differently, a system
is confronted by the necessity, as a precondition for
its continued existence, of maintaining and renewing

---

[44]Parsons and Smelser, op. cit., pp. 16-19. These four concepts
were originally developed by Robert F. Bales for the analysis of small
groups and further developed by Parsons, Shils and Bales. See Robert
F. Bales, Interaction Process Analysis: A Method for the Study of Small
Group (Cambridge, Massachusetts: Addison-Wesley Press, 1950) and Talcott
Parsons, Robert F. Bales, and Edward A. Shils, Working Papers in the
Theory of Action. (Glencoe, Illinois: The Free Press, 1953).

the motivational and cultural patterns which are
integral to its interaction as a system.[45]

Talcott Parsons applied these four concepts to a special area of
social system -- a system of law -- to analyze the function of a system
of law and changed them for (1) legitimation, (2) interpretation,
(3) sanctions, and (4) jurisdiction. Although the latter four terms may
be applicable, without modification, to the analysis of social function
of a set of accounting principles, two terms "interpretation" and
"jurisdiction" may well be changed for "application" and "administration."

The first problem concerns the basis of legitimation of a set of
accounting principles. The question is why, in the value or meaning sense,
should the business enterprise conform to a set of accounting principles
in developing accounting information and why should the business enterprise fulfill the informational expectation of all interest groups with
whom it interacts? What, in other words, is the basis for the gratification of informational needs. In order for a set of accounting principles
to function in our society, it must be accepted as legitimate by all
interest groups. This is the problem of general acceptance. Is it
legitimate simply because some authority says so without further justification? In this problem a set of accounting principles relates itself
first to accounting theory since accounting theory gives the criterion
by which the validity of a set of accounting principles may be judged.
The basis of this legitimation depends also upon the value system,
personality, and expectations of each interest group. This problem

---

[45]Parsons, Bales, and Shils, op. cit., pp. 183-85.

area is mainly concerned with the formation and revision of a set of accounting principles.

The second problem concerns the interpretation or application of a set of accounting principles. In the nature of the case, a set of accounting principles must be formulated in general terms. The general statement may not cover all of the cases of the particular situation for which a special method is applied since it is universalistic. Or there may be two or more methods which follow from the same principle. That is, the implication of a principle may differ from transaction to transaction. A particular method must be selected when a principle is applied to a particular situation. This means that the interpretation problem of accounting principles is related to the application of a set of principles by a business enterprise in the process of developing and communicating accounting information.

The third problem is that of the consequences, favorable or unfavorable, that follow from conforming to the principles to a greater or lesser degree. These consequences will vary according to the degrees of non-conformity and according to the circumstances in which the deviation occurs. Under a set of accounting principles as a rule for social control, the question of whether or not conformity is achieved cannot be a matter of indifference. This is a problem of sanctions. Without sanctions a set of accounting principles as a rule for social control cannot perform its social function.

Finally, the fourth problem is that of jurisdiction or administration, which deals with the following questions: (1) What authority should have jurisdiction over a given business enterprise in applying a set of accounting principles? (2) To which business enterprise does a given set of accounting principles apply? In other words, this is the problem of maintaining and administering a set of accounting principles as a system for social control.

The foregoing brief discussion of the four concepts as a framework of analysis should enable the identification of the following problems to be discussed in this study:

(1) Legitimation:
1. to identify interest groups for whose service a set of accounting principles has been formulated,
2. to analyze the degree of conformity with accounting theory, and
3. to identify those who have been taking initiative in the formation of a set of accounting principles.

(2) Application:
1. to analyze how accountants in business enterprises have been applying a set of accounting principles in the process of developing accounting information, and
2. to analyze how independent auditors have been interpreting a set of accounting principles in the process of expressing their judgment with respect to the fairness of presentation of accounting information.

(3) Sanctions:
1. to identify what types of sanctions have been used to support a set of accounting principles, and
2. to identify those who have been applying the given sanctions against the violator of a set of accounting principles.

(4) Administration:
1. to analyze what authority has had jurisdiction for the effective administration of a set of accounting principles, and
2. to analyze to which business enterprise a given set of accounting principles has been applied.

The above problems will be discussed in Chapters III, IV, and V to show how each set of accounting principles has performed its conflict-minimizing function in the Japanese society.

CHAPTER II

A HISTORY OF THE DEVELOPMENT OF ACCOUNTING
PRINCIPLES IN JAPAN

A historical perspective is necessary for a meaningful comprehension
of the interrelationship between social developments and accounting
principles. This is one of the basic assumptions of this study. In
accordance with this assumption, as noted in Chapter I, this chapter
provides a brief historical description of the development of the
Japanese industrial society and accounting principles and clarifys
certain relationships among the subject matters to be discussed in the
subsequent chapters. Chapters III, IV, and V will provide the analysis
of each set of accounting principles in terms of Talcott Parsons' framework.

The First Stage: Groping for Uniformity in Financial Reporting (1890-1947)

Predecessors to A Statement of Business Accounting Principles, such
as the Commercial Code, the Working Rules for Financial Statements, and
the Tentative Standards for Financial Statements of Manufacturing
Companies, may not themselves properly be called accounting principles.
They are included in the study, however, for the following reasons: First,
until the pronouncement of A Statement of Business Accounting Principles
in 1949, they performed substitutive functions for it and had a great
influence on its formation, directly or indirectly. Second, since the
establishment of business accounting principles, the Commercial Code
has been performing a supplementary function and the interactions are
too important to be omitted from consideration.

Enactment and Amendments of the Commercial Code. The more than
two thousand years of Japanese history reveals a period of unusual
combinations of upheaval and continuity. The two major upheavals
occurred in 1868 and 1945. The first, called the Meiji Ishin (Meiji
Restoration), gave birth to modern Japan as a follower of advanced
western countries, though many distinctive characteristics of modern
Japan may clearly be traced back as far as the late Tokugawa period.[1]
The Meiji Restoration required Japan to deal with two very difficult
problems. One problem was to revise the several inequitable treaties,
which the Tokugawa was forced to sign under military duress of such
powers as the United States, England, Russia, and Holland. The other
problem was to enact a modern, uniform legal system to secure the legal
status of the Japanese people and to promote the industrial development
of Japan.[2] Although the first problem was directly related to foreign
affairs and the second dealt mainly with the domestic problems, both
areas of concern were closely interrelated. As a first step toward a
solution of these problems, the Meiji Government began the task of
codifying a series of modern laws, such as a Constitution, a Civil Code,
a Commercial Code, and a Criminal Code.

---

[1]Thomas C. Smith, Political Change and Industrial Development in
Japan: Government Enterprise, 1868-1880 (Stanford, California: Stanford
University Press, 1965), p. 1.

[2]Kikuo Nakamura, Kindai Nihon no Hoteki-Keisei - Shinpan (Legal
Formation of Modern Japan - new edition) (Tokyo, Japan: Yushindo, 1963),
pp. 3-10 and Takeyoshi Kawashima, Nihonjin no Ho-Ishiki (Legal Consciousness of the Japanese People) (Tokyo, Japan: Iwanami-Shoten,
1967), pp. 1-4.

The codification of the Japanese Commercial Code was begun in 1881 by a German, Hermann Carl Friedrich Roesler, who was a legal advisor to the Ministry of Justice. The first Commercial Code, which is commonly known as the "Old Commercial Code," was promulgated in 1890 and scheduled to become effective on January 1, 1891. Even before the promulgation of the Old Commercial Code, the Meiji Government enacted a series of regulations concerning merchant ships, banks, railways, and exchanges. They were for the most part of administrative character. Their main purpose was to guide the sound development of business activities and promote the use of the corporate form by business enterprises. Of these regulations, the National Bank Act (1872) and its related regulations had a great influence on the development of the corporate financial reporting system in Japan since (1) they contained the first accounting provisions and the uniform financial statements for the national banks were designed in 1877 based upon an Appendix to the Regulation for National Bank Reporting, and (2) the national banks were the first corporate forms of business organization - Kabushiki-Kaisha (stock corporations) - and promoted the development of corporations in Japan.[3]

---

[3]For the details of these regulations, see the following literature: Masao Fukushima, "Zaisan-Ho--Ho-Taisei Junbiki" (Property Law in the Preparatory Period of the Legal System) in Nobushige Ukai, et al. (eds.), Nihon Kindai-Ho Hattatsushi, I (Historical Development of Japanese Modern Laws, I) (Tokyo, Japan: Keiso-Shobo, 1958), pp. 78-86.

Toshihiko Kato, "Ginko Seido--Ho-Taisei Junbibi" (Bank System in the Preparatory Period of the Legal System) in Nobushige Ukai, et al. (eds.), Nihon Kindai-Ho Hattatsushi, V (Historical Development of Japanese Modern Laws, V) (Tokyo, Japan: Keiso-Shobo, 1958), pp. 137-154.

As early as 1889, opposition to the enforcement of the Civil Code and the Commercial Code began to be voiced. For example, concern was expressed at the disregard of indigenous customs and business operations. As a result of this opposition, the Diet decided in 1892 to postpone the enforcement of both codes until December 31, 1896. Conditions in the business world, however, permitted no further delay in the enforcement of those parts of the Old Commercial Code concerning companies, bills, and bankruptcy and they were declared in effect on January 1, 1893.

After the Diet decided to postpone the Civil and Commercial Codes, the Meiji Government created a new committee, called Hoten Chosa-Kai (Law Research Committee), to prepare new drafts of'the Civil and Commercial Codes. Because the redrafting by the Committee could not be completed on schedule, the date of enforcement of the Old Commercial Code again was postponed. The Committee's work was finally completed in December, 1897, but the Diet was dissolved, because of the political situation of that time, before any action was taken on the Commercial Code. As a result of these circumstances, the anomalous situation developed that the whole of the Old Commercial Code was placed in operation for approximately one year (July 1, 1898 through June 15, 1899).

Kamekichi Takahashi, Meiji Taisho Sangyo Hattatsushi (Historical Development of Japanese Industries in Meiji and Taisho Eras) (Tokyo, Japan: Kashiwa Shobo, 1966), pp. 76-81.

Ichiro Katano, "Nihon Zaimushohyo Seido no Tenkai to Kadai" (Development of Corporate Financial Reporting in Japan and Its Problems), Kigyokaikei (Accounting), Vol. 18, No. 2, (February, 1966), pp. 10-23.

In 1898 the final revised draft, prepared by the Law Research Committee, was approved by the Diet with a few minor modifications.[4] The New Commercial Code contained the following accounting provisions in Book I (General provisions): (1) maintaining trade (or accounting) books (Article 25), (2) preparation of Zaison-Mokuroku (an inventory - a detailed list of all the assets and liabilities) and Taishaku-Taisho-Hyo (a balance sheet) (Article 26-1), and (3) a valuation of properties for an inventory based upon their respective values at the preparation date (article 26-2). Special accounting provisions for Kabushiki-Kaisha (stock corporation), which were contained in Book II, Chapter IV (Stock Corporation), required (1) submitting the following documents by Torishimariyaku (directors) to Kansayaku (statutory auditors); (a) Soneki-Keisan-Sho (an income statement), and (3) Junbikin oyobi Rieki matawa Risoku no Haito ni kansuru Gian (a statement of proposals pertaining to the legal reserve and the distribution of profit or interest during construction) (Article 190), (2) keeping the above documents with the report of the statutory auditors at the main office of the company for the use by shareholders (Article 191), (3) submitting the above documents to the ordinary general meeting of shareholders for their approval and giving publicity to the approved balance sheet (Article 192), (4) retaining a legal reserve from profits and premium on the issuance of stock in excess of par value (Article 194), and (5) prohibiting dividend payment before the full recovery of loss and the regular

---

[4]The New Commercial Code was promulgated as Law No. 48 in March, 1899 and became effective on June 16, 1899.

periodical retention of the legal reserve (article 195).

The New Commercial Code remained unamended for more than ten years although it was not presumed to be free from defects. During this period of enforcement of the Code, many questions were raised regarding the interpretation of individual articles and the inadequacy of the Code was blamed for the emergence of many financially-unsound companies after the Russo-Japanese War. In 1907, a committee was established to revise the Code. An amended draft was approved by the Diet and became effective on October 1, 1911. Although the amended Code was hardly more than an emergency remedy, the following two provisions represented important improvements: (1) the clarification and expansion of directors' responsibilities, and (2) the revision of the general valuation basis for properties from a market-price basis to a lower-than-market-price basis.

During the thirty-year period following the amendment of the Commercial Code, especially after the World War I, the Japanese economy made great progress. The number of big business firms increased and a new trend to separate management from ownership became prominent. Under these circumstances, the actual operation of the Commercial Code, especially those provisions concerning "corporations," revealed many abuses. As a result, the Commercial Code was extensively amended and promulgated in 1938 to cope with the great changes in economic conditions. The following revisions dealt with the tendency toward separation of management from ownership of the corporation: (1) stengthening of the authority of shareholders' meeting (Articles 196, 245, 246, and 375 etc.), (2) the election of non-shareholder director(s) was permitted (Article

254), and (3) the election of non-shareholder statutory auditor(s) was started (Articles 254 and 280). Several significant revisions of accounting provisions were made: (1) a cost-less-depreciation basis for the fixed assets used in business operation was adopted (Article 34-2), (2) recognition of deferred assets, such as (a) organization expense, (b) bond discount, and (c) interest during construction was authorized (Articles 286, 287, and 291-3), and (3) there was general improvement in ways of giving publicity to the financial statements.[5]

In 1938, a law pertaining to the operation of the amendment to the Commercial Code was enacted. Article 49 of that law provided that the manner in which an inventory, a balance sheet, and an income statement of a stock corporation are to be prepared and other forms shall be prescribed by ordinance.[6] Although no ordinance had been passed until the enactment of the Regulation for Corporate Balance Sheets and Income Statements in 1963, it should be noted that the Commercial Code possessed the potential power to prescribe detailed accounting provisions in the framework of law.

Working Rules for Financial Statements by the Ministry of Commerce and Industry. Between the two major upheavals in 1868 and 1945, there were several momentous events which accelerated the industrial develop-

---

[5]For the explanation of "interest during construction," see Toshio Iino, "Accounting Principles and Contemporary Legal Thought in Japan," The International Journal of Accounting Education and Research, Vol. 2, No. 2, (Spring, 1967), p. 67n.

[6]Sumio Fukuda, The New Commercial Code of Japan, (Tokyo, Japan: The Tokyo News Service, Ltd., 1948), p. 371.

ment in Japan. They were the wars which Japan fought with foreign
countries during these eighty years: the Sino-Japanese War (1894-95),
the Russo-Japanese War (1904-5), the First World War (1914-18), and
the Second World War (1941-45). These wars provided the motivating
power for the development of capitalism in Japan. According to the
Marxist's usage of term, the industrial development in Japan during
this period may be characterized as progress along the road of capital-
istic industrialization leading to imperialism.[7] Of these wars, except
the Second World War which destroyed the entire Japanese economy, the
effects of the First World War on the industrial development in Japan
were most profound for two reasons: (1) the war brought an unexampled
prosperity to Japan, and (2) the termination of the war revealed many
difficult economic problems from which Japan suffered for a long time.

The sudden slump of stock prices in March, 1920 halted the boom
and led to the collapse of raw silk and rice prices, the temporary
closing of several banks, and the bankruptcy of some business firms.
The reluctant attitudes of business leaders in developing a sound solution to the economic difficulties, coupled with the unsound financial
policy of the government, made it difficult for the Japanese economy to

---

[7]Mitsuhaya Kajinishi, et al., Nihon ni okeru Shihonshugi no Hattatsu
(The Development of Capitalism in Japan) (Tokyo, Japan: Tokyo University
Press, 1958), pp. 95-103.

alleviate the effects of the depression for several years.[8] Before the

Japanese economy could recover fully from the depression, a great earth-

quake around the Tokyo area (1923), the bank crisis (1923), and the

world-wide panic (1929) buffeted the Japanese economy in succession.

Large political states, such as Russia, Great Britain, and the United

States, could weather the impact of world depression for they had their

own sources of supply for most raw materials and their own consumer

markets. But a small country, such as Japan, dependent on other lands

for most of its raw materials, and on China, India, and the Occident for

a vital part of its export market, seemed entirely at the mercy of the

tariff policies of other nations.[9] Foreign markets for export were also

essential for Japan to support her expanded population of more than sixty

millions in the narrow islands of Japan. Japan's answers to higher

---

[8]Kamekichi Takahashi describes the attitudes of business leaders
in Japan at that time as follows:
    The financial adjustments of business firms after the
    depression in 1920 were not implemental in a normal
    way but temporized by concealing losses and reporting
    paper profits to avoid losing credit standing. Many
    business leaders dreamed of a windfall recovery of
    economic conditions in a short period of time. This type
    of patching was also supported by bankers.
(Kamekichi Takahashi, Taisho Showa Zaikai Hendo-Shi -Jo- [The Changing
Japanese Business World in Taisho and Showa Eras, I] [Tokyo, Japan:
Tokyo Keizai Shinpo-Sha, 1954], p. 431.)
Taisho Era in Japan started in 1912 and ended in 1925, and Showa Era
started in 1926.

[9]Edwin O. Reischauer, Japan -- Past and Present (3rd ed. rev.)
(Tokyo, Japan: Charles E. Tuttle Company, Inc., 1964), p. 164 and
Kajinishi, et al., op. cit., pp. 229-30.

protective tariffs by foreign powers and to a trend of international

economy, such as the formation of a broad economic bloc by Great Britain,

were (1) to follow the old, historical program of colonial expansion, and

(2) to develop a nation-wide movement toward industrial rationalization.

The first answer resulted in an effort to win, by a colonial expan-

sion, the sources of raw materials and the markets needed to make Japan

self-sufficient and invulnerable as a world power. This was advocated

first by the reactionary and militaristic groups but gradually obtained

public support. The government initiated a powerful movement of indus-

trial rationalization at home by establishing advisory councils such as

the Commerce and Industry Council (1927) and the Economy Council (1928).

In 1930, the Hamaguchi Cabinet reorganized the Commerce and Industry

Council into the Temporary Industry Council and argued the necessity for

the industrial rationalization.[10]

Following the reorganization of the Council, the government created

the Temporary Industrial Rationalization Bureau in the Ministry of Commerce

---

[10]Prime Minister Yuko Hamaguchi addressed at the first general
meeting of the Temporary Industry Council on February 3, 1930 as follows:
.... As all of you know, the necessity for the industrial
rationalization was well recognized in the powerful industrial nations such as the United States and Germany and
the governments as well as peoples of these countries have
endeavored to secure the successful conversion of the wartime economy into the peacetime economy.
In Japan, however, the adjustment of the wartime
economy has not been completed. Many lines of rapidly
expanded industries, stimulated by the increased demands
during the war, are now at a disadvantage since the domestic
market is open to the menace of keen competitions with
European countries and the United States on the one hand
and the foreign export markets obtained during the wartime
are gradually being recaptured on the other hand. If we
neglect the fundamental rearrangement of our industries at
this time, we could not expect future prosperity for our
country in the keen competitive international economy.

and Industry in May, 1930 to implement its industrial rationalization
policy. The Temporary Industrial Rationalization Bureau was composed
of two divisions. Division I, which included experts from the related
areas, concentrated on fundamental research for rationalization. Division II, which was composed of officers from the Ministry of Commerce
and Industry, dealt mainly with practical problems for business control
and export promotion. Under Division I of the Bureau, several standing
and temporary committees were established such as the Production Management Committee, the Financial Management Committee, the Consumption
Economy Committee, the Control Committee, and the Product Standardization Research Committee.[11]

We have many things to do for the reconstruction of our
industries. First of all, the industrial rationalization is
a matter of great urgency.... In view of the present status
of our industries, I believe that the control of business
enterprise, the thorough improvement of efficiency, the improvement of industrial finance, and the encouragement of
the buy-Japanese products-policy are among the most urgent
problems for the industrial rationalization movement. I
submit these questions to your council for your advices....
(quoted in Nihon Ginko, Chosa Kyoku [The Bank of Japan, Research Bureau],
Nihon Kinyu-Shi Shiryo -- Showa-Hen, VII [The Data on the Financial
History of Japan -- Showa Era Section, VII] [Tokyo, Japan: Ministry
of Finance, Printing Bureau, 1963] , pp. 440-41.)

[11]Yoshio Ando, Showa Keizai-Shi eno Shogen -Jo- (A Witness to the
Economic History of Showa Era, I) (Tokyo, Japan: Mainichi-Shinbun-Sha,
1965), pp. 116-30. Yu Noguchi, Nihon Shihon-Shugi Keiei-Shi -- Senzen-Hen
(The Development of Japanese Capitalism from the Viewpoint of Business
History -- Pre-war Section) (Tokyo, Japan: Ochanomizu-Shobo, 1960),
p. 160.

One of the main tasks assigned to the Financial Management Committee was improvement and unification of financial statements of business enterprises. Although financial statements, such as an inventory, a balance sheet, and an income statement, were being prepared periodically by companies based upon the accounting provisions in the Commercial Code, their form vaired from company to company and they did not provide a true and fair picture of business activities. After four years of deliberation, the Committee published the Working Rules for Financial Statements in August 1934. Their purpose was stated as follows:

> A balance sheet, an inventory, and an income statement, which present an integrated result of business accounting, are essential data for reviewing the performance of a business enterprise. Although working rules and forms for financial statements used in special business, such as banking, insurance, electricity, and railway, are prescribed in special regulations, no general working rules have been established for other industries and financial statements prepared by companies are of wide variety. Most financial statements are not very helpful in obtaining for readers true information on business activities because of incompleteness in reporting and window-dressing. If an attempt to improve and develop the business did not include an improvement and unification of financial statements, the business enterprise could not expect a successful improvement of its business operation and shareholders and creditors would suffer from unexpected losses. This is the reason for the necessity for true and fair presentation of financial statements not only for the improvement of private enterprises but also for the sound development of national economy.[12]

The Working Rules for Financial Statements were published as an important method to promote the industrial rationalization movement by the improvement of financial statements. The Committee strongly urged all

[12]Quoted in Ichiro Katano, "Nihon Zaimushohyo Seido no Tenkai to Kadai -5-" (Development of Corporate Financial Reporting in Japan and Its Problems -5-), Kigyokaikei (Accounting), Vol. 18, No. 9, (September, 1966), p. 28.

business enterprises to follow these working rules in the preparation of
financial statements based upon the Commercial Code although they were
not promulgated as law. The Working Rules for Financial Statements
included (1) Working Rules for the Balance Sheet, (2) Working Rules for
the Inventory, and (3) Working Rules for the Income Statement with illustrations of financial statements to be used by industrial and trading
companies. In addition to these rules, the Committee published the
Working Rules for Assets Valuation in February, 1936, designed substantially to improve financial statements. All of these rules supplemented
the incomplete accounting provisions contained in the Commercial Code.

After the Manchurian Incident, the industrial rationalization movement was further accelerated by more direct measures. Cartels were
formed in many lines of major industries. Mergers were promoted in the
iron and steel and banking areas. These measures were adopted by the
government and based on the Major Industries Control Law which was promulgated in 1931.[13] The industrial rationalization movement, which was
initiated by the government to allow the Japanese economy to recover
from the depression, promoted the concentration of capital in large
economic units and then the rapid expansion of the Zaibatsu (economic
cliques), such as Mitsui, Mitsubishi, Sumitomo, and Yasuda. With the

[13]For the legal background of the government control over the
Japanese industries, see Yoshio Kanazawa, "Sangyo-Ho -- Ho-Taisei
Saihenki" (Industrial Law in the Rearrangement Period of the Legal
System) in Nobushige Ukai, et al. (eds.), Nihon Kindai-Ho Hattatsushi,
IV (Historical Development of Japanese Modern Laws, IV) (Tokyo,
Japan: Keiso Shobo, 1958), pp. 275-319. For the economic background,
see Ando, op. cit., pp. 245-67.

expansion of the munitions industry after the Incident, several new
Zaibatsu concerns were formed in the chemical, machine tools, and mining
industries. Thus, the industrial rationalization movement played an
unexpected role in transferring the Japanese economy from a peacetime,
free economy to a wartime, controlled economy.

Tentative Standards for Financial Statements of Manufacturing Companies by the Planning Board. The economic development in Japan since
the Meiji Restoration had been much influenced by the political developments at home and abroad. The war years of 1937-45 were the most fateful
period in the entire history of Japan. The formation of the sterling
bloc by Great Britain and its allied nations based upon the Ottawa agreement in 1932 was followed by the formation of other economic blocs, such
as the dollar bloc by the United States, the gold bloc by France, and
the East European block by Germany. The formation of several economic
blocs did not unfortunately provide for peaceful coexistence but rather
seemed to promote international conflicts.[14] Under these circumstances,
the Japanese yen bloc was expanded after the China Incident near Peking
in North China in July, 1937 by military extremists without either the
knowledge or the expressed approval of the Japanese government.[15]

After the outbreak of war in Europe in 1939, the United States began
to aid Britain and took a more positive stand against Japanese aggression

[14]Mitsuhaya Kajinishi, et al., Nihon Shihonshugi no Botsuraku, III
(The Decline of Japanese Capitalism, III) (Tokyo, Japan: Tokyo University
Press, 1963), p. 614.

[15]Reischauer, op. cit., p. 187.

in China. The old policies of verbal protests and non-recognition of Japanese conquests were supplemented by economic sanctions, which hurt Japan far more than verbal protests. The economic sanctions by the United States began with the denunciation of the 1911 U.S. - Japan Trading Treaty in July, 1939. Shipments of machine tools and scrap iron were stopped in 1940. Japanese assets abroad were frozen. With the co-operation of the British and the Dutch, shipments of oil were suspended. Imports of scrap iron and oil were vital to the Japanese economy, especially to the war machine production.[16] Thus, Japan was becoming economically isolated.

Two choices were open to Japan. It could bring the war in China to an end or it could expand the yen bloc to Manchukou, Inner Mongolia, China, and even to South-East Asia. Despite the early localization policy of the Japanese government concerning the China Incident, the war in China was expanded endlessly. After four years of war with China, the Japanese government had a chance to terminate the war in conversations between Secretary of State Hull of the United States and Japanese Ambassador Nomura in March, 1941, which Ambassador Kurusu also joined in November. Japan, however, lost the chance to terminate the war with China, and mutual misunderstandings between the United States and Japan led to a new war, which should never have been fought, on December 7, 1941.[17]

---

[16]Ibid., pp. 189-91 and Mitsuhaya Kajinishi, et al., Nihon Shihon-Shugi no Botsuraku, IV (The Decline of Japanese Capitalism, IV) (Tokyo, Japan: Tokyo University Press, 1964), p. 920.

[17]Jerome B. Cohen, Japan's Economy in War and Reconstruction (Minneapolis, Minnesota: University of Minnesota Press, 1949), p. 48.

With the expansion of the war, the government adopted strong policies of centralizing its control over the entire economy. In October, 1938, the Kikaku-In (Planning Board) was established as a central government agent for planning and controlling a wartime economy. The economic policy of the Japanese government was crystalized in Kokka So-Doin Ho (National General Mobilization Law), which was drafted by the Planning Board and promulgated in 1938, over considerable opposition by Japanese businessmen. This law provided for the control and utilization of all human and goods resources for the purposes of "national defense." The law was to be enforced by Imperial Order, that is, by a sole decision of the cabinet, and no action of the Diet was required. Under its authority a great variety of ordinances were issued regulating all phases of economic life in Japan.[18] Of these ordinances, Kaisha Keiri Tosei-Rei (Corporate Accounting Control Ordinance) should be noted as it provided the groundwork for the publication of the Tentative Standards for Financial Statements of Manufacturing Companies by the Planning Board in 1941.[19]

The Corporate Accounting Control Ordinance had two important features. The first feature of the ordinance was the advocacy of a new concept of

---

[18]Ibid., p. 11 and E. B. Schumpeter, "Industrial Development and Government Policy," in E. B. Schumpeter (ed.), The Industrialization of Japan and Manchukuo 1930-40 (New York: The Macmillan Company, 1940), p. 821.

[19]The Corporate Accounting Control Ordinance was promulgated as Imperial Order No. 680 in October, 1940, under the authority of Article 11 of the National General Mobilization Law. It included six chapters: (1) general provisions, (2) dividends payment and special reserve, (3) salaries of officers and employees, (4) expenses and funds management, (5) accounting examination, and (6) miscellaneous provisions.

the corporation in a new totalitarian economic order.[20] The second fea-

ture was the requirement for corporations to prepare an inventory, a

balance sheet, an income statement, and a cost report in accordance with

provisions of a cabinet order and to evaluate the assets, which were to

be listed in the inventory, as prescribed by a cabinet order (Article 36).

When the Corporate Accounting Control Ordinance was enforced in October,

1940, however, neither the Working Rules for Financial Statements by the

Ministry of Commerce and Industry of 1934 nor an ordinance based upon the

revised Commercial Code of 1938 was enacted. Thus, the government needed

to establish a set of new accounting standards as a cabinet order to

enforce the Ordinance and requested the Planning Board to prepare such

a set of standards. The Uniform Financial Statements Council, which was

established in the Planning Board, released the "Tentative Manual for

Cost Accounting of Manufacturing Companies" in August, 1941, and the

"Tentative Standards for Financial Statements of Manufacturing Companies"

in November, 1941. The Tentative Standards for Financial Statements of

[20]Yasubei Hasegawa, "Keiri Tosei no Zenbo" (An Entire Picture of
Accounting Control), Waseda Shogaku (Waseda Commercial Review), Vol. 16,
No. 4, (January, 1941), p. 4. Article 2 of the Ordinance reads:
Corporation shall understand that the main purpose of
business management be to share responsibilities for
national economy to achieve the nation's objectives
and observe the following matters on accounting;
  1. Funds shall be applied in the most effective
     way and any misuse of human and goods
     resources shall be avoided.
  2. Amount of expenses and depreciation for fixed
     assets shall be adequate.
  3. Amount and payment methods of salaries of
     officers and employees shall be adequate.
  4. Distribution of profits shall be adequate
     to secure the accumulation of corporate
     funds.

Manufacturing Companies included "Tentative Standards for Balance Sheets."

"Tentative Standards for Inventories," and "Tentative Standards for Income

Statements."

As with the Working Rules for Financial Statements published by the

Ministry of Commerce and Industry, this statement of Tentative Standards

was not issued as a cabinet order as originally scheduled. The Tentative

Standards were, however, the last of the series of devices designed by

the government for the central control of the economy in wartime: The

National General Mobilization Law -- The Corporate Accounting Control

Ordinance -- The Tentative Standards for Financial Statements of Manu-

facturing Companies. In the year previous to the publication of the

Tentative Standards by the Planning Board, the Ministry of the Navy and

the Ministry of the Army published pamphlets entitled "The Manual for

Preparing Financial Statements in the Factories of Munitions for the Navy"

and "The Working Rules for Financial Statements of the Factories of

Munitions for the Army." The purpose of these pamphlets was for both

Ministries to exercise direct control over the munitions factories.

The Second Stage: Establishment and Improvement of A Statement of Business

Accounting Principles (1947-1962).

Instructions for the Preparation of Financial Statements of Manu-

facturing and Trading Companies by General Headquarters, Supreme Com-

mander for the Allied Powers (GHQ, SCAP). The second, but the most

drastic, upheaval in Japanese history occurred on August 14, 1945 when

Japan accepted the terms of the Potsdam Proclamation which suggested to the Japanese people the path of reason rather than the control by the self-willed militaristic advisers.[21] Following the acceptance of the Potsdam Proclamation, the first page of the history of the new Japan began with the occupation by the Allied Powers, actually by the United States. The occupation by the Allied Powers lasted for six and a half years until the peace treaty with forty-eight nations went into effect on April 28, 1952. During the period of occupation, the authority of the Emperor and Japanese Government to rule the state was subject to the Supreme Commander for the Allied Powers (SCAP).[22] This meant that all phases of Japanese life were governed by the orders, instructions, and memoranda issued by SCAP and that the Japanese government was but an agency to reproduce and execute them as its own laws and ordinances.

The basic policies of occupation by the Allied Powers at the initial stage were directed by the terms of the "Potsdam Proclamation" and the "United States Initial Post-Surrender Policy For Japan," which was prepared jointly by the State, War, and Navy Departments, approved by the President, and sent to the late General Douglas MacArthur, Supreme

---

[21]For the details of political situations in Japan before the acceptance of the Potsdam Proclamation, see Robert J. C. Butow, Japan's Decision to Surrender (Stanford, California: Stanford University Press, 1954).

[22]U.S. Department of State, Occupation of Japan -- Policy and Progress (Publication 2671, Far Eastern Series 17) (Washington, D.C., n. d.), p. 62.

Commander for the Allied Powers, on August 29, 1945.[23] The reconstruc-

tion plan for the Japanese economy after the war was based upon three

basic policies stated in the "United States Initial Post-Surrender Policy

For Japan:" (1) Economic Demilitarization, (2) Promotion of Democratic

Forces, and (3) Resumption of Peaceful Economic Activity. Although these

three policies are interrelated with one another, the second one greatly

influenced the reconstruction and improvement of the business accounting

system in Japan after World War II.

Under the caption, "Promotion of Democratic Forces," the "United

States Initial Post Surrender Policy for Japan" states:

> Encouragement shall be given and favor shown to the develop-
> ment of organizations in labor, industry, and agriculture,
> organized on a democratic basis. Policies shall be favored
> which permit a wide distribution of income and of the owner-
> ship of the means of production and trade.
>
> Those forms of economic activity, organization and leadership
> shall be favored that are deemed likely to strengthen the peace-
> ful disposition of the Japanese people, and to make it difficult
> to command or direct economic activity in support of military
> ends. To this end it shall be the policy of the Supreme Commander:
> (a) To prohibit the retnetion in or selection for places of
>   importance in the economic field of individuals who do
>   not direct future Japanese economic effort solely towards
>   peaceful ends; and
> (b) To favor a program for the dissolution of the large
>   industrial and banking combinations which have exercised
>   control over a great part of Japan's trade and industry.[24]

In this statement, "the large industrial and banking combinations" meant

the so-called "Zaibatsu." The Zaibatsu was regarded by the authorities of

the Allied Powers as among the groups principally responsible for the war

---

[23]Ibid., pp. 53-55 and pp. 73-81.

[24]Ibid., pp. 78-79.

and as a primary factor in the Japanese war potential.[25] In other words, it was the _Zaibatsu_ who, in concert with the Japanese military, organized and participated in the war of imperialist aggression.[26] Therefore, it was considered essential to depose the _Zaibatsu_, break their stranglehold on economic enterprise, and give the ordinary businessman a stake in a democratic nation in order to reorganize Japan on a peaceful basis.

The program to dissolve the _Zaibatsu_ began with the release by SCAP of the memorandum "Dissolution or Liquidation of Major Financial or Industrial Enterprise," dated October 20, 1945 (SCAPIN-162).[27] While SCAP expected the _Zaibatsu_,such as Mitsui, Mitsubishi, Sumitomo, and Yasuda, to implement the dissolution program by themselves, it began its own activity by gathering information on these firms and releasing a memorandum "Reports to be Made by Certain Business Firms," dated October 25, 1945 (SCAPIN-177).[28] The SCAPIN-177 reads:

1. It is directed that the following named financial, commercial and industrial firms in Japan provide the information specified in inclosure 1 and inclosure 2. Mitsui Honsha,

[25]U.S. Department of State, _Report of the Mission on Japanese Combines -- Part I: Analytical and Technical Data_ (Publication 2628, Far Eastern Series 14) (Washington, D.C., March, 1946), p. vii.

[26]Economic and Scientific Section, GHQ, SCAP, _Mission and Accomplishments of the Occupation in the Economic and Scientific Fields_ (Tokyo, Japan: Economic and Scientific Section, September 26, 1949), p. 20.

[27]The abbreviation "SCAPIN" will be used hereafter for "Supreme Commander for the Allied Power's Instruction." Every SCAPIN has a consequutive number. For the text of SCAPIN-162, see General Headquarters, Supreme Commander for the Allied Powers, _SCAPINS -- from 4 September, 1945 to 8 March,1952_, (Tokyo, Japan: General Headquarters, Supreme Commander for the Allied Powers, 20 March, 1952), p. 25.

[28]_Ibid._, pp. 27-29.

Mitsubishi Honsha, Sumitomo Honsha, Yasuda Hazensha,
Kewasaki and Co., Nissan and Co., Asano Honsha, Fuji
Industrial Co., Shibusawa Dozoku and Co., Nippon Nitro-
genous Fertilizer Mfg. Co., Furukawa and Co., Okura and
Co., Nomura and Co., Riken and Co., Nisso Co.
Similar reports will be required from other firms to be
added to the above list from time to time.

2. Inclosure 1 will be used in reporting an industrial or
   commercial enterprise. Inclosure 2 will be used in
   reporting a bank or other financial institution.
3. It is considered that submittal of such information
   should be completed within 45 days from date of receipt
   of this directive. As noted in inclosed forms, each
   section of report will be submitted separately as completed.
4. (Omitted)

The following excerpt from the Inclosure 1, which was to be used in
reporting commercial and industrial companies, provides a major clue for
the explanation for the release by the General Headquarters (GHQ), SCAP
of a pamphlet entitled "Instructions for the Preparation of Financial
Statements of Manufacturing and Trading Companies" in 1948:

1. Each of thereporting companies will submit a separate
   report for itself and for each of its subsidiaries on
   financial and other allied matters as more fully
   described in the following paragraphs.
2. For the purpose of this directive, a subsidiary is
   defined as any corporation, partnership, or association for the purpose of doing business in which the
   reporting company is directly or indirectly the owner
   of, or enjoys other beneficial interest in 10% or
   more of any one class of stock or indebtedness outstanding, or exercises control to the extent of 10%
   or more over voting controlling operations or policy.
3. a. All reports will be prepared in English according
   to the principle and in the form of the best accounting practices current in the United States.
4. (Omitted)
5. (Omitted)
6. The report will be divided into sections, each section
   to correspond in numbering and in content with the
   following subparagraphs.
   a. Section 1. EARNINGS.
   b. Section 2. BALANCE SHEET.
   c. Section 3. CAPITALIZATION.
   d. Section 4. CONTROL.
   e. Section 5. REALESTATE, PLANT & EQUIPMENT.
   f. Section 6. INVESTMENT.

g. Section 7.   CURRENT ASSETS.
h. Section 8.   CURRENT LIABILITIES.
i. Section 9.   SALES
j. Section 10. COST OF SALES.
k. Section 11. MANAGEMENT FEES.
l. Section 12. PUBLIC STATEMENTS.

7. If reporting company cannot comply with any of the terms of this directive or the attached annex, a report of non-compliance will be submitted together with the reasons therefor. Reference will be made in such report to the corresponding paragraph in this letter of instructions.

8. (Omitted)

To the fifteen holding companies listed in SCAPIN-177, a memorandum "Establishment of a Schedule of restricted Concerns," dated December 8, 1945 (SCAPIN-403), added Hitachi Ltd., Manchuria Investment Securities Co. Ltd., and Nichiden Industrial Co. along with 336 subsidiaries or affiliates of 18 holding companies. The change gave evidence of SCAP's growing need for information on combine structures, mainly as a result of data submitted in response to SCAPIN-177.[29]

Financial statements submitted by the "restricted" companies to the GHQ, SCAP were said to be deplorable and proved of little use to the authority. As the number of the restricted companies increased to 643 by the end of April, 1946, the officials of the Research and Statistics Division, Economic and Scientific Section, thought it absolutely necessary to establish some regulations for the preparation of financial statements.[30]

_____

[29]T. A. Bisson, Zaibatsu Dissolution in Japan (Berkeley and Los Angeles: University of California Press, 1954), p. 81.

[30]Takeo Suzuki, "Seigen-Kaisha Ichiranhyo Settei ni Kansuru Oboegaki" (Memorandum Concerning the Establishment of a Schedule of Restricted Concerns), Nihon Kanri Horei Kenkyu (Japan Occupation Law Review), Vol. 1, No. 6, (September 1, 1946), p. 46. The schedule eventually listed a total of 1,203 companies in which the Zaibatsu held direct stock interest. (Economic and Scientific Section, GHQ, SCAP, op. cit., p. 21.)

William G. Hessler, CPA, of the Research and Statistics Division asked

the late Gen Murase to make the first draft of such regulations. First,

Gen Murase translated into English two Japanese statements on accounting.

They are: (1) "Tentative Standards for Financial Statements of Manufactur-

ing Companies" by the Planning Board (1941) and (2) "The Manuals for

Costing in Manufacturing Companies" by the Planning Board (1942). Murase,

then, wrote the first draft by comparing these translated statements

with statements of American accounting principles, such as A Statement

of Accounting Principles by Sanders, Hatfield, and Moore (1938) and

Accounting Principles by the American Accounting Association (1936,

1941).[31] According to Murase, in three weeks Hessler and Murase pre-

pared a pamphlet entitled "Instruction for the Preparation of Financial

Statements of Manufacturing and Trading Companies" based upon Murase's

first draft in 1947.[32]

The introduction of the GHQ "Instructions" states its purpose as
follows:

> The primary purpose of this manual of instructions is to assist
> Japanese companies in the preparation of the type of clear,
> intelligible financial reports required by SCAP authorities
> from time to time in connection with SCAP's effort to establish
> in Japan a sound, democratic, industrial economy.

---

[31]Thomas Henry Sanders, Henry Rand Hatfield, and Underhill Moore,
A Statement of Accounting Principles (New York: American Institute of
Accountants, 1938) The Executive Committee of the American Accounting
Association, "A Tentative Statement of Accounting Principles Affecting
Corporate Reports," The Accounting Review, Vol. XI, No. 2, (June, 1936),
pp. 187-191. The Executive Committee of the American Accounting Associa-
tion, "Accounting Principles Underlying Corporate Financial Statements,"
The Accounting Review, Vol. XVI, No. 2, (June, 1941), pp. 133-39.

[32]Gen Murase, "Nichi, Ei, Bei Sangoku ni okeru Kaikei-Genoku Seitei
no Yurai" (A Brief History of the Establishment of Accounting Principles
in Japan, England, and the United States), Kigyokaikei (Accounting), Vol.
6, No. 1, (January, 1954), p. 112.

A secondary purpose is to lay the foundation for improving
and standardizing Japanese commercial and industrial accounting practices. Statements furnished to SCAP in the past
have disclosed deplorable shortcoming in accounting practices
and procedures. Japanese business concerns will find it
desirable to make necessary changes in their own classification of ledger accounts to enable them to complete the prescribed statements from the periodic trial balances drawn
from their accounting records.33

Thus, the first step toward the democratization of the Japanese economy,

that is, the dissolution of the Zaibatsu companies started with the col-

lection by SCAP of accounting information on these companies.

Establishment of A Statement of Business Accounting Principles. The

second step designed to democratize the Japanese economy was to promote

a wide distribution of income and the ownership of the business enterprise.

The securities, held by the holding companies and the designated persons

(the Zaibatsu families), were to be transferred to the Holding Company

Liquidation Commission which was established to perform the liquidation

program in April, 1946.34 The shares transferred by the holding companies

and the designated persons numbered 164 million shares with paid-up value

of 7.4 billion yen.35 In addition to this Commission, other governmental

agencies, such as the Ministry of Finance, the Closed Institution Liquida-

tion Commission, and the Fair Trade Commission, were required to dispose

---

33Research and Statistics Division, Economic and Scientific Section,
GHQ, SCAP, Instructions for the Preparation of Financial Statements of
Manufacturing and Trading Company (Tokyo, Japan: Research and Statistics
Division, Economic and Scientific Section, GHQ, SCAP, 1947), pp. 1-2.

34For the English text of "The Holding Company Liquidation Commission Ordinance" (Imperial Ordinance No. 233), see Bisson, op. cit.,
pp. 245-51.

35Holding Company Liquidation Commission, Nihon Zaibatsu to sono
Kaitai (Japanese Zaibatso and Their Dissolution) (Tokyo, Japan: Holding
Company Liquidation Commission, 1951), p. 454.

of about 9 billion yen worth of securities appropriated to the payment

of property taxes or transferred based upon the provisions of the Anti-

Trust Law. In 1947, the Securities Coordinating Liquidation Committee

was established to promote disposal operations of securities in a demo-

cratic manner. Employees and local residents of the companies were

given priority in the purchase of securities.

Most of Japan's largest companies faced bankruptcy, as a result of

extensive war losses, at the end of the war. To avoid the ruin of the

national economy, several business enterprise laws were enacted in 1946

requiring a special type of financial reorganization without bankruptcy.

Some 4,990 companies submitted to this reorganization procedure. These

companies, called "Special Accounting" companies, needed to issue nearly

50 billion yen of new capital stock.[36] Under these circumstances, the

development of a sound and democratic securities market became urgent.

Since Japan became westernized, however, the banks and the government

have been the only important sources of external capital available to

the Japanese enterprises and most Japanese people have not been accustomed

to making direct investment through the securities market. In response

to the request of SCAP, the "security democratization" movement was ini-

tiated by the Japanese government and many associations of businessmen.[37]

[36]Economic and Scientific Section, GHQ, SCAP, op. cit., p. 22.

[37]In a press conference on October 4, 1946, Edward G. Welsch, Chief
of the Antitrust and Cartels Division, GHQ, urged Japanese people to
make every effort in purchasing of temporarily government-owned securities
for the democratic prosperity of the Japanese economy. (quoted in Takeo
Suzuki, "Shoken no Minshuka" [Security Democratization] Nihon Kanri
Horei Kenkyu [Japan Occupation Law Review] , No. 20, [June 1, 1948] , p. 106.)

The fair protection of the investors and fair transactions in securities were among important prerequisities to the development of a sound and democratic securities market for the public. To this end a Securities Exchange Act was first promulgated in March, 1947, but was not enforced until it was entirely revised in 1948. The revised Act came into operation in May, 1948. The Securities Exchange Act of Japan was modelled on the 1933 Securities Act and 1934 Securities Exchange Act in the United States although the economic background of the enactment of these Acts in both countries was not identical. The purpose of the Act was to permit and facilitate fair issuance and transfer procedures, as well as other transactions in securities, and to provide for the orderly exchange of securities to make possible a rational administration of the national economy in addition to protecting the investors (Article 1). The importance of an informed shareholders group, both present and potential, for the sound development of the national economy was first recognized by this Act.

As Tetsuzo Ota noted, the development of a sound, democratic securities market should be backed up by the establishment of an effective auditing system.[38] Article 193 of the old Securities Exchange Act suggested the possibility of an audit of financial statements by the public accountants in the public interest. This Article allowed two choices for the public accountants as auditors: <u>Keirishi</u> (Registered Public Accountants) or <u>Konin-Kaikeishi</u> (Certified Public Accountants).

---

[38]Tetsuzo Ota, "Shoken-Shihon Sei no Fukki to sono Jyoken" (Conditions for the Resumption of Security Capital Market), in Yasutaro Harai (ed.) <u>Keiei-Keiri to Konin-Kaikeishi</u> (Business Accounting and Certified Public Accountants) (Tokyo, Japan: Kunimoto Shobo, 1949), p. 12.

As mentioned earlier, the Commercial Codes of Japan have required all
stock corporations to have __Kansayaku__ (Statutory Auditors) since the first
enforcement. Statutory auditors, however, have not necessarily made the
substantial audits which the Commercial Code expected of them. Apart
from the Commercial Code, the Registered Public Accountant Law was enforced in 1927 to promote the development of the accounting profession
in Japan. During the years from 1927 through 1948, more than twenty-five
thousand accountants registered as Registered Public Accountants under
this law. Most of them were deficient as to their qualifications,
independence, and discipline compared with Certified Public Accountants
and Chartered Accountants in the United States and England.[39]

In addition to the security democratization, a major influx of
foreign capital was regarded as another essential requirement for the
reconstruction of the post-war Japanese economy. To meet these requirements, the revision of the old system of registered accountants seemed
to be incomplete. After deliberations by the Investigation Committee on
a Public Accountants System, which was established in the Ministry of
Finance, the Japanese government decided to establish a completely new
CPA system comparable to that of the United States. Thus, the Certified
Public Accountants Law was promulgated as Law No. 103 in July, 1948. By

---

[39]Although the earliest activities of professional accountants in
Japan perhaps date back to the beginning of the twentieth century, the
profession was legally recognized by the Registered Public Accountants
Law in 1927. For the development of the Registered Public Accountants,
see Shigeru Uchiyama, "Nihon Konin-Kaikeishi Seido" (Certified Public
Accountants System in Japan), in __Kaikei-Kansa__ (Auditing) (Tokyo, Japan:
Shunjusha, 1951), pp. 167-76 and Kiyoshi Kurosawa, __Kaikeigaku__ (Account-
ing) (Tokyo, Japan: Chikura Shobo, 1947), pp. 120-24.

the enactment of the Securities Exchange Act and the Certified Public Accountants Law, financial statements prepared by the listed stock corporations were required to be audited by Certified Public Accountants. This was one of the causes for the establishment in 1949 of A Statement of Business Accounting Principles which constitutes "generally accepted accounting principles" in Japan.

The movement toward the establishment of accounting principles was initiated by a study group of Japanese accounting educators and businss-men. They had a prepatory meeting in February, 1948, to establish an Accounting System and Education Commission.[40] In March, 1948, the study group submitted the following recommendation on business accounting to the Prime Minister Ashida:

> The improvement of business accounting system is one of the most urgent tasks for the democratic reconstruction of the Japanese economy. Since business accounting practices in Japan, as compared with those in the Western Countries, are far behind, it is presently difficult to understand financial conditions and results of operations of business enterprises.

---

[40] In the Fall of 1947, the late Michisuke Ueno[x] and Kiyoshi Kurosawa[xx] were requested by the Economic and Scientific Section, GHQ, SCAP to conduct research on the following problems:
1. Improvement of "The GHQ Instructions for the Preparation of Financial Statements of Manufacturing and Trading Companies."
2. Establishment of a standard bookkeeping system for small and medium sized business firms.
3. Preparation of standard textbooks on bookkeeping and accounting.

Following this request, they organized a study group of accounting educators and businessmen. (Kiyoshi Kurosawa, "Kaikei-Gensoku no Kaisei Mondai" [Some Problems on the Amendment to the Business Accounting Principles], Kaikei [Accounting] Vol. 66, No. 1, [July, 1954] , pp. 8-9.)
   x Professor of Accunting at Tokyo University and Chairman of the Investi-gation Committee on Business Accounting System.
  xx Professor of Accunting at Yokohama National University and a chief drafter of A Statment of Business Accounting Principles.

Unless business accounting is modernized and a scientific
foundation for the sound development of the Japanese economy
is established, it is difficult to find a basis for
the industrial reconstruction by the induction of foreign
capital and it is impossible for business accounting to contribute anything to the solution of the closely related
problems, such as prices stabilization, business finance
rationalization, security democratization, protection of public
investors, fair taxation, and the utilization of accounting
information for the improvement of labor relations. Therefore,
the establishment of an Accounting System and Education Commission is promptly required to improve business accounting and
conduct basic research on the fundamental reform of accounting
education. It is also necessary to establish an organization
to execute and diffuse the research products of the Commission.[41]

This recommendation was accepted by the Ashida Cabinet in June, 1948, and

the Investigation Committee on Business Accounting System was established

in July, 1948, in the organizational structure of the Economic Stabili-

zation Board which was attached to the cabinet.[42] After a year's

deliberation, the Committee, consisting of many noted men from the ranks

of accounting professors, businessmen, and top-ranking governmental

officials, released in July, 1949, as an interim report, two pamphlets

entitled A Statement of Business Accounting Principles and Working Rules

for Preparing Financial Statements.

Although the authorities of GHQ, SCAP suggested the preparation of

the "Working Rules for Preparing Financial Statements," the Committee

did not limit its work to the preparation of the "Working Rules" but it

---

[41]Quoted in Michisuke Ueno, "Waga Kuni Keizai Saiken ni okeru
Kaikeigaku no Igi" (The Significance of Accunting for the Reconstruction
of the Japanese Economy), Kaikei (Accounting), Vol. 56, No. 1, (February,
1949), pp. 9-10.

[42]The name and organization of the Committee was later changed to the
Business Accounting Standards Deliberation Council in May, 1950, and still
later to its present name, the Business Accounting Deliberation Council
when it became a consultative body to the Ministry of Finance in August,
1952.

spent much time in discussing business accounting principles. A Statement

of Business Accounting Principles is the first written prounouncement of

so-called "generally accepted accounting principles" which Certified

Public Accountants must observe when they audit financial statements and

express their opinions on them based upon the Securities Exchange Act

and the Certified Public Accountants Law. The movement for the improve-

ment and unification of the Japanese financial reporting system after

World War II thus was based upon the Securities Exchange Act, the Certified

Public Accountant Law, and A Statement of Business Accounting Principles.

In addition, the Securities and Exchange Commission (SEC) of Japan, which

was established in 1948 based upon the Securities Exchange Act, released

in September, 1950, "Regulation for Wording, Form, and Preparation Method

of Financial Statements" -- often abbreviated as "SEC Regulation for

Financial Statements" -- which became effective in January, 1951.[43] The

Japanese SEC Regulation for Financial Statements was enacted by adopting

the basic ideas of A Statement of Business Accounting Principles to imple-

ment the Securities Exchange Act. All Japanese stock corporations, which

offered shares of stock or debentures with a value of more than 50 million

yen, except corporations engaged in special lines of business such as

banking, electric power and gas, and railroad, were required to follow

the SEC Regulation in the preparation of their financial statements to

[43]For the comparative study of the Securities and Exchange Commis-
sions in the United States and Japan, see Makoto Yazawa, "Kosei Torihiki
Iinkai to Shoken Torihiki Iinkai" (The Fair Trade Commission and the
Securities and Exchange Commission), Nihon Kanri Horei Kenkyu (Japan
Occupation Law Review), No. 25, (March 1, 1949), pp. 42-50.

be submitted to the SEC of Japan.[44]

Revision of the Commercial Code. The Commercial Code of Japan was

not revised during World War II. The suggestion to revise the Commercial

Code after World War II was made by GHQ, SCAP based upon the report of

the Edwards Mission which states as follows:

> While Japanese corporation law fails to contain many of the
> basic restraints typical of Western Law, it does contain
> certain safeguards seemingly calculated to protect the stock-
> holder. In practice, however, these requirements have been
> loosely drawn and as far as Zaibatsu enterprises are concerned
> even more loosely enforced. In effect, the Japanese commercial
> code has imposed no significant restraints upon Zaibatsu enter-
> prise.
>
> As the result, the relationships between stockholders and manage-
> ment in the Zaibatsu-controlled corporations is a distillation
> of the most objectionable features to be found in other economies.
> To begin with, the stockholders of any corporation are sharply
> divided into two groups -- those who control, and others. In
> practice the identity of the two groups is never in question.
> Both groups look upon the corporation as being the property of
> Zaibatsu stockholders. The non-controlling stockholders purchase
> their securities almost entirely on the basis of the reputation
> of the controlling group.[45]

As one of the measures to strengthen the non-controlling shareholders'

position, the installment method of paying shares at the time of incor-

poration was changed to the lump-sum payment method in 1948.[46] This

---

[44]Since the SEC Regulation of Japan was more detailed and uniform
than a series of SEC regulations in the United States, the enactment of
the SEC Regulation was criticized as a violation from the Commission's
original functions. See Koichi Sato, "Shoken Torihiki Kisoku Dai-Juhachi-
Go no Hihanteki Kaisetsu" (Critical Comments on the SEC Regulation),
Waseda Shogaku (Waseda Commercial Review), No. 91, (March, 1951), pp.
21-41.

[45]U.S. Department of State, op. cit., p. 22.

[46]Article 171 of the Japanese Commercial Code before the revision
in 1948 reads:
The issuing price of the shares shall not be less than their
face value.

revision itself was a rather technical one but it caused the fundamental revision in 1950.

In April, 1948, an Investigation Committee to prepare for the Revision of the Commercial Code was established in the Justice Office to conduct research of many problems arising from the revision of the code in 1948 such as the adoption of an authorized capital system and non-par stocks.[47] The Legal Institution Deliberation Council, which assumed the responsibility of the Investigation Committee in August, 1949, released "A Revised Tentative Statement of the Partial Revision of the Commercial Code" in December, 1949. Based upon this statement the government promulgated the "Law Concerning the Partial Revision of the Commercial Code" in 1950.[48] The important revisions in 1950 were: (1) the strengthening of shareholders' position, (2) the rationalization of managerial organization by the establishment of the board of directors, and (3) the facilitation of corporation finance by the adoption of an authorized capital system and by making possible the issuance of non-par value stocks.[49]

The amount of the first payment shall not be less than one-fourth of the amount of the shares. Where shares have been issued above their face value, the amount in excess of the face value shall be paid in simultaneously with the first payment.

[47]Takeo Suzuki and Teruhisa Ishii, _Kaisei Kabushiki-Kaisha-Ho Kaisetsu_ (Comments on the Revised Stock Corporation Act) (Tokyo, Japan: Nihon Hyoronsha, 1950), P. 2.

[48]This law was promulgated as Law No. 167 in May, 1950 and became effective in July, 1951.

[49]Makoto Yazawa and Tsuneo Ootori, "Kaisha-Ho no Sengo no Tenkai to Kadai -I-" (The Development of the Corporation Act after World War II and its Problems -I-), _Hogaku Seminar_ (Jurisprudence Seminar), No. 142, (January, 1968), pp. 4-5. See also Suzuki and Ishii, _op. cit._, pp. 7-16.

Although the valuation basis of assets was not changed in 1950,
revisions of accounting provisions in the Commercial Code were made on
several points.[50] In addition to organization expense, bond discount, and
interest during construction, commission and expenses for issuance of new
capital shares were included in the category of deferred assets (Article
286-2). The second point of the revision was the division of the legal
revenue reserve and the legal capital reserve. In the old Commercial Code
the legal reserve was required to be accumulated until it should amount to
one-fourth of the stated capital. The revised Commercial Code required each
stock corporation to retain at least one-twentieth of the profit for the
current period until it amounted to one-fourth of the stated capital (Article 288). The Code also required the following be set aside as the legal
capital reserves: (1) paid-in capital from the issuance of par-value stock
in excess of par value, (2) paid-in capital from the issuance of non-par
stock in excess of stated value, (3) net amount resulting from a revaluation
of assets, (4) paid-in capital from reduction in value assigned to outstanding stock, and (5) paid-in surplus from amalgamation (Article 288-2).

In relation to the strengthening of shareholders' position, greater
disclosure of accounting information was required for shareholders. The
Commercial Code required the directors of stock corporations to prepare
schedules of the documents mentioned in Article 281 (an inventory, a balance
sheet, a business report, an income statement, and a statement of proposals

[50]For the revision of the accounting provisions of the Commercial
Code in 1950, see Iino, op. cit., pp. 66-67 and 69-70.

pertaining to the legal reserves and to the distribution of profit or
interest during construction) within four months after the closing date
of accounts for each accounting period and keep them at the main office
of the company (Article 293-5). The schedules were to state the business
operations and financial condition of the company in detail, specifying
(1) the change in the stated capital and reserves, (2) all transactions
with the directors, statutory auditors, and shareholders, (3) security
offered, (4) the loans of money made if the company were non-financial,
(5) the acquisition of shares of other companies, and (6) the disposition
of any fixed assets (Article 293-5). All shareholders were allowed to
inspect or make copies from the schedules (Article 293-5).

Revision of A Statement of Business Accounting Principles. Despite the
wish that the basic ideas of A Statement of Business Accounting Principles
should be respected and incorporated as much as possible into laws, such as
the Commercial Code and the Corporate Income Tax Law, there still remained
a gap between A Statement of Business Accounting Principles and the revised
Commercial Code and the Corporate Income Tax Law. As far as the Commercial
Code is concerned, it was technically difficult for the Code to incorporate
the ideas of A Statement of Business Accounting Principles into the revised
Code since the most part of the draft of the revised Code was already completed when the Statement was released in 1949.[51] A reconciliation of A
Statement of Business Accounting Principles and the Commercial Code, however,
was vital in Japan since A Statement of Business Accounting Principles was

---

[51]Takashi Yoshida, "Kigyo-Kaikei-Gensoku no Zaimushohyo-Taikei to
Shoho" (Financial Statements Listed in A Statement of Business Accounting
Principles and the Commercial Code), Kansa (Auditing Review), (February,
1951), p. 23.

not viewed as the Commercial Custom Law and the provisions of the Commercial

Code were not supplemented by A Statement of Business Accounting Principles.[52]

In other words, A Statement of Business Accounting Principles could not

affect greatly the accounting practices unless its ideas were incorporated

into laws.

In September, 1951, the Business Accounting Standards Deliberation

Council released "A Statement of Opinions on Reconciliation of the Commercial

Code and A Statment of Business Accounting Principles." The purpose of the

statement was to clarify the differences between them and indicate a direction

of the future amendment of the Commercial Code from the viewpoint of the

Business Accounting Principles. The published opinions discussed fourteen

controversial problems which needed to be reconciled. They were: (1) account-

ing books, (2) balance sheets and income statements, (3) inventory and valua-

tion basis for the regular, closing balance sheet, (4) fiscal year and interim

distribution of dividends, (5) statutory auditor and audit by a CPA based upon

the Securities Exchange Act, (6) preparation of financial documents, (7) approval

of financial documents, (8) valuation of assets, (9) organization expense,

(10) deferred assets, (11) treasury stock, (12) capital reserve, (13) extra-

ordinary loss, and (14) schedules relating financial documents. The Statement

of Opinions on Reconciliation of the Commercial Code and A Statement of Busi-

ness Accounting Principles thus provided for a foundation for the revision of

the Commercial Code in 1962.[53] A Statement of Business Accounting Principles,

---

[52]Iino, op. cit., P. 66.

[53]Makoto Yazawa and Tsuneo Ootori, "Kaisha-Ho no Sengo no Tenkai to
Kadai -II-" (The Development of the Corporation Act after World War II and
Its Problems -II-), Hogaku Seminar (Jurisprudence Seminar), No. 143,
(February, 1968), P. 51.

however, could not remain unchanged until the Commercial Code was changed

in 1962. To be "generally accepted accounting principles," the business

accounting principles were not allowed to be discrete from the laws.[54]

In July, 1951, the first legal audit by CPAs based upon the Securities

Exchange Act started and the SEC Regulation for Financial Statements was

applied to the listed stock corporations. In advance of the enforcement of

the SEC Regulation, Keizai-Dantai Rengokai (Federation of Economic Organiza-

tions), a national association of private, industrial groups, published a

statement entitled "An Opinion on the Revision of A Statement of Business

Accounting Principles" in August, 1950, and requested the narrowing of the

differences among accounting provisions of the Commercial Code, the Corporate

Income Tax Law, and A Statement of Business Accounting Principles.[55] The

statement of the Federation of Economic Organization states:

> The contents of A Statement of Business Accounting Principles
> and the Working Rules for Preparing Financial Statements by
> the Investigation Committee on Business Accounting Systems do
> not harmonize with the prevailing accounting practices because
> the Committee introduced consciously the accounting conventions
> and systems developed in the United States for educational pur-
> pose. On the other hand, there are serious discrepancies among
> accounting provisions of the Commercial Code, the Corporate
> Income Tax Law, and the Interim Report of the Committee because
> these laws were revised without taking into consideration the
> ideas of A Statement of Business Accounting Principles. If

---

[54]Kurosawa, op. cit., P. 3.

[55]Keizai-Dantai-Rengokai, Keizai-Dantai-Rengokai Jyunen-Shi -Jo-
(The First Ten Years of the Federation of Economic Organizations, I)
(Tokyo, Japan: Keizai-Dantai-Rengokai, 1962), pp. 227-28.

the SEC Regulation were enforced before the reasonable reconciliation of these laws and accounting principles, confusion
and friction would be inevitable....[56]

The statement also requested clarification of the meaning of principles and

interpretation of terms for better application of business accounting prin-

ciples to practices. The proposals expressed in the statement of the Federa-

tion of Economic Organizations, however, were not accepted by the SEC Regula-

tion. Its actual application in relation to the first legal audit since

July, 1951, raised many questions as to the interpretation of the regulation.

This was the practical reason for the revision of A Statement of Business

Accounting Principles.

Under these circumstances, the First Section of the Business Accounting

Deliberation Council began its preparation to revise business accounting

principles in September, 1952. According to Kiyoshi Kurosawa, Chairman of

the First Section, the possibility of or necessity for the fundamental revision

of A Statement of Business Accounting Principles was discussed in the process

of preparatory research. The final revision, however, was partial and not

very important since the Council believed that A Statement of Business Account-

ing Principles was a social institution and that an arbitrary, drastic

revision was not feasible.[57] One of the most important features of the revision

was that comments were given to eighteen items by the Deliberation Council to

clarify the meaning of the statement.

---

[56]Keizai-Dantai-Rengokai, Keizai-Dantai-Rengokai Jyunen-Shi -Ge- (The
First Ten Years of the Federation of Economic Organizations, II) (Tokyo, Japan:
Keizai-Dantai Rengokai, 1963), p. 43. For the details of the statement and
comments on it, see Kiyoshi Kurosawa, "Keidanren no Kaikei-Gensoku no Kaisei
ni kansuru Iken ni tsuite" (Comments on "An Opinion on the Revision of A
Statement of Business Accounting Principles" by The Federation of Economic
Organization), Kaikei (Accounting), Vol. 58, No. 3, (September, 1950), pp. 131-
35.

[57]Kiyoshi Kurosawa, "Shusei-Kaikei-Gensoku Soron" (General Comments
on the Revised Statement of Business Accounting Principles), Sangyo-Keiri
(Financial and Cost Accounting) Vol. 14, No. 8, (August, 1954), p. 44.

The Third Stage: Reconciliation of the Commercial Code and A Statement of Business Accounting Principles (1962 -   )

Revision of the Commercial Code. Since the revision of the Commercial Code in 1950 was suggested by GHQ (SCAP), and completed in a relatively short period of time, the refinement of accounting provisions in the Commercial Code was limited to a few items. When the legal audit by CPAs was switched from the preparatory audit of the accounting system to the regular audit of financial statements in January, 1957, the reconciliation of the accounting provisions of the Commercial Code and the SEC Regulation for Financial Statements became urgent. As mentioned earlier, the SEC Regulation for Financial Statements, which was enacted based upon Article 193 of the Securities Exchange Act, adopted the basic ideas of A Statement of Business Accounting Principles. The contents of the SEC Regulation, therefore, do not necessarily harmonize with the accounting provisions in the Commercial Code. As a result of the differences among accounting provisions of the Commercial Code and the SEC Regulation, the contents of financial statements for the SEC Regulation purpose are different from those for the Commercial Code purpose.

This situation needed prompt improvement for two reasons, that is, the legal and practical reasons. Akinobu Ueda, an official of the Civil Affairs Bureau, Ministry of Justice, states:

"The SEC Regulation for Financial Statements lacks a basic law for the substantial provisions while it prescribes the wording and form of financial statements. If the Commercial Code were a basic law for the substantial provisions of the SEC Regulation, the part of the SEC Regulation, which does not conform with the Commercial Code, would be invalid. If the substantial provisions of the SEC Regulation were based upon the logic, the SEC Regulation would not violate the Commercial Code. In the latter case, two sets of financial statements should be prepared based upon the Commercial Code and the SEC Regulation and either one set of financial statements could not substitute the other."[58]

It was quite evident from the legal theory that the SEC Regulation was not supported by the Commercial Code and that the Commercial Code was not supplemented by A Statement of Business Accounting Principles. It then follows that the listed stock corporations which were under the control of the Security Exchange Act, should have prepared two sets of financial statements. Most companies, however, had been preparing only one set of financial statements based upon the SEC Regulation. The accounting provisions of the Commercial Code were virtually ineffective.[59]

Under these circumstances, the legal Institution Deliberation Council's Commercial Code Section began preparations in March, 1958, for the revision of the accounting provisions of the Commercial Code. The Commercial Code Section decided the several important issues to be discussed for the revision in July, 1958, and publicized them. By April, 1960, the Commercial Code Section completed the discussion of all issues, but it found that most members of the Commercial Code Section had different opinions on each issue. Thus, the Civil Affairs Bureau of the Ministry of Justice released "A Tentative Statement of the Revision of Accounting Provisions Applied to Stock Corporations in the Commercial Code" in August, 1960, to invite comments or suggestions from lawyers,

---

[58]Akinobu Ueda, "Shoho no Kaisei ni tsuite" (On the revision of the Commercial Code) in Seiji Tanaka, et al., Shoho Kaisei ni tomonau Shomondai (Some Problems on the Revision of the Commercial Code), (Tokyo, Japan: Ikkyo Shuppan, 1962), p. 19.

[59]Masanori Kuroki, Shin-Shoho ni motozuku Kaisha Kessan Jitsumu (Corporate Accounting Practices based upon the New Commercial Code) (Tokyo, Japan: Chuo-Keizai-Sha, 1963), p. 4.

professors of law, and businessmen. About seventy statements of comments

on "Tentative Statement" were submitted to the Ministry of Justice.[60] Influ-

enced by these valuable comments and suggestions, the Legal Institution Delib-

eration Council prepared "A Draft of Law to Revise A Part of The Commercial

Code" in February, 1962. The draft was approved by the Japanese Diet in

April, 1962.[61]

The distinctive characteristics of the revision of the Commercial Code

in 1962 may be summarized in four points: (1) it radically changed the

principles of asset valuation -- from a lower-than-market-price basis to a

historical cost (Article 285--285-7); (2) it enlarged the scope of the defer-

red assets classification and added four new items, such as preliminary (start-

up) expenses, development expenses, experimental and research expenses, and

---

[60]Yazawa and Ootori, op. cit., p. 50. Keizai-Dantai-Rengokai, for example,
submitted the following statement in November, 1960:
.... In the modern big business, the responsibility of the management
for the maintenance of business has increased. Therefore, the proper
income determination assuming the continuity and safety of the business enterprise should be emphasized. Although the "Tentative Statement"
emphasizes the income determination by adopting the basic ideas of "A
Statement of Business Accounting Principles," there remains much emphasis
on the accounting for net worth. Because of the co-existence of two
basically different accounting ideas, confusion of the business accounting practices might be inevitable. Since the "Tentative Statement"
prescribes the complicated transactions in detail and enforces a
standardized accounting treatment, it seems to neglect a good business
management and sound accounting conventions....
(Quoted in Hiroshi Suekawa [ed.] , Shiryo Sengo Nijyunen-Shi -- Horitsu [Data on
the Twenty-Year History After the War -- Laws] [Tokyo, Japan: Nihon Hyoronsha,
1966] , p. 606.)

[61]The revised Commercial Code was promulgated on April 20, 1962, as Law
No. 82 and became effective on April 1, 1963.

bond expenses (Article 286-2, 286-3, and 286-5); (3) it recognized "provisions" as items to be listed in the liabilities section of a balance sheet (Article 287-2); and (4) it expressly specified the maximum amount of profits available for dividends (Article 290).[62]

Enactment of the Regulation for Corporate Balance Sheets and Income Statements. Related to the Amendmant of the Commercial Code in 1962, the Ministry of Justice released in March, 1963, "The Regulation for Corporate Balance Sheets and Income Statements" which prescribed the manner of preparing balance sheets and income statements to be submitted to the general meeting of shareholders. This was an Ordinance No. 31 of the Ministry of Justice and it was enacted pursuant to Article 49 of the Law Pertaining to the Operation of the Amendment to the Commercial Code in 1938. In parallel with the deliberation of the revision of the Commercial Code, the Civil Affairs Bureau of the Ministry of Justice sponsored a study of the regulation by a small group of members in the Commercial Code Section, Legal Institution Deliberation Council. The Civil Affairs Bureau informally invited comments and suggestions, such as the Federation of Economic Organizations and the Tokyo Chambers of Commerce and Industry.[63]

The purpose of the regulation was to make accounting provisions of the Commercial Code effective and then improve the public reporting system of financial statement. Since the regulation applies to balance sheets and

---

[62]Iino, op. cit., p. 70.

[63]Kuroki, op. cit., p. 12.

income statements which are prepared based upon Article 281 of the Commercial Code (Article 1), all stock corporations should follow the regulation in the preparation of balance sheets and income statements for the shareholders' meeting. The regulation is composed of four chapters: (1) general provisions, (2) balance sheet, (3) income statement, and (4) miscellaneous provision. Concerning the binding power of the regulation, there has been no unanimous opinion between lawyers and accountants. Most Japanese lawyers have considered the regulation as a set of compulsory provisions which should be observed by all corporations. Some accountants, however, have considered the regulation as a set of instructive provisions which is not applicable or enforceable for all corporations.[64] In practice, however, nearly all Japanese corporations have been preparing their balance sheets and income statements as prescribed by the Regulation since the Fall of 1963.

Revision of A Statement of Business Accounting Principles. When the Investigation Committee on Business Accounting System released A Statement of Business Accounting Principles in 1949, the Committee in the foreword expressed the nature of accounting principles in the following terms:

1. Business Accounting Principles are the summaries of those generally accepted as fair and proper among accounting conventions developed in practices of business accounting, and they are standards which should be observed when all business enterprises practice accounting even though they are not forced to do so by law or ordinance.
2. Business Accounting Principles are the standards which Certified Public Accountants should observe when they audit financial statements based upon the Certified Public Accountant Law and the Securities Exchange Act.

---

[64]Kiyoshi Kurosawa, "Kigyo-Kaikei-Gensoku to Zaimu-Shohyo-Kisoku" (A Statement of Business Accounting Principles and the Regulation for Financial Statement) in Katsuji Yamashita (ed.) Keisan-Shorui-Kisoku no Mondaiten (Some Problems on the Regulation for Corporate Balance Sheets and Income Statements) (Tokyo, Japan: Chuo-Keizai-Sha, 1965), p. 21.

3. Business Accounting Principles should be respected in
case that laws and ordinance affecting business accounting,
such as the Commercial Code, Tax Laws, and Price Control
Ordinance, be established, amended, or abolished in the
future.

This foreword shows that A Statement of Business Accounting Principles is a

compound of two things, differing in their nature: general and special or

natural and artificial. The first paragraph of the quoted foreword des-

cribes the general nature of the "autogenous" type of accounting principles.

If there are accounting conventions which can generally be accepted as

fair and proper in a society, their summaries may naturally constitute a

set of accounting principles. In Japan, however, it is doubtful whether

the naturally developed accounting conventions existed when A Statement of

Business Accounting Principles was established. It seems to the author that

there were few naturally developed accounting conventions which could be

identified as accounting principles. Because of the non-existence of such

conventions, the Committee considered it necessary to add the second nature

to the newly established accounting principles.

The second and third paragraphs are an expression of the Committee's

wish that the accounting principles should be institutionalized through the

provisions of laws and ordinances.[65] As far as the second paragraph is con-

cerned, the Committee's wish was promptly satisfied by the enactment of the

SEC Regulation for Financial Statements and the audit standards in 1950. It

took thirteen years, however, before the Commercial Code was revised in 1962

[65]Kiyoshi Kurosawa, "Kaikei-Kijyun no Kakuritsu to Iji ni tsuite"
(Establishment and Maintenance of Accounting Standards), Sangyo-Keiri (Financial and Cost Accounting), Vol. 9, No. 5, (May, 1949), pp. 7-9.

by adopting the basic ideas of A Statement of Business Accounting Principles.

During this period of thirteen years the ideas of A Statement of Business

Accounting Principles has penetrated, being supported by the Securities

Exchange Act, into accounting practices of big business enterprises.[66] In

addition to the declaration of its wish expressed in the third paragraph of

the foreword, the Business Accounting Deliberation Council (the present name

of the Investigation Committee on Business Accounting System since 1952)

published "A Statement of Opinions on Reconciliation of the Commercial Code

and A Statement of Business Accounting Principles" (1951), "A Statement of

Opinions on Reconciliation of the Tax Law and A Statement of Business Account-

ing Principles" (1952), and a series of opinions on reconciliation of A State-

ment of Business Accounting Principles and the related regulations.[67] In

view of the gradual penetration of the ideas of A Statement of Business Account-

ing Principles into accounting practices and the requests expressed in a series

of opinions of the Business Accounting Deliberation Council, the Commercial Code

was revised in 1962 and the Regulation for Corporate Balance Sheets and Income

Statements was released in 1963 by the Ministry of Justice.

---

[66]Yazawa and Ootori, op. cit., p. 49 and Saichi Chu, "Kigyo-Kaikei
Gensoku no Za" (The Position of A Statement of Business Accounting Principles),
Kaikei (Accounting), Vol. 87, No. 1, (January, 1965), pp. 83-84.

[67]The Business Accounting Deliberation Council issued the following series
of opinions.
Series of Opinion No. 1, "On Composition of Financial Statements" (1960)
Series of Opinion No. 2, "On Form of Financial Statements" (1960)
Series of Opinion No. 3, "On Depreciation of Tangible Fixed Assets" (1960)
Series of Opinion No. 4, "On Evaluation of Inventories" (1962)
Series of Opinion No. 5, "On Deferred Assets" (1962)

As mentioned in the previous sections, the accounting provisions in
the revised Commercial Code were considerably improved from the accounting
viewpoint.[68] Despite an effort of reconciliation from the Commercial Code
side, several significant discrepancies still remained unbridged between
them. This means that some of the requests from accountants were not
accepted by the Commercial Code because of the differences in purposes of
the Commercial Code and A Statement of Business Accounting Principles. If
accounting principles were to be institutionalized in a way other than
being incorporated in the provisions of laws and regulations, they would
be free from the revision. Since A Statement of Business Accounting Principles in Japan, however, chose another way of institutionalization, its revision
was inevitable in view of the compulsory nature of the Commercial Code. In
November, 1963, the Business Accounting Deliberation Council revised a part of
A Statement of Business Accounting Principles which did not harmonize with
the new provisions in the Commercial Code. The fundamental revision for its
further refinement was postponed.

The foregoing description of the historical development of accounting
principles in Japan is summarized in Figure 2 (page 87). The most basic
law governing accounting practices in Japan has been the Commercial Code.
In 1934, the Working Rules for Financial Statements was released by the
Ministry of Commerce and Industry to improve financial reporting practices
by supplementing the accounting provisions of the Commercial Code. The Tentative Standards for Financial Statements of Manufacturing Companies was

---

[68]For the detailed evaluation of the revised Commercial Code, see
Iino, op. cit., pp. 76-80.

was released in 1941 by the Planning Board to supplement the Corporate Accounting Control Ordinance of 1940. Neither the Working Rules nor the Tentative Standards, however, were enforced by law as originally scheduled.

A Statement of Business Accounting Principles was released by the Investigation Committee on Business Accounting System as the first written pronouncement of "generally accepted accounting principles." Although it was supported by the Securities Exchange Act, A Statement of Business Accounting Principles was not enacted as a law by the Japanese Diet.

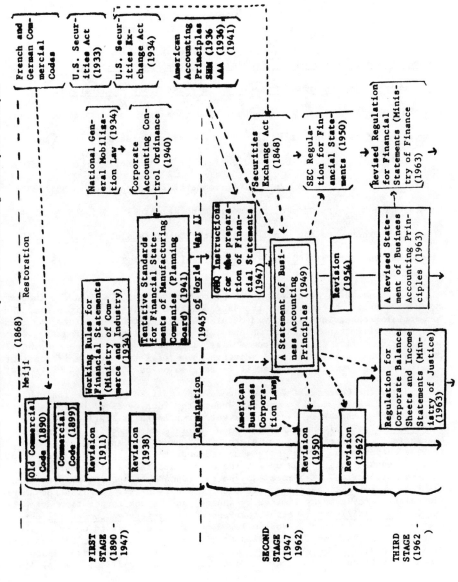

FIGURE 2   Historical Development of Accounting Principles in Japan

CHAPTER III

AN ANALYSIS OF ACCOUNTING PRINCIPLES
AT THE FIRST STAGE OF THEIR DEVELOPMENT (1890-1947)

An Analysis of the Accounting Provisions in the Commercial Code

General Purpose of the Commercial Code and Stock Corporation. The

Commercial Code of Japan was the basic law governing business traders and

commercial transactions since 1890.[1] The general purpose of the Commercial

Code was to promote sound business activities by protecting the property

rights of both parties engaged in the commercial transactions. Besides a

natural person, four types of business corporations were allowed to be

"traders." They were the Gomei-Kaisha, the Goshi-Kaisha, the Kabushiki-

Kaisha and the Kabushiki-Goshi-Kaisha (Article 43).[2] The discussion in this

---

[1]The Commercial Code defines the term "trader" as a person who in his own name carries on commercial transactions as a business (Article 4). The commercial transactions are divided into two categories: absolute and relative commercial transactions. An absolute commercial transaction is a transaction which by its nature is commercial, irrespective of the person who carries it on (Article 263). A relative commercial transaction is considered as a commercial transaction when it is carried on by a trader (Article 264).

[2]Since the Commercial Code of Japan was codified under the influence of the French and German Commercial Codes, the four types of business corporations do not necessarily have equivalent terms in Anglo-American usage. Gomei-Kaisha is a literal translation of societe en nom collectif in the French law. It corresponds to "partnership" under the Anglo-American Law, but it is a corporation. Goshi-Kaisha corresponds to societe en commandite and "limited partnership." But unlike the Anglo-American "limited partnership," it is a corporation. Kabushiki-Kaisha corresponds to societe anonyme under the French law; Aktiengesellschaft under the German law. English and American equivalents are "company limited by shares" and "stock corporation" respectively. Kabushiki-Goshi-Kaisha corresponds to societe en commandite par actions under the French. No similar type of company exists under Anglo-American law. (The Code Translation Committee of the League of Nations Association of Japan, The Commercial Code of Japan, annotated, I [Tokyo, Japan: The League of Nations Association of Japan, 1931], pp. 70-71, p. 129, p. 158, and p. 394)

section is confined to an analysis of the accounting provisions applicable
to the Kabushiki-Kaisha (stock corporation) because it has been the typical
and most important of the four legal forms of business corporations in Japan.

According to the Japanese Commercial Code, the stock corporation consisted of three elements: (1) the general meeting of shareholders (2) the
directors, and (3) the statutory auditors. This reflected the impact of the
democratic idea of politics upon the business organization in that each element was expected to perform a different function for the continuous operation
of the corporation (Articles 157-189). Whereas the author identified in
Chapter I seven interest groups in the business enterprise, the Commercial
Code of Japan identified one additional interest group in addition to the
three groups of persons who represented three elements previously mentioned.
The fourth interest group was a person or a group of persons engaging in commercial transactions with a stock corporation as a trader (Article 3). This
group of persons was generally called "creditor(s)" in the legal usage of the
term. The Commercial Code thus recognized four relationships between the
stock corporation and (1) the shareholders, (2) the directors, (3) the statutory auditors, and (4) the creditors. This means, as a Japanese jurist once
noted, that the legal form of the stock corporation can exist only when the
relationships among the corporation itself, shareholders group, management
group, and creditors group are properly regulated. He held that the notion of
proper regulation was based upon a legal philosophy which includes the three
types of Aristotelian justice -- justice of exchange or commercial justice,

distributive justice, and general or universal justice.[3]

Accounting Provisions in the Commercial Code. In addition to the
general accounting provisions concerning the trade (or accounting) books,
which were applicable to all kinds of traders, the stock corporation was
subject to the special accounting provisions of the Code.[4] The special
accounting provisions applicable to the stock corporation may be divided
into three groups: (1) provisions concerning financial documents, (2) provisions concerning the concept and valuation of assets, and (3) provisions
concerning profits available for dividends.

Concerning the financial documents, Article 281 of the Commercial Code
stated:

> The directors shall submit to the statutory auditors at least
> two weeks before the day set for an ordinary general meeting of
> shareholders the following documents:
> (1) An inventory
> (2) A balance sheet
> (3) A business report
> (4) An income Statement
> (5) A statement of proposals pertaining to the legal
>   reserve and the distribution of profit or interest
>   during construction.

---

[3]Kotaro Tanaka, "Kabushiki-Kaisha-Ho Jyosetsu" (An Introduction to the
Stock Corporation Law) in Kotaro Tanaka (ed.), Kabushiki-Kaisha-Ho Koza, I
(Stock Corporation Law Handbook, I)(Tokyo, Japan: Yuhikaku, 1955), p. 22,
pp. 1-32.

[4]The general accounting provisions are concerned with the trade (or
accounting) books (Article 25-28 in the 1899 Code or Articles 32-36 in the
1938 Code.) Article 32 of the 1938 Commercial Code states:
Every trader shall keep books and shall record therein in an
orderly and clear manner his daily transactions and all matters
which may tend to affect his property....
Article 33 of the 1938 Code states:
At the time of commencement of business and once in each year
at a fixed date, every trader shall prepare a comprehensive
inventory of movables, immovables, claims and obligations and
of all other properties as well as a balance sheet.
In the case of a corporation, the documents mentioned in the
preceding paragraph shall be prepared at the time of its incorporation and at the end of each fiscal year....

The primary concern of the Commercial Code was to protect the right of creditors regardless of the legal form of the business organization. In the stock corporation, special emphasis was given to the protection of the rights of creditors since the possible loss of a shareholder was limited to the amount paid for the shares (Article 200) while the corporate assets were the only resources available for the creditors. The inventory and balance sheet were considered indispensable media for disclosing the financial position of the stock corporation and its ability to meet liabilities. This idea of the Commercial Code was nothing more than a tradition attributable to the Ordonnance de Commerce of 1673.[5]

The stock corporation was a business association of several persons seeking to make a business profit. Most of the individuals, however, had less personal contact with the daily business operations.[6] The stock corporation was a legal entity independent from its shareholders (owners of the corporation) and was administered by a relatively small number of individuals. The proper regulation of the relationships between the shareholders and the corporation was another area of concern of the Commercial Code.[7] That is, the Commercial Code required the directors of a stock corporation to prepare

---

[5]Toshio Iino, "Accounting Principles and Contemporary Legal Thought in Japan," The International Journal of Accounting Education and Research, Vol. 2, No. 2, (Spring, 1967), pp. 67-68.

[6]A. C. Littleton, Accounting Evolution to 1900 (New York: Russell & Russell, 1966), p. 206. This book was originally published by American Institute Publishing Co., Inc. of New York in 1933.

[7]Eisuke Yoshinaga, "Keisan Shorui" (Accounting Documents) in Kotaro Tanaka (ed.) Kabushiki-Kaisha-Ho Koza, IV (Stock Corporation Law Handbook, IV)(Tokyo, Japan: Yuhikaku, 1956), p. 1478.

a business report and an income statement which revealed to the shareholders an accurate picture of results of operations. These documents,
coupled with a balance sheet, were supposed to disclose the efficiency of
capital utilization and the amount of profits available for dividends. In
addition, the directors of a stock corporation were required to prepare a
statement of proposals pertaining to the disposal of profits and submit it,
with the four documents (an inventory, a balance sheet, a business report,
and an income statement) and a report of the statutory auditors, at the
ordinary general meeting of shareholders for approval by the shareholders
(Article 283).

Each of the first four documents was initially useful in showing the
financial position and results of operations of the stock corporation from an
accounting point of view. From the viewpoint of legal theory, however, they
were supplementary to the statement of proposals pertaining to the disposal
of profits. Because the relations between the corporation and the directors
were subject to the provisions set forth in certain legal mandates (Article
254) and the directors were elected at the general meeting of shareholders,
the directors were required to submit the five documents at the general
meeting of shareholders in order to disclose their responsibility or accountability for business operations of the corporation.[8] Approval by shareholders
of these documents discharged the responsibilities of the directors as
trustees. To the average shareholders, the right to dividends, which was a

---

[8]Since most of the Japanese stock corporations adopted a six-month period
for an accounting period, the general meeting of shareholders was held twice
a year. The term of office of the directors could not exceed three years.

right to share in the profits, was one of the most important rights he possessed.[9] As a result, the primary concern of shareholders was the amount of dividends which they could be paid. Therefore, they were especially interested in the proposed disposal of profit figures shown in the statement of proposals. The four documents -- an inventory, a balance sheet, an income statement and a business report -- provided the essential data for the shareholders to judge the adequacy of the proposals submitted by the directors and audited by the statutory auditors. If the shareholders believed it necessary to examine the documents and the audit report in detail, they could appoint special inspectors to make a detailed examination of the documents (Article 238).

The most important problems encountered in the preparation of a balance sheet were the concept and valuation of assets. Although no clear description of assets can be found in the Commercial Code, assets were considered from the legal point of view as debt-paying media. This Japanese Commercial Code concept of an asset was evidenced by its referral to assets only in relation to the preparation of an inventory and a balance sheet (Article 33) and its failure to allow the traders to list any type of deferred asset in the balance sheet until the revision of the Code in 1938. Two Japanese professors explain the Commercial Code's basic concept of assets in the following terms:

_____

[9] Dow Votaw, Modern Corporations (Englewood Cliffs, New Jersey: Prentice-Hall, Inc., 1965), p. 68.

The fixed assets and deferred assets may be the same in their nature from the income determination viewpoint. It is, however, questionable whether the latter should be listed on the asset side of the balance sheet since they have neither service potential nor realizable value, whereas the former is no doubt admitted as assets because it has both attributes. According to the traditional theory of the Commercial Code, a primary concern of accounting provisions in the Commercial Code has been to require every corporation to disclose its financial position, especially its realizable value when it is liquidated. The Commercial Code has thus emphasized the principle that only those assets which have realizable value should be listed in the balance sheet....[10]

When the Commercial Code was revised in 1938, the concept of a deferred asset was introduced into the accounting provisions in the Code. The 1938 revised Commercial Code recognized (1) organization expense, (2) bond discount, and (3) interest during construction as deferred assets (Articles 286, 287, and 291). From the accounting viewpoint, the term "deferred, like the term "accrued," was related to the concept of matching for rational, periodic income determination.[11] Although deferred assets were neither tangible nor realizable, they were usually considered as unavoidable cost of launching an enterprise and raising capital, and were essentially homogeneous in their significance to the enterprise. According to Paton and Littleton, "neither lack of specific assignability nor legal unavailability for paying debts warrants the conclusion that the costs in question represent balance-sheet items of doubtful propriety."[12] The basic legal concept of assets,

---

[10]Seiji Tanaka and Kinya Kubo, "Kabushiki-Kaisha no Kaikei-Ho" (Accounting Law for the Stock Corporation) in Seiji Tanaka, et al., Kaisha-Kaikei-Hoki Shokai (A Comprehensive Study of the Accounting Law for the Corporations) (Tokyo, Japan: Shunjusha, 1959), p. 75.

[11]W. A. Paton and A. C. Littleton, An Introduction to Corporate Accounting Standards (Iowa City, Iowa: American Accounting Association, 1964), p. 16. This book was originally published by the American Accounting Association in 1940.

[12]Ibid., p. 32.

however, was in opposition to this accounting interpretation of deferred

assets. Why then did the Japanese Commercial Code recognize three types

of deferred assets?

The Civil Affairs Bureau of the Ministry of Justice, which prepared

a draft of the revised Code, attempted to justify the recognition of

deferred assets in the following terms:

> It has been a convention in accounting practice to list the
> expense items mentioned in Article 281 as organization expense
> on the asset side of the balance sheet. This new article was
> added to recognize such items as deferred assets for legal pur-
> pose although it is still questionable whether the recognition
> of organization expense as a deferred asset is legitimate. For
> the safe maintenance of the financial foundation of the corpora-
> tion, however, the amortization of such expense within a rather
> short period of time is required.
>
> The reason for the recognition of bond discount as a deferred
> asset is the same as that used for the organization expense.[13]

Although this explanation is not clear by itself, there seems to have been

two reasons why the Commercial Code recognized deferred assets. The first

was that it had gradually become accepted accounting practice to defer some

types of expenses for the purpose of smoothing profits and losses. The

Working Rules for Financial Statements by the Ministry of Commerce and

Industry in 1934, for example, recommended that the following items be listed

on the asset side of the balance sheet under the caption of "Miscellaneous

Accounts": (1) bond discount and bond issue expenses, (2) interest during

construction, (3) development expenses, and (4) organization expenses. The

second reason was related to the effort directed to the protection of the

basic right of shareholders. If all the expenses of this nature were assigned

to the accounting period in which they incurred, the corporation would report

---

[13]Shiho-Sho Minji-Kyoku (Civil Affairs Bureau, the Ministry of Justice),
Shoho Kaisei Horitsu-An Riyusho (A Commentary on the Draft of the Revised
Commercial Code)(Tokyo, Japan: Shimizu-Shoten, 1937), pp. 156-57.

a large amount of loss for the period. Because the Japanese corporation
was prohibited from distributing dividends before the full recovery of
losses (Article 290), the Commercial Code recognized three types of deferred assets as an exception to its basic concept of assets in order to enable
a stock corporation to pay dividends in its early years of life. Since
deferred assets were fictitious assets from the viewpoint of disclosing
assets value, the recognition by the Commercial Code of the deferred assets
represented a compromise of the Code with the accounting practices.[14]

The fundamental idea of the Commercial Code that the creditors should
be protected had a great influence on its basis of asset valuation. The
1899 Commercial Code of Japan had only one general provision concerning
asset valuation (Article 26-2) which stated:

> The valuation of assets for the preparation of an inventory shall
> be based upon their value at the preparation date of the inventory.

This provision was changed to a lower-than-market-price basis in 1911 and

changed again in 1938 to:

> The valuation of assets for the preparation of an inventory shall
> not exceed tha value at the preparation date of the inventory,
> except for the fixed assets used in business operations, which may
> be valued at the amount of the acquisition cost or manufacturing
> cost less reasonable value diminution (Article 34).

In addition to this general provision, the 1938 Commercial Code added a new

provision for asset valuation by the stock corporation (Article 285):

> The valuation of fixed assets used in business operation shall not
> exceed the amount of the acquisition cost or manufacturing cost.
> The valuation of marketable securities shall not exceed the average
> price prevailing during the one month immediately prior to the date
> inventory is prepared.

---

[14]Makoto Yazawa, Kigyo-Kaikei-Ho Kogi (Lectures on Business Accounting
Law)(Tokyo, Japan: Yuhikaku, 1958), p. 34..

This change of the asset valuation basis in the Commercial Code from

a market-price basis to a lower-than-market-price basis for the general

assets and a cost-less-depreciation basis for the fixed assets indicates

that the relative degree of protection for creditors was strengthened.[15]

The Commercial Code emphasized that only those assets which have realizable

value should be listed in the inventory and should be disclosed in the

balance sheet from the viewpoint of protection for creditors. The evaluation

of assets at their realizable value, however, does not necessarily conform

to this point of view because excess dividends may be made from the "paper

profits" which results when the realizable value of assets is higher than

their acquisition costs. A lower-than-market-price basis is a much "safer"

principle than a market-price basis. The lower-than-cost-basis for the

fixed assets in business operations in the corporation was enforced for two

reasons: (1) the difficulty in finding a reliable market price data for

the fixed assets used in business operations, and (2) the desire to conform

with the basic purpose of the Commercial Code to protect both creditors and

shareholders.

In relation to the protection of creditors, the Civil Affairs Bureau

of the Ministry of Justice noted that the purpose of the new provision in

Article 285 was to prevent the stock corporation from paying excessive divi-

dends from unrealized profits and ensure that the financial foundation of

the corporation would be much firmer.[16] In view of the bitter deflationary

[15]Although there are two kinds of market price; the realizable value and
the replacement cost, "market price" used in the Commercial Code was interpreted as the "realizable value."

[16]Shiho-Sho Minji-Kyoku, op. cit., p. 156.

experience from which the Japanese economy suffered in 1930 and 1931, on the other hand, there was a common fear among Japanese businessmen of capital impairment and a difficulty in continuing the payment of dividends under a lower-than-market-price basis. When the market prices of the fixed assets are considerably lower than their acquisition costs, the strict application of a lower-than-market-price basis to the fixed assets inevitably reduces the dividend paying ability of the corporation because of the large degree of capital impairment.[17]

The central accounting issue in a corporation concerns the amount of profits available for dividends.[18] This was also true for the Commercial Code since the interests of creditors and shareholders conflict at this point. Concerning dividends, Article 290 of the 1938 Commercial Code stated:

> No dividend may be paid until a capital impairment caused by a loss has been made good and the reserve mentioned in the first paragraph of Article 288 has been deducted. Creditors of the corporation may require the refund of dividends when they are paid in violation of the preceding provision.[19]

According to this provision, the amount of profits available for dividends was calculated by the following formula, if there were no accumulated profits available for dividends:

> The amount of profits available for dividends = the profits for the current period - the legal reserve for the current period - capital impairment, if any.......................(1)

---

[17]Yasubei Hasegawa, "Shoho Kaisei ni tomonau Kaisha-Keisan no Shomondai" (Some Problems on the Corporate Accounting Arising from the Revision of the Commercial Code), Kaikei (Accounting), Vol. 42, No. 3, (March, 1938), p. 9.

[18]Littleton, op. cit., p. 206.

[19]The first paragraph of Article 288 reads: The corporation shall retain at least one-twentieth of the profit for the current period until it shall amount to one-fourth of the stated capital.

The calculation of the profits for the current period depended upon the balance sheet, however, since the profit was defined in the Commercial Code as the excess of corporate net worth over stated capital and legal reserve.[20] Profit for the current period was calculated as follows:

Profits for the current period = (assets - liabilities) - stated capital - accumulated legal reserve..........................(2)

The amount of profits available for dividends was calculated by the following formula which is usually called the "comparison of net worth method."

The amount of profits available for dividends = (assets - liabilities) - stated capital - legal reserve - capital impairment, if any..(3)

The accounting provisions for asset valuation were first applied in the preparation of the inventory or listing of assets. The inventory was prepared by the "count and price" method.[21] These provisions also applied to the balance sheet. The balance sheet prepared in accordance with the requirements of the Commercial Code were based upon the inventory. The balances of assets and liabilities at the end of the accounting period were ascertained by this method. The balance of the stated capital, however, could not be calculated by the "count and price" method if there were any change in the amount of the stated capital during the prieod. This change in the stated capital had to be disclosed by the systematically recorded data. The income statement in the Japanese Commercial Code was said to be a by-product of two calculations of capital, the "count and price" and the "syste-

---

[20]Tanaka and Kubo, op. cit., p. 147.

[21]A. C. Littleton and V. K. Zimmerman, Accounting Theory: Continuity and Change (Englewood Cliffs, New Jersey: Prentice-Hall, Inc., 1962), pp. 73-74.

matic record" methods, or a schedule of the profits calculated in the
balance sheet.[22] This means that the amount of profits to be entered into
a statement of proposals pertaining to the disposal of profits did not
come from the income statement but came from the balance sheet. In other
words, the accounting system in the Japanese Commercial Code, which was
influenced by the Franco-German laws, emphasized the inventory and did not
necessarily rely on the Anglo-American type of income statement.

Application, Sanctions, and Administration of the Commercial Code.
According to a historical study by Ichiro Katano of corporate financial
reporting in Japan, the accounting system introduced in the national banks
is considered to have been the first step toward a modern accounting system
for the corporation in Japan.[23] The national banks of Japan were established
in 1873 and were developed by using the national banking system of the United
States as a model. The accounting system in the national banks, however,
was designed by Alexander Allan Shand from Great Britain and was based on his
book, Ginko-Boki-Seiho (The Detailed Method of Bank Bookkeeping) which was
published by the Ministry of Finance of Japan in 1873. Until the partial
enforcement of the Old Commercial Code in 1893, the financial reporting
system of the national banks had a great influence on the financial reporting
practices of commercial and industrial corporations in Japan. That is, most
corporations usually prepared two financial statemsnts: (1) a combined state-

[22]Iwao Iwata, "Shoho ni okeru Keiri Taikei" (Accounting System in the
Commercial Code), Kaikei (Accounting), Vol. 56, No. 1, (February, 1949), p. 39.

[23]Ichiro Katano, "Nihon Zaimushohyo Seido no Tenkai to Kadai" (Development of Corporate Financial Reporting in Japan and Its Problems), Kigyokaikei
(Accounting), Vol. 18, No. 2, (February, 1966), p. 11.

ment of income and profit appropriation, and (2) a balance sheet before profit appropriation or a balance sheet after profit appropriation.[24]

The partial enforcement of the Old Commercial Code, which required a stock corporation to prepare the five financial documents mentioned in the previous section, posed two problems.[25] The first problem was the change in the nature of the balance sheet. The balance sheet had long been based upon the systematically recorded data but the inclusion by the Commercial Code of the inventory in financial documents made the balance sheet independent of the systematically recorded data. The second problem was the separation of a combined statement of income and profit appropriation into an income statement and a statement of proposals pertaining to the disposal of profits.

The case of Nihon Yusen Corporation, which adapted its financial statements system to the requirement of the Commercial Code, may well illustrate this problem.[26] The following is a comparison of the old and new financial statements system of the Nihon Yusen Corporation.

(Before the Enforcement of the Commercial Code)

1. a statement of profit and loss accounts (a combined statement of income and profits appropriation)
2. a balance sheet (a balance sheet after profits appropriation)
3. a statement of self-insurance reserve account (a special type of statement of earned surplus)
4. a statement of big repairs reserve account (a special type statement of earned surplus)

---

[24] Ichiro Katano, "Nihon Zaimushohyo Seido no Tenkai to Kadai -3-" (Development of Corporate Financial Reporting in Japan and Its Problems -3-), Kigyokaikei (Accounting), Vol. 18, No. 5, (May, 1966), pp. 10-12.

[25] In the Old Commercial Code, the term "an accounting statement" was used for "an income statement" (Article 218).

[26] Ibid., pp. 21-27. Nihon Yusen Corporation is one of the oldest marine transportation companies in Japan.

(After the Enforcement of the Commercial Code)

1. an accounting statement
    section 1 a statement of profit and loss accounts
               (an income statement)
    section 2 a statement of self-insurance reserve account
               (a special type provision statement)
    section 3 a statement of big repairs account (a special
               type provision statement)
2. a balance sheet (a balance sheet before profits appropriation)
3. an inventory (a list of assets before profits appropriation)
4. a statement of proposals pertaining to the disposal of profits

This illustration serves as evidence of the legal power of the Commercial

Code. Most Japanese stock corporations, such as the Nihon Yusen Corporation,

seem to have reorganized their financial statement systems to comply with

the requirements of the Commercial Code. The financial statements of the

Nihon Yusen Corporation provided for detailed accounting information because

it was incorporated in 1885 and had been operated under the control of the

Ministry of Agriculture and Commerce.

The presentation of financial statements by many Japanese stock corpora-

tions, however, was generally less informative since the Commercial Code

contained no prescriptions concerning the manner of preparation of financial

statements. The following quotation from the Edwards Mission's report

explains the common practice of financial reporting in Japan:

> The financial statements submitted to Japanese stockholders
> are curiosities in obscurity and evasion. By way of illustration,
> the stated assets of Yasuda Kogyo, as carried on the 1944 balance
> sheet, are reproduced below:

	In thousands of Yen
Plant and property	740
Investments	444
Other fixed assets	11
Cash	5
Bank deposits	1,691

Receivables	1,865
Inventories	617
Deferred charges	358
Other current assets	34,679
Total assets	40,410

The absence of reserves for depreciation, of an indication of the basis for valuation of assets, of a description of the nature of receivables, and of any provisions for bad debts would be major deficiencies in themselves; but the lumping of more than 75 per cent of the assets under the caption "other current assets" deprives the balance sheet of any real value which it might otherwise have.[27]

Concerning the income statements presentation, the same report stated:

The profit and loss statement of Japanese corporations are as obscure as their balance sheets. The 1944 statement of the same Yasuda Kogyo (with some rearrangement of items) appears as follows:

INCOME ITEMS	¥1,000	
Sales	4,863	
Income from investments	2,403	
Miscellaneous other income		
(including return from tax reserves)	250	
Total income		7,521
EXPENSE ITEMS		
Cost of sales (including depreciation)	4,666	
Taxes paid	208	
Miscellaneous other expenses	1,573	
Total expenses		6,447
Net earnings		1,074
Dividends paid	670	
Other deduction	342	
Total deductions		1,012
Carried to surplus		62

---

[27]U. S. Department of State, Report of the Mission on Japanese Combines -- Part I: Analytical and Technical Data (Publication 2628, Far Eastern Series 14)(Washington, D. C., March, 1946), p. 26. Yasuda Kogyo, manufacturer of nails, is one of the stock corporations held by the Yasuda Zaibatsu.

The statement needs no detailed comment. The blanketing
of all expenses into "cost of sales" and "miscellaneous other
expenses" is sufficient to prevent it from serving much useful
purpose.[28]

Despite its importance from the legal viewpoint, most Japanese corpora-

tions omitted the presentation of the inventory by adding a sentence at the

end of the balance sheet: "the content of the inventory is the same as that

shown in the assets section of this balance sheet."[29] This did not neces-

sarily mean that the inventory was prepared from the balance sheet. Accord-

ing to the requirements of accounting provisions of the Commercial Code,

the inventory should be prepared first. In other words, the inventory was

a schedule to support the balance sheet. Most Japanese corporate executives

did not want to show a detailed picture of financial position and the results

of operations even to the shareholders of their companies. When asked to

explain the meaning of obscure items in the financial statements of their

companies at the general meeting of shareholders, corporate executives fre-

quently could not offer an explanation without resort to supplementary infor-

mation not available to the shareholders.[30]

The Japanese Commercial Code required the statutory auditors to examine

the financial documents which the directors proposed to submit to a general

meeting of shareholders and report their opinion upon them at the shareholders'

general meeting (Article 275). The statutory auditors were to be elected by

the shareholders to safeguard their interests in the company (Article 254 and

[28]Ibid., pp. 26-27.

[29]Ryohei Kato, "Gorikyoku Zaimu-Junsoku to Jitsumu-Kanshu tono Kosaku
-II-" (The Working Rules for Financial Statements by the Ministry of Commerce
and Industry and the Accounting Practices -II-)., Kaikei (Accounting), Vol. 38,
No. 5, (May, 1936), p. 73.

[30]U. S. Department of State, op. cit., p. 26.

280). The statutory auditor system in the Japanese Commercial Code had its origin in the German Commercial Code ef 1870.[31] Unlike the United Kingdom system, there was no legal requirement that the statutory auditors be profes- sional accountants. In most cases, the statutory auditors did not have adequate, active staff members. The statutory auditors could scarcely be considered independent of the directors since in fact they were designated by the directors or by the company's largest creditors group. Therefore, the Japanese statutory auditors were not in a position to conduct a fair and independent audit of the financial statements. The institution of the statutory auditors in Japan was a good illustration of a seemingly sound institution being misused for the ends of management.[32]

The intent of the Japanese Commercial Code to protect the rights of both creditors and shareholders was clearly reflected in the accounting provisions of the Code although the provisions were few in number and defec- tive in substance from an accounting point of view. These accounting pro- visions do not seem to have been properly applied to the accounting practices used by the Japanese stock corporations. One reason for this phenomenon was the lack of supporting working rules for the preparation of financial state- ments. Another reason was the attitude of the corporate executives to the disclosure of financial data. It is quite evident that most Japanese cor- pcrate executives to the disclosure of financial data.

---

[31] Chuhei Yamamura, "Kansa-Yaku Seido" (The Statutory Auditors System) in Kotaro Tanaka (ed.), Kabushiki-Kaisha-Ho Koza, III (Stock Corporation Law Handbook, III)(Tokyo, Japan: Yuhikaku, 1956), p. 1178.

[32] U. S. Department of State, op. cit., p. 23.

The reluctance to disclose financial information is not so surprising because of the unique structure of Japanese industrial society. Most leading stock corporations in Japan were affiliated, directly or indirectly, with the Zaibatsu. According to the official report of the Japanese Holding Company Liquidation Commission, the big ten Zaibatsu controlled 881 stock corporations in all lines of business through their 65 holding companies.[33] Table 1 (page 127) indicates that a relatively large portion of the paid-in capital of all Japanese stock corporations was supplied by the big nine or ten Zaibatsu. Especially the degree of control by these Zaibatsu over the banking, trust, and insurance areas was considerable. The banks affiliated with the Zaibatsu were also the main suppliers of industrial funds in Japan. As Table 2 (page 128) indicates, the amount of industrial funds supplied by banks increased at a very high rate while the rate of increase in funds from sale of capital stocks was low or remained unchanged. These figures indicate that most Japanese investors preferred indirect investment through banks rather than direct investment in the capital stock market. Even investors who preferred the direct investment, the so-called "non-controlling" shareholders, purchased their securities almost entirely on the basis of the reputation of the group controlling their companies.

---

[33]Holding Company Liquidation Commission, Nihon Zaibatsu to sono Kaitai (Japanese Zaibatsu and Their Dissolution)(Tokyo, Japan: Holding Company Liquidation Commission, 1951), pp. 188-89. The big ten Zaibatsu in Japan were: Mitsui, Mitsubishi, Sumitomo, Yasuda, Ayukawa, Asano, Furukawa, Okura, Nakajima, and Nomura.

An Examination of the Working Rules for Financial Statements by the Ministry
of Commerce and Industry

General Nature of the Working Rules for Financial Statements. The
Working Rules for Financial Statements were released in 1934 by the Ministry
of Commerce and Industry as an important method to promote the industrial
rationalization movement in Japan. While the Japanese Commercial Code prescribed some accounting provisions to protect the rights of shareholders and
creditors, financial reporting practices based upon the Code were deficient
in disclosing a true and fair picture of business operations. This situation needed prompt improvement not only to enforce rigid observance of the
intent of the Commercial Code but also for the sound development of individual enterprises and the national economy.

The Working Rules for Financial Statements were composed of (1) Working
Rules for the Balance Sheet, (2) Working Rules for the Inventory, and (3) Working Rules for the Income Statement. The Working Rules for the Balance Sheet
indicated their relationship to the Commercial Code in the following terms:

> The prescribed rules shall be applied to balance sheets prepared
> in accordance with and based upon Article 26 of the 1911 Commer-
> cial Code. The rules shall also be applied to balance sheets
> prepared by business enterprises other than a stock corporation.[34]
>
> The prescribed rules shall be applied to the balance sheet sub-
> mitted at the general meeting of shareholders of the stock corpora-
> tion. The balance sheet to be publicized in accordance with
> Article 192 of the 1911 Commercial Code shall be the same as the
> balance sheet mentioned in the previous sentence so far as circum-
> stances permit....[35]

---

[34] The Working Rules for the Balance Sheet, Rule 1.

[35] Ibid., Rule 2.

Rule 1 of the Working Rules for the Inventory and Rule 1 of the Working Rules for the Income Statement revealed their relationships to the Commercial Code in the same terms. Although the Japanese Commercial Code required all stock corporations to prepare five financial documents, a business report and the statement of proposals pertaining to the disposal of profits were not financial statements in a strict accounting sense. The primary purpose of the Working Rules for Financial Statements by the Ministry of Commerce and Industry was, therefore, to supplement the accounting provisions in the Commercial Code. This meant that the improvement and unification of financial statements for the industrial rationalization movement were not separated from the general application of the accounting provisions in the Commercial Code.

The Working Rules for the Balance Sheet. The Working Rules for the Balance Sheet were composed of 102 rules with the following fifteen sections: (1) general rules, (2) form, (3) fixed assets, (4) investment, (5) special assets, (6) working assets, (7) current assets, (8) miscellaneous accounts (debit), (9) long-term liabilities, (10) short-term liabilities, (11) miscellaneous accounts (credit), (12) provisions, (13) capital, (14) contingent liabilities, (15) consolidation of balance sheets. The Working Rules for the Balance Sheet were mainly concerned with the classification and presentation of assets, liabilities, and capital in the balance sheet. Provisions concerning the contents and valuation of properties were delegated to the Working Rules for Assets Valuation, the Working Rules for the Inventory, and the Working Rules for the Income Statements (Rule 7).[36]

Concerning the classification of properties, the Working Rules stated:

All properties and capital shall be classified based upon
criteria such as type, structure, function, and purpose. Each
caption of the classified groups shall disclose its substance.
Tangible and intangible assets, liabilities and capital shall
be clearly separated. Assets shall be classified in terms of
liquidity, realizability, and security, and liabilities in terms
of their payment date.[37]

As far as criteria for asset classification are concerned, the Working Rules

reflected the basic idea of assets reflected in the Commercial Code. Assets

were classified into: (1) fixed assets, (2) investment, (3) special assets,

(4) working assets, (5) current assets, and (6) miscellaneous accounts.

Liabilities were classified into: (1) long-term liabilities, (2) short-

term liabilities, (3) provisions, and (4) miscellaneous accounts. The

presentation of assets and liabilities in the balance sheet followed this

same order. According to Tetsuzo Ota, a chief drafter of the Working Rules,

the Working Rules adopted this order of presentation at the strong urging

of the committee members representing the Zaibatsu companies.[38] This order

of presentation of the classified groups of assets -- fixed assets first

and miscellaneous accounts last -- emphasized the great interest in the

security of investments in the corporation.

---

[36]The Working Rules for the Assets Valuation, which consisted of 66
rules, was released in February, 1936 by the Ministry of Commerce and
Industry to supplement the Working Rules for the Financial Statements.

[37]Ibid., Rule 5.

[38]The Japanese Accounting Association, "Taishaku-Taisho-Hyo Junsoku
Tokyu" (Symposium on the Working Rules for the Balance Sheet), Kaikei (Accounting), Vol. 46, No. 5, (May, 1940), p. 90.

The accounting rules dealing with the assets referred to in the
Working Rules were different from those of the Commercial Code in two
ways: (1) the scope of assets, and (2) the appropriate valuation basis.
It was in 1938 that the Japanese Commercial Code first recognized three
types of deferred assets, i.e., organization expense, bond discount, and
interest during construction. The Working Rules for the Balance Sheet
recognized, under the caption of "miscellaneous accounts," the following
five types of deferred assets: (1) bond discount, (2) bond expenses,
(3) interest during construction, (4) development expenses, and (5) organization expenses.[39] Bond discount, bond expenses, and development expenses
were quite new concepts of an asset which were not mentioned in the Japanese
Commercial Code. The terms "interest during construction" and "organization
expenses" were employed in the Commercial Code but they were not closely
related to the concept of an asset. The Working Rules recognize these two
items as deferred assets as long as they were properly treated in accordance
with the provision of the Commercial Code. Influenced by the Commercial
Code's basic idea of assets, the Working Rules required that these deferred
assets be amortized as promptly.

All rules for the asset valuation were prescribed in the 1936 Working
Rules for Assets Valuation. The Working Rules for Assets Valuation defined three important asset valuation terms as follows:

   a) Cost. Cost means acquisition cost, that is, it includes the
      purchase price of an asset and all expenditures incurred in
      preparing it for use. The concept of cost consists of both
      purchase cost and production cost....

----

[39]The Working Rules for the Balance Sheet, Rules 55, 56, 57, and 59.

b) Value. Value means the price of the asset at the time of
    valuation and at the place of its location. If a market
    price is available for the asset, it shall be applied. If
    a market price is not available, the asset shall be valued
    by careful estimation....
c) Book value. Book value means the amount recorded in the
    accounting books at the valuation date. The book value of
    an asset acquired during the current period is usually equal
    to its cost, but the book value of assets acquired in the
    prior periods is adjusted by proper procedures for such things
    as additional expenditures, depreciation, and change in valua-
    tion methods.[40]

Following these definitions, the Working Rules for Assets Valuation pre-

scribed eight rules for asset valuation:

a) Land shall be valued at cost.
b) Buildings, machinery, and equipment shall be valued at a cost-
    less-depreciation basis.
c) The recognition of intangible fixed assets such as goodwill
    shall be limited to those which have substantial value and
    they shall be valued on a cost-less-amortization basis.
d) Securities shall be divided into two classes in terms of the
    purpose for holding them. Those securities held for a long
    term shall be valued at their costs if cost is lower than
    current market prices. The temporarily held securities shall
    be valued on a lower-than-market-price basis.
e) Working assets, such as raw materials, finished goods, and
    merchandise, shall be valued at "cost or market, whichever is
    lower."
f) Receivables shall be valued on a book-value-less-uncollectible-
    amount basis.
g) Other assets shall be valued in the light of their nature.
h) All liabilities shall be valued at their book value.[41]

In general, the basic principle underlying the eight rules was the lower-than-

market-price basis which was adopted by the Japanese Commercial Code in 1911

although the Working Rules introduced a partial-cost basis.

---

[40]The Working Rules for Assets Valuation, Rule 2.

[41]Ibid., Rule 3.

The Working Rules for the Inventory. The Working Rules for the
Inventory were composed of 40 rules with five sections: (1) general rules,
(2) form, (3) assets, (4) liabilities, and (5) net worth. One of the most
important characteristics of the Working Rules was to have placed properly
in a system of financial statements for the stock corporation the inventory
which the Japanese Commercial Code had required all stock corporations to
prepare for the purpose of protecting creditors.[42] The Working Rules for
the Inventory defined the inventory as a detailed list of all the assets
and liabilities (Rule 3).

The inventory was prepared after confirming the quantity and amount of
every asset and liability by physical examination and by an examination of
original documents (Rule 6). All assets and liabilities thus confirmed
were classified as precisely as possible under the designated captions.
This means that the inventory prescribed in the Working Rules was more than
merely a summary of the balances in the recorded accounts and presented an
independent statement from the records in the accounting books.

In the inventory, the difference between the total amount of assets and
the total amount of liabilities was referred to as "net worth" (Rule 39).
From the creditors' point of view, the amount of net worth was an important
figure indicating a margin of safety for them. Thus, the inventory was presented in the following form: Assets - Liabilities = New Worth. In addition, the inventory prescribed in the Working Rules required the reporting

[42]Ichiro Katano, "Nihon Zaimushohyo Seido no Tenkai to Kadai -V-"
(Development of Corporate Financial Reporting in Japan and Its Problems -V-),
Kigyokaikei (Accounting), Vol. 18, No. 9 (September, 1966), p. 38.

of "uncalled capital" below the amount of net worth (Rule 12). Under the

Japanese Commercial Code, a corporation could legally come into existence

when more than one-fourth of the total amount of the authorized capital

stock was paid in by shareholders. After the incorporation, the directors

of the stock corporation could call for additional payment from the share-

holders to the original issuing price of shares whenever they believed

that the corporation needed more capital funds. The difference between the

issuing price of shares and the actual, first payment by the shareholders

was referred to as the "uncalled capital."

Despite opposition by committee members representing accounting educa-

tors, the Working Rules for Financial Statements sanctioned the accounting

practice of listing "uncalled capital" on the asset side of the balance

sheet and adding it to the amount of net worth in the inventory because of

the strong urging of the Japanese bankers.[43] This accounting practice had

long been Japanese custom although it was not accepted as good accounting

practices in western countries.[44] The "uncalled capital" was legally regarded

as an obligation of the shareholders to the company. Since the amount and

time of call, however, were uncertain, to regard it as an asset and show the

gross amount of "capital stock authorized" on the equity side of the balance

sheet was questionable. There seems to be no reason for the distinctive

Japanese treatment since this same uncertainty prevailed in all societies.

Until the uncalled capital is actually called by the directors of the com-

pany, it does not represent outstanding capital stock.

---

[43]The Japanese Accounting Association, op. cit., p. 91.

[44]Research and Statistics Division, Economic and Scientific Section, GHQ, SCAP, Instructions for the Preparation of Financial Statements of Manufacturing and Trading Companies, (Tokyo, Japan: Research and Statistics Division, Economic and Scientific Section, GHQ, SCAP, 1947), p. 29.

The <u>Working</u> <u>Rules</u> <u>for</u> <u>the</u> <u>Income</u> <u>Statement</u>. The Working Rules for

the Income Statement totaled 38 with the following seven sections: (1) gen-

eral, (2) form, (3) manufacturing cost accounting, (4) sales income account-

ing, (5) operating income accounting, (6) net income accounting, and (7) ap-

propriation of net income. Before the enforcement of the Japanese Commercial

Code, the preparation of a combined statement of income and profit appropria-

tion was common accounting practice. The Japanese Commercial Code, as men-

tioned earlier, divided this combined statement into an income statement and

a statement of proposals pertaining to the disposal of profits, but it did

not prescribe the content and form of the income statement. One of the main

objectives of the Working Rules for the Income Statement was to present the

content and form of the income statement.

Concerning the presentation of the income statement, the Working Rules

required:

> The income statement shall be divided into the following sections
> indicating the different types of business activities. These
> sections may be combined, or no separation may be needed, so far
> as the statement discloses clearly the results of operations:
> (a) Sections for the manufacturing company;
>   the first section   ...   Manufacturing cost accounting
>   the second section ...   Sales income accounting
>   the third section   ...   Operating income accounting
>   the fourth section ...   Net income accounting
> (b) Sections for a trading company;
>   the first section   ...   Sales income accounting
>   the second section ...   Operating income accounting
>   the third section   ...   Net income accounting
> In the case of a company that operates more than one line of
> business or has a secondary business, the income statement,
> with the same sectional arrangement as described above, may
> be prepared for each business.[45]

---

[45]The <u>Working</u> <u>Rules</u> <u>for</u> <u>the</u> <u>Income</u> <u>Statement</u>, Rule 4.

The first important features of the Working Rules for the Income Statement was the adoption of the "multiple-step" income statement: the income statement, designed for the use by the manufacturing company, consisted of four sections and the income statement for the trading company was composed of three sections. The adoption of the multiple-step type of income statement was not new. The arrangement of the sections in the income statement, however, was unique. The "manufacturing cost accounting" sections was designed to present the cost of products finished during the current period (Rule 9). According to the common accounting practice, a manufacturing cost report is prepared as a schedule to support the income statement and is not included in the income statement. The Working Rules for the Income Statement, as mentioned earlier, were closely related to the Japanese Commercial Code. They were also designed as an important means to rationalize business operations. The inclusion of the "manufacturing cost accounting" section in the income statement was a device to meet the informational needs required for industrial rationalization within the framework of the financial statements prescribed by the Commercial Code.

The "sales income accounting" section reported the income from the sales of rpoducts, by-products, or merchandise (Rule 20). In this section, "cost of goods sold" and "selling expenses," such as salesmen's commissions, salesmen's salaries, and advertising expenses, were deducted from "sales revenue" to arrive at "sales income." The "operating income accounting" section was designed to show the ordinary income from the broad business activities other than sales activities (Rule 28). The concept of "operating income" in the Working Rules was broader than the "operating income" concept commonly used in

American accounting practices in that the former contained the so-called "non-operating income" and "non-operating expenses" items, such as interest income, dividends received, interest expenses, and amortization of bond discount and expenses, as well as general and administrative expenses. "Operating income" was calculated by adding to or subtracting from "sales income" the ordinary items. In the "net income accounting" section, extra-ordinary items, i.e., gains or losses from (a) the sale or abandonment of fixed assets, (b) the sale of securities, and (c) the write-off of fixed assets and securities, were added to or deducted from the "operating income" to arrive at "net income" (Rule 34). By inclusion of "net income accounting," the Working Rules supported the "all-inclusive type of income statement

Based upon the financial statements system of the Japanese Commercial Code, the Working Rules for the Income Statement distinguished conceptually the process of income determination from the process of appropriation of net income. Concerning the presentation of "accounting for appropriation of net income," the Working Rules stated:

> Although accounting for appropriation of net income is separate
> from the development of the income statement, it will be disclosed
> as a part of the income statement for the sake of convenience.[46]

This statement obscured the basic views of the Working Rules in distinguish-ing between the income statement and "accounting for appropriation of new income."[47] The income statement illustrated in the Working Rules was a dynamic schedule showing an entire picture of income from its production to its disposi-

---

[46]Ibid., Rule 5.

[47]Katano, op. cit., p. 34.

tion since it contained the "accounting for appropriation of net income."

As analyzed above, the Working Rules for Financial Statements by the Ministry of Commerce and Industry went into considerable detail because its purpose was to improve the public financial reporting system of all business enterprises. The content of the Working Rules was educational and theoretical rather than practical on the one hand, and accounting-oriented rather than law-oriented on the other hand probably because they were drafted primarily by two leading Japanese accounting professors, the late Ryozo Yoshida and Tetsuzo Ota. Ryozo Yoshida was one of the pioneers who introduced American accounting theory into Japan even though many western bookkeeping techniques were already introduced during the last half of the nineteenth century from England, France, Germany, and the United States.[48] In 1910 Ryozo Yoshida published the first accounting book in Japan, entitled Accounting. It was largely under the influence of the Anglo-American accounting thoughts of L. R. Dicksee, G. Lisle, and H. R. Hatfield.[49] The Working Rules for Financial Statements were a product of the efforts of Japanese accountants to put new Anglo-American accounting thought into the old Franco-German form.

---

[48]For the details of the early history of double-entry bookkeeping in Japan, see Kojiro Nishikawa, "The Early History of Double-entry Bookkeeping in Japan," in A. C. Littleton and B. S. Yamey (eds.), Studies in the History of Accounting (Homewood, Illinois: Richard D. Irwin, Inc., 1956), pp. 380-87.

[49]Wasaburo Kimura, Nihon ni okeru Boki Kaikeigaku no Hatten (Development of Bookkeeping and Accounting in Japan) (Tokyo, Japan: Choryusha, 1950), pp. 36-37. Of these three the influence of Hatfield's book is said to have been most direct and greatest. Henry Rand Hatfield, Modern Accounting, (New York: D. Appleton and Company, 1909).

Since there were objections against the legal enforcement of the
Working Rules even among committee members, their application was not enforced. The Working Rules for Financial Statements were much too detailed
to be applied to accounting practice. Many Japanese accounting educators,
however, admitted that the effect of the Working Rules for both accounting
education and the improvement of financial reporting practices in Japan was
profound. Ichiro Katano, for example, states:

> The corporate financial reporting in Japan, which began in 1873 with
> the introduction of the Anglo-American type of "combined accounting
> for income and profit appropriation," absorbed about twenty years
> later the Franco-German type of "accounting for properties" and
> emphasized the protection of creditors. After forty year of experience,
> these two types of financial reporting were reconciled and integrated
> into the Working Rules for Financial Statements by the Ministry
> Commerce and Industry in 1934 as a model for the Japanese financial
> reporting system for stock corporations. Since the Working Rules
> had both historical background and practical experience, their effect
> on the rationalization of accounting in Japan was profound. They
> were dominant in accounting thought until A Statement of Business
> Accounting Principles was established after World War II.[50]

An Investigation of the Tentative Standards for Financial Statements of Manufacturing Companies by the Planning Board

General Nature of the Tentative Standards for Financial Statement. The
nature of the Tentative Standards for Financial Statements of Manufacturing
Companies, released by the Planning Board in 1941, was considerably different from that of the Working Rules for Financial Statements issued by
the Ministry of Commerce and Industry. The difference in nature between the
Tentative Standards and the Working Rules seem to have stemmed from the
varying purposes for which they were expected to serve under the different

---

[50]Katano, op. cit., p. 41.

economic and political conditions. The Tentative Standards for Financial

Statements, as noted in Chapter II, were released as an important means

of the central control of the national economy during wartime. Although

control by the government over the munitions industry began in 1939, the

scope of central control by the government was enlarged to include general

manufacturing companies by the publication of the Tentative Standards for

Financial Statements. The primary purpose of the Tentative Standards was

to implement the policies of the Corporate Accounting Control Ordinance.

The Tentative Standards required manufacturing companies to present finan-

cial statement information which was used as the basic data for establishing

a fair profit distribution policy, determining price policy, and formulating

financial policy for the national economy.[51]

As with the Working Rules for Financial Statements by the Ministry of

Commerce and Industry, the Tentative Standards for Financial Statements of

Manufacturing Companies were composed of (1) the Tentative Standards for the

Balance Sheet, (2) the Tentative Standards of the Inventory, and (3) the

Tentative Standards for the Income Statement. Concerning the Relationship

to the Commercial Code, however, the Tentative Standards for Financial State-

ments contained neither positive nor negative provisions. This means that

the Tentative Standards emphasized the need for closer relationship with

the Corporate Accounting Control Ordinance of 1940, although they did not

explicitly declare their severance from the Commercial Code.[52]

---

[51]Shuho Nakagawa, "Kikakuin Zaimushohyo Junsoku no Seikaku" (The Nature of the Tentative Standards for Financial Statements by the Planning Board), Kaikei (Accounting), Vol. 50, No. 5, (May, 1942), p. 60.

[52]The Working Rules for Financial Statements by the Ministry of Commerce and Industry declared positively their relationship to the Commercial Code. The Working Rules for Financial Statements of the Factories of Munitions by the Ministry of the Army in 1940 denied explicitly their relationship to the Commercial Code.

The Tentative Standards for the Balance Sheet. The Tentative Standards

for the Balance Sheet were composed of 49 standards or rules and were

classified under five chapters: (1) general standards, (2) assets,

(3) liabilities, (4) capital, and (5) contingent liabilities. The number

of standards was less than half those proposed by the Working Rules for the

Balance Sheet. They were mostly of an administrative, directive nature and

contained no statement which could properly be called "principles" or

"standards." Concerning the classification of balance sheet items, the

Tentative Standards provided only the following uniform classification

without noting the criterion for the classification:

Debit (Assets)
1. Uncalled Capital
2. Fixed Assets
   (1) Tangible Assets
       Land
       Buildings
       Structures
       Machinery and equipment
       Vessels
       Vehicles and delivery
          equipment
       Tools, furnitures, and
          fixtures
       Construction in process account
   (2) Intangible Assets
       Patent
       Surface right and mining right
       Good will
       Organization expenses
       Experimental and research
          expenses
   (3) Long-term Investment
       Investment in controlling
          companies
       Long-term investment
3. Current Assets
   (1) Inventories
       Material
       Supplies

Credit (Liabilities and Capital)
1. Capital
   (1) Capital Stock
   (2) Legal Reserve
   (3) Voluntary Reserve
2. Liabilities
   (1) Long-term Liabilities
       Debentures
       Long-term Loans
   (2) Short-term Liabilities
       Short-term Loans
       Accounts payable
       Prepayments received
       Deposits received
       Other liabilities
          payable
       Deferred revenue
       Temporary receipt
   (3) Provisions
3. Profit
   (1) Profit Carried forward
       from the Previous Period
   (2) Profit for the Current
       Period

    Semi-products
    Products
    Work-in-process
    By-products and scrap
    (2) Quick Assets
    Securities
    Short-term credit
    Accounts receivable
    Accrued revenue
    Prepaid expenses
    Cash in bank and cash on hand
4. Deferred Assets
    (1) Bond Discount
    (2) Interest during Construction
5. Loss
    (1) Loss Carried forward from the
         Previous Period
    (2) Loss for the Current Period

Whereas the Working Rules for the Financial Statements left much room

for exercising judgment in applying the rules, the Tentative Standards for

Financial Statements suggested clearly prescribed procedures. The following

provisions dealing with the accounting for an affiliated company, for example,

present a sharp contrast between the Working Rules and the Tentative Standards.

> Affiliated companies are those companies which are connected with
> one another by common ownership and control. Parent company, sub-
> sidiary company, and sister companies, in general terms, constitute
> affiliation.[53]

> Under the caption of "Investment in Controlling Company," the
> amount of stocks possessed for the control purpose shall be
> entered. If a company possessed more than one-third of the total
> number of shares of any company, the company shall be regarded
> as a controlling company.[54]

The Tentative Standards for the Balance Sheet required that the amount of

assets and liabilities in the balance sheet be equal to that in the inventory

(Standard 5). This established the dependence of the balance sheet upon the

---

[53]The Working Rules for the Balance Sheet, Rule 23.

[54]The Tentative Standards for the Balance Sheet, Standard 19.

inventory. Although the Tentative Standards for the Inventory prescribed
that the valuation of properties to be listed in the inventory should be
based upon the Tentative Standards for Assets Valuation (Standard 5), the
latter was not published as originally scheduled. Thus, the Tentative
Standards for the Balance Sheet remained incomplete.

The Tentative Standards for the Inventory. The Tentative Standards for
the Inventory included 37 standards. Unlike the Working Rules for the
Inventory by the Ministry of Commerce and Industry, the Tentative Standards
for the Inventory contained no substantive provisions. Their primary concern
was to prescribe a standard form for the inventory. Except for the "Loss"
section on the debit side of the "Capital" and "Profit" sections on the credit
side of the balance sheet, the presentation of properties in the inventory
was the same as that used in the balance sheet. The prescribed inventory was
designed to show the details of assets and liabilities, and did not contain
the "net worth" section. This was a traditional type of the inventory except
for the inclusion of "uncalled capital" as an asset.

The Tentative Standards for the Income Statement. The Tentative Standards
for the Income Statement contained 21 standards, whereas the Working Rules for
the Income Statement contained 38 rules under seven sections. One of the
most important features of the Tentative Standards for the Income Statement was
the adoption of the "single-step" income statement: The income statement
consisted of a "profit" section and a "loss" section. Although there was no
explanation for the adoption of the "single-step" income statement, the primary reason seems to have been pragmatic. That is, to be followed as
thoroughly as possible, the Tentative Standards had to be simple and practica-
ble.

Concerning the presentation of the income statement, the Tentative

Standards provided:

The income statement items shall be presented in accordance with the following classification. Each group of items may be sub-divided:[55]

Losses	Profits
1. Inventories, the beginning balance	1. Inventories, the ending balance
2. Inventories, purchased	2. Fixed assets, produced
3. Labor	3. Sales
4. Manufacturing overhead	4. Interest and dividend income
5. General administration and selling	5. Profit on revaluation of assets
6. Interest expense	6. Profit on disposition of assets
7. Loss on reduction of assets value	7. Miscellaneous profit
8. Loss on disposition of assets	
9. Miscellaneous loss	

The six items (No. 1 through No. 4 in the "Losses" section, and Nos. 1 and 2

in the "Profits" section) were elements used for the calculation of cost of

goods sold. The Tentative Standard allowed them to be presented under the

heading of "cost of goods sold" if the company kept cost records based upon

the Manual for Cost Accounting issued by the Ministry of the Army and the

Ministry of the Navy (Standard 19). The income statement prescribed in the

Tentative Standards was extremely simple as compared to that required by the

1934 Working Rules for the Financial Statement. It was also simpler than the

balance sheet presentation required by the Tentative Standards.

The foregoing analysis reveals that the Tentative Standards for Financial

Statements by the Planning Board prescribed the minimum requirements for

financial statements. They were designed to serve a limited purpose. The

Japanese government needed the financial information from manufacturing

---

[55]The Tentative Standards for the Income Statement, Standard 4.

companies to exercise its control over the national economy under wartime
circumstances. None of the Tentative Standards for the Balance Sheet,
the Inventory, and the Income Statement were supported by basic principles
or standards. In the Paton and Littleton usage they were not a statement
of "accounting standards" but a statement of "standardized accounting."[56]

Summary

From the legal point of view, the shareholders, the directors, and the
statutory auditors were the insiders of the stock corporation because the
corporation could not come into existence as a legal entity without these
three groups. The tendency toward the separation of the management from the
owners did not basically change this idea of the Japanese Commercial Code,
although the regulations concerning the relationship between the management
group and the shareholders group were changed in 1938 to maintain a balance
of justice between them. The outsiders of the corporation in the Commercial
Code were designated in a broad sense as creditors. In addition to creditors
in a narrow sense, suppliers of goods and services, laborers, and even
government were considered as creditors. From the viewpoint of the Commercial
Code, the relationship between the corporation and its creditors was an
external relation and the relationship between the corporation and its shareholders was an internal one. Thus, the protection of the creditors became
the primary concern of the Commercial Code. The protection of the shareholders was secondary.

The accounting provisions in the Japanese Commercial Code were prescribed in accordance with this basic idea of the Commercial Code. The
accounting provisions, which emphasized the inventory and the balance sheet

---

[56]Paton and Littleton, op. cit., p. 5.

rather than the income statement, were not illogical by themselves judging from the purpose of the Japanese Commercial Code. In other words, the accounting provisions in the Japanese Commercial Code were supported by the "static" view of accounting which held that the primary concern of the Commercial Code was to determine the value of the corporation at a certain point of time by the "count and price" method. Although there was a considerable increase in the separation of management and ownership during this period (1890-1947), a large proportion of Japanese corporations were under the control of the Zaibatsu as Table 1 shows (Page 127). For these companies the substantive separation of the two groups was not apparent and even the decisions by the so-called "absentee shareholders" with respect to purchasing stock were not based upon financial information but rather upon the reputation of the management of such companies.

During the period analyzed in this chapter, rather incomplete public financial reporting based upon the accounting provisions of the Commercial Code was common. The Financial Statements published by most Japanese corporations were not particularly informative because the accounting provisions were few in number and deficient in substance. The need to present more informative financial statements was first recognized by the Japanese government in relation to the industrial rationalization movement of the 1930's. The Working Rules for Financial Statements issued by the Ministry of Commerce and Industry in 1934 were an historical product of a series of movements toward the improvement and unification of Japanese financial reporting. One of the most important features of the Working Rules for Financial Statements was the introduction of Anglo-American accounting thought into the framework of traditional law.

The income statement prescribed in the Working Rules was a comprehensive type of income statement based upon the "matching concept." The "multiple-step" income statement was analytical and informative. If the Working Rules had been promulgated as a law or regulation to supplement the Commercial Code as originally scheduled, the public financial reporting in Japan would have been significantly improved. They were too educational and detailed to be applied practically. The basic ideas of accounting developed in the Working Rules, however, were generally accepted by accountants. The author believes that the Working Rules laid the cornerstone of the modern, public financial reporting in Japan.

The nature of the 1941 Tentative Standards for Financial Statements by the Planning Board represented a great contrast to the Working Rules for Financial Statements of 1934. They did not contain statement which could be called "standards" or "principles." Under the emergency conditions of wartime, the government needed financial information on all manufacturing companies in order to exert control over them. This was necessary because all manufacturing companies were related, directly or indirectly, to the war potential of Japan. This accounts for the simplicity of the Tentative Standards for Financial Statements. They represented minimum requirements for disclosing financial information by the manufacturing companies and were a statement of "standardized accounting" designed for the exclusive use of the government.

TABLE 1   Paid-in Capital of Stock Corporations Owned
or Controlled by the Big Ten Zaibatsu

(Money Amounts in
Millions of Yen)

	1937			1946		
	Paid-in Capital Owned by the Big Nine Zaibatsu[x] (A)	Total Paid-in Capital of All Stock Corporations (B)	A/B (%)	Paid-in Capital Owned by the Big Ten Zaibatsu (A)	Total Paid-in Capital of All Stock Corporations (B)	A/B (%)
Financing:						
Banking	309	1,419	21.8	508	1,007	50.4
Trust	32	73	43.6	35	41	85.4
Insurance	74	147	50.5	102	168	60.3
Total	415	1,639	25.3	645	1,216	53.0
Heavy Industries:						
Mining	516	1,453	35.5	1,551	3,071	50.5
Metal	134	911	14.7	1,599	3,830	41.8
Machinery	331	1,048	31.6	4,086	6,019	67.9
Shipbuilding	25	264	9.5	203	1,614	12.5
Chemicals	254	1,389	18.3	1,142	2,969	38.5
Total	1,260	5,065	24.9	8,581	17,503	49.0
Light Industries:						
Paper	20	364	5.8	25	535	4.7
Ceramics	139	298	46.6	176	315	55.8
Textiles	111	1,075	10.3	243	1,289	18.8
Fishery & Foods	87	718	12.1	124	1,183	10.4
Others	47	554	8.4	205	1,266	16.2
Total	404	2,991	13.5	773	4,588	16.8
Others:						
Electric Power & Gas	96	2,649	3.6	21	3,826	0.5
Land Transportation	82	1,278	6.4	52	933	5.6
Marine Transportation	91	476	19.2	609	992	61.4
Real Estate & Warehouse	134	635	21.2	176	599	29.4
Commerce	189	2,920	6.5	552	2,724	20.3
Total	592	7,958	7.4	1,410	9,074	15.5
Grand Total	2,671	17,653	15.1	11,409	32,381	35.2

Source: Holding Company Liquidation Commission, Nihon Zaibatsu to sono
Kaitai Shiryo (Data on the Dissolution of Japanese Zaibatsu)
(Tokyo, Japan: Holding Company Liquidation Commission, 1950),
pp. 468-69 and pp. 472-73.

[x]Nakajimi Zaibatsu was excluded since it was not yet established
by 1937.

TABLE 2   Net Supply of Industrial Funds
in Japan (Increase or Decrease)

(Money Amounts in
Millions of Yen)

	Sources of Industrial Funds					Total
	Capital Stocks	Debentures	Loans from Banks	Loans from other Financial Institutions	Loans from Govern- ment	
1936	996	-68	498	45	91	1,562
1937	1,986	-7	1,438	345	-29	3,733
1938	2,286	357	1,337	639	-20	4,598
1939	2,330	750	3,079	576	195	6,930
1940	2,940	609	3,636	577	-109	7,653
1941	3,523	1,225	3,014	391	-112	8,041
1942	3,930	1,362	4,697	322	207	10,518
1943	3,956	1,368	5,644	620	596	12,184
1944	2,303	2,098	18,800	-4,145	169	19,225
1945	3,082	325	46,466	-640	1,172	50,405

Source: Nihon Ginko Tokei Kyoku (Statistics Department, the Bank of
Japan), Honpo Keizai Tokei -- 1964 (Economic Statistics of
Japan -- 1964) (Tokyo, Japan: Statistics Department, the
Bank of Japan, 1965), Table 14, pp. 31-32.

CHAPTER IV

AN ANALYSIS OF ACCOUNTING PRINCIPLES
AT THE SECOND STAGE OF THEIR DEVELOPMENT (1947-1962)

Instructions for the Preparation of Financial Statements of Manufacturing
and Trading Companies by GHQ, SCAP

Legitimation. A pamphlet entitled "Instructions for the Preparation
of Financial Statements of Manufacturing and Trading Companies" was issued
in 1947 by the Research and Statistics Division, Economic and Scientific
Section of the General Headquarters, Supreme Commander for the Allied
Powers (GHQ, SCAP). As described in Chapter II, the issuance of this
pamphlet was based upon a memorandum "Report to be made by Certain Business
Firms" (SCAPIN-177) issued by GHQ, SCAP.

Despite the requirement of SCAPIN-177 that all reports be prepared
in English according to the principles and in the form of the best accounting practice current in the United States, the financial statements
furnished by the Zaibatsu companies to SCAP were not completely in accord
with such accounting principles and practices. This indicated that the
usual accounting practices followed by most Japanese corporations were
different in many respects from those used in the United States. Recognition of this difference was the primary reason why the "Instructions for
the Preparation of Financial Statements of Manufacturing and Trading
Companies" (this title hereafter will be abbreviated to "GHQ Instructions")
was released. The GHQ Instructions were specifically designed to gather
information on the Zaibatsu companies which SCAP authorities needed to
implement their occupation policies of dissolving the Zaibatsu. They were
not Japanese accounting principles or rules. The GHQ Instructions, how-

ever, were applied to the Japanese "restricted" companies mentioned in Chapter II and had a great influence on the establishment of A Statement of Business Accounting Principles in 1949.

The 73-page pamphlet of GHQ Instruction consisted of the following five sections of text with illustrations of six different statement forms: (1) Introductory Statement, (2) Instructions with respect to the Detailed Balance Sheet, (3) Instructions with respect to the Detailed Profit and Loss Statement, (4) Instructions with respect to the Surplus Reconcilement Statement, and (5) Instructions with respect to Plan for Distribution of Accumulated Undivided Profits.

The GHQ Instructions was not a statement of "principles" or "standards." Rather it was a manual of detailed instructions for the preparation of financial statements in conformity with the accepted accounting practices in occidental countries.[1] In other words, the GHQ Instructions suggested the manner of presenting accounting information in the financial statements and the necessary changes in classification of ledger accounts for a specific reporting purpose. Following some brief notes on the six financial statements, the GHQ Instructions stated:

> In conclusion of this introduction it seems desirable to state certain rules that are absolutely fundamental to the preparation of clear, intelligible financial statements. These rules must never be violated:
> a. Let each item in the statement represent one particular type of asset, liability, income, or expense. Never combine items of dissimilar character.

---

1. Research and Statistics Division, Economic and Scientific Section, GHQ, SCAP, Instructions for the Preparation of Financial Statements of Manufacturing and Trading Companies (Tokyo, Japan: Research and Statistics Division, Economic and Scientific Section, GHQ, SCAP, 1947), p. 1.

b. Let each item be given a title clearly descriptive of its character.

c. Let item titles and titles of major classifications conform to accepted accounting terminology. (The English titles of the items listed in the exhibits included in this manual do conform to accepted standardized accounting terminology as developed in occidental countries.)

d. Let each item be shown under its proper heading, or major classification. The major classification of Exhibits C and D are shown in Exhibits A and B. Every asset and every liability of any manufacturing or trading concern will fall properly under one, and only one, of the major classifications shown in Exhibit A.

e. All statements must be headed with the name of the company and the period of date for which the statement is prepared.[2]

These were all fundamental rules designed for the meaningful presentation

of accounting information in financial statements.

Although six different statement forms were illustrated, (1) the

balance sheet, (2) the profit and loss statement, (3) the surplus recon-

cilement statement, and (4) the plan for disposition of accumulated

undivided profits were the major financial statements. The other two

statements were (1) a summary balance sheet and (2) a summary profit

and loss statement. Of the four basic financial statements, "the plan

for disposition of accumulated undivided profits" was not common to

Anglo-American accunting practice because of differences in the concept

of "net profit" and in the treatment of "dividends." As noted in Chapter

III, all Japanese corporations were required to prepare "a statement of

proposals pertaining to the disposal of profits" and to submit it at the

general meeting of shareholders since the directors' proposals needed

---

[2] Ibid., pp. 6-7.

approval by the shareholders. In addition to "dividends," some items, such as corporate income tax, provisions for legal reserve, and bonuses to officers based upon profits, were considered to be dispositions of profits rather than expenses under the Japanese Commercial Code. In western legal and accounting practice there is no need to indicate in the financial statements the dividend plans of the company followed prior to the declaration of a dividend.[3] Acceptance of the Japanese concept of "net profit," however, necessitated in inclusion of the plan for disposition of accumulated undivided profits in the periodical financial statements of a company.[4]

Concerning the presentation of the balance sheet, the GHQ Instructions stated:

It is perhaps well to emphasize that nothing should appear on the asset side of the balance sheet except such items as are in fact assets. It has in the past sometimes been the practice to show accumulated losses and unpaid capital on the asset side of the balance sheet. Such items are in no sense assets, and must not appear among assets.[5]

The GHQ Instructions also defined the term "asset" as:

Any expenditure which gives rise to something of asset value on hand at the balance sheet date, or any expenditure the burden of which should properly be borne by a future period, are proper items to show among assets.[6]

Since the GHQ Instructions did not explain what was meant by "asset value," this definition of an asset was somewhat tautological.

---

[3]Ibid., p. 5.

[4]Ibid., p. 6.

[5]Ibid., p. 9. The term "unpaid capital" used in this quotation is a synonym for "uncalled capital" discussed in Chapter III.

[6]Ibid., p. 10.

The GHQ Instructions' definition of an asset, however, reflected the common concept of an asset developed in American accounting literature, emphasizing "cost" rather than "value," and presented a sharp contrast to the traditional concept of an asset in the Japanese Commercial Code.[7] In other words, the GHQ Instructions defined an asset from a dynamic point of view of accounting.

The Edwards Mission on Japanese Combines reported several deficiencies in Japanese practices of preparing financial statements as mentioned in the previous chapter.[8] The GHQ Instructions recommended prompt correction of these deficiences. Most Japanese stock corporations wrote off depreciation and depletion against the asset account instead of maintaining "allowance for depreciation and depletion" accounts. Concerning the

---

[7]As noted in Chapter II, the GHQ Instructions were influenced by American accounting principles. The similarity in the concept of an asset between them is an evidence of the later's influence. See the following literature:

The executive Committee of the American Accounting Association, "A Tentative Statement of Accounting Principles Affecting Corporate Reports," The Accounting Review, Vol. XI, No. 2 (June, 1936), pp. 188-89.
Thomas Henry Sanders, Henry Rand Hatfield, and Underhill Moore, A Statement of Accounting Principles (New York: American Institute of Accountants, 1938), p. 58.
W. A. Paton and A. C. Littleton, An Introduction to Corporate Accounting Standards (Chicago, Illinois: American Accounting Association, 1940), pp. 25-26.
The Executive Committee of the American Accounting Association, "Accounting Principles Underlying Corporate Financial Statements," The Accounting Review, Vol. XVI, No. 2, (June, 1941), pp. 134-35.

[8]The Edwards Mission on Japanese Combines was sent to Japan in January, 1946, by the State and War Departments jointly. Its assignment was to recommend to the two departments standards, policies, and procedures for dissolving the great Japanese combines which are collectively known as the Zaibatsu.

presentation of fixed assets in the balance sheet, the GHQ Instructions stated:

> For purposes of statements to be transmitted to SCAP and to conform to accepted procedures, it is necessary to show all Fixed Assets at cost (except where fixed assets have been revalued as provided in the Enterprise Reconstruction Measures procedure) and to show the aggregate reserves for depreciation up to the balance sheet date as deductions from the Fixed Assets at cost.... It is strongly recommended that all companies set up their ledger accounts in this way and discontinue the practice of crediting depreciation provisions to the fixed asset accounts.[9]

Although the presentation of the accumulated allowance for depreciation in the explanation column of the balance sheet was recommended by the 1934 Working Rules for Financial Statements, this recommendation had not been accepted by most of Japanese stock corporations.

Another example of the deficiencies in the balance sheet presentation was the Japanese custom of showing "uncalled capital" on the asset side of the balance sheet. This custom was accepted by both the 1934 Working Rules for Financial Statements and the 1941 Tentative Standards for Financial Standards. The SCAP's opinion on this problem was expressed in the following terms:

> ..., the purpose of the balance sheet is to show on the one side the company's assets, and on the other side, the company's liabilities and its net worth. Net worth is capital paid in plus undivided profits (or minus the accumulated deficit) and represents the owner's equity in the assets. It may therefore be said that while there might be some justification for setting up as an asset unpaid subscriptions which have been called, there would certainly never be justification for the Japanese practive of treating uncalled capital as an asset, thereby inflating both the total asset figure and the total net figure.[10]

---

[9]Research and Statistics Division, GHQ, SCAP, op. cit., p. 17.

[10]Ibid., pp. 30-31.

As discussed in Chapter III, the practice to treat the "uncalled capital" as an asset was deceptive since the amount and time of the call were uncertain until action was taken by the directors of the company.

The GHQ Instructions required the Japanese stock corporations to prepare a surplus reconcilement statement. This requirement was the most important feature of the GHQ Instructions in that for the first time a surplus statement was introduced into Japanese accounting practice. In Chapter III, the author noted that the directors were required to submit five documents at the general meeting of shareholders in order to disclose their responsibility or accountability for business operations of the company. Approval by the shareholders of these documents discharged the responsibilities of the directors as trustees. This observation, however, probably needs a brief supplementary note. The Commercial Code of Japan required the directors to prepare the statement of proposals pertaining to the disposal of profits. This statement was an expression of the directors' plan concerning the disposition of profits. It was not an accounting statement in the sense of a report of historical events. Even approval by the shareholders of the statement of proposals could not make it an accounting statement unless a statement of the actual disposition of profits was prepared. None of the five financial documents prescribed by the Japanese Commercial Code disclosed the historical facts concerning the disposition of profits. In other words, the directors' responsibility for the disposition of profits was not disclosed by these financial documents.

This was apparently a deficiency in Japanese accounting practice from the viewpoint of full disclosure of the directors' responsibility.

A Japanese accountant once reported a case of Japanese financial reporting
where the amount of retained earnings carried forward from the previous
period as shown in the statement of proposals pertaining to the disposal of
profit for the current period differed from the amount of retained earnings
carried forward to the current period.[11] The difference between the two
figures was not reported in the financial statements. This practice was
said to have been common among many Japanese corporations. The preparation
of the surplus statement could possibly preclude the use of such a deceptive
practice by Japanese companies.

Application, Sanctions, and Administration. The primary purpose of the
GHQ Instructions was "to assist Japanese companies in the preparation of the
type of clear, intelligible financial reports required by SCAP authorities
from time to time in connection with SCAP's efforts to establish in Japan a
sound, democratic, industrial economy."[12] The GHQ Instructions were not one
of the SCAPINs but a manual to supplement the SCAPIN-177 which was issued by
SCAP on October 25, 1945. That is, the phrase "financial reports required
by SCAP" in the statement quoted above meant "financial reports required by
the SCAPIN-177." The SCAPIN-177 required the 15 largest holding companies
in Japan to submit financial reports to SCAP. The number of the Japanese
companies, which were required to submit their financial reports to SCAP,
amounted to 1015 by the summer of 1947 when the GHQ Instructions were published.[13] Whenever they submitted their financial statements to SCAP since

---

[11]Ryohei Kato, "Gorikyoku Zaimu-Junsoku to Jitsumu-Kanshu tono Kosaku
-II-" (The Working Rules for Financial Statements by the Ministry of Com-
merce and Industry and the Accounting Practices -II-), Kaikei (Accounting),
Vol. 38, No. 5, (May, 1936), pp. 91-92.

[12]Research and Statistics Division, GHQ, SCAP, op. cit., p. 1.

[13]SCAP issued 27 SCAPINS, including SCAPIN-177, by July 28, 1947 to
designate 1015 Japanese companies as "restricted companies."

1947, these companies were required to prepare their financial reports in conformity with the GHQ Instructions.

As mentioned earlier, the financial reports of the Japanese companies were based upon the accounting provisions of the Japanese Commercial Code and were not intelligible to the American officers of SCAP. To the accountants of Japanese companies, on the other hand, the accounting procedures of the GHQ Instructions were quite confusing despite an effort of Hessler and Murase, who drafted the GHQ Instructions, to reconcile the traditional Japanese accounting practices with modern American accounting practices. Although the GHQ Instructions were not a directive of SCAP, accountants of the Japanese companies tried to prepare financial statements in conformity with the GHQ Instructions. It is regretable that no evidence or literature exists to indicate the degree to which the submitted financial statements conformed with the GHQ Instructions.

The application of the GHQ Instructions were limited to the financial statements submitted by approximately one thousand "restricted" companies to SCAP. The GHQ Instructions, however, undoubtedly had a great influence upon the improvement of Japanese accounting practices after World War II because these companies were the leading companies in all areas of industry in Japan and SCAP had responsibility for the effective administration of the GHQ Instructions. In historical perspective, it appears that the most important feature of the GHQ Instructions was that they promoted within a relatively short period of time an improvement in Japanese accounting practices by orienting them to American accounting practices. As mentioned in Chapter III, American accounting thoughts were introduced

into Japan around 1910 and partially incorporated into the 1934 Working
Rules for Financial Statement. They were not wholly accepted by practicing accountants until 1947. If the GHQ Instructions had not been released,
the modernization or Americanization of Japanese accounting practices
would have been delayed.

A Statement of Business Accounting Principles

Institutional Basis of Legitimation. The application of the GHQ
Instructions was limited to the Zaibatsu companies, which were designated
as "restricted" by SCAP, because the purpose of the GHQ instructions
was to gather financial information on the Zaibatsu companies. After the
release of the GHQ Instructions, SCAP authorities suggested that two
Japanese accounting professors prepare a Working Rules for Preparing
Financial Statements, which could be applied generally to all business
enterprises in Japan in order to promote a further improvement in
Japanese accounting practices. Based upon a preliminary study by a group
of Japanese accounting educators and businessmen, which was organized
by Michisuke Ueno and Kiyoshi Kurosawa, the Japanese government established an Investigation Committee on the Business Accounting System in
July, 1948, as a part of the organizational structure of the Economic
Stabilization Board. A Statement of Business Accounting Principles
was released in July, 1949, by the Committee which consisted of twenty
members from the rank of accounting professors, businessmen, and top-
ranking governmental officials.

As mentioned in Chapter II, the democratization of the Japanese
economy after World War II was implemented in two steps. The first step

was the dissolution of the <u>Zaibatsu</u> companies and the second was the

fostering of wide distribution of the income and ownership of business

enterprises. The 1947 GHQ Instructions was related to the first step

which was carried out primarily by SCAP authorities. The second step

toward the democratization of the Japanese economy was largely carried

out by the Japanese government. The publication of <u>A Statement of

Business Accounting Principles</u> was concerned with the second step. In

advance of the publication of <u>A Statement of Business Accounting Princi-

ples</u>, the way for the democratization of investment in securities was

paved by the enactment of the Securities Exchange Act in 1947 and the

Certified Public Accountants Law in 1948. As will be discussed in

detail later, these two things provide an most important clue for a

correct understanding of the nature of <u>A Statement of Business Accounting

Principles</u>: (1) That <u>A Statement of Business Accounting Principles</u> was

released by a government-appointed committee in the Economic Stabiliza-

tion Board, which was attached to the cabinet and (2) that <u>A Statement of

Accounting Principles</u> was released to supplement the Securities Exchange

Act and the Certified Public Accountants Law.

Although <u>A Statement of Business Accounting Principles</u> did not refer

explicitly in its text to the interest groups for whose service it was

formulated, its foreward implied the identification of several interest

groups, such as management, shareholders, creditors, and government. The

foreward, entitled "On the establishment of A Statement of Business Account-

ing Principles," stated its purpose in the following terms:

> Since business accounting systems in Japan, as compared with
> those in the Western countries, have much room for improve-
> ment and lack uniformity, it is presently difficult for the

readers of financial statements to understand financial
conditions and results of operations of business enterprises. In order to realize the sound development of
business enterprises in our country and to promote the
benefits of the whole society, any difficulty should be
removed as quickly as possible. Further, for the
rational solution of the current problems, such as the
influx of foreign capital, rationalization of business
enterprises, justification of taxation, democratization
of investment in securities, and proper industrial
financing, which are essential to the reconstruction of
the Japanese economy, the improvement and unification
of the business accounting system are urgent problems
to be undertaken.
Therefore, Business Assounting Principles are to be
established aiming at the establishment and maintenance
of the standards of business accounting, and consequently
offering a scientific basis for the democratic and sound
development of the national economy of Japan.

The identification of the interest groups by A Statement of Business

Accounting Principles was broader than that provided by its predeces-

sors, such as the Commercial Code, the 1934 Working Rules for Financial

Statements, and the 1941 Tentative Standards for Financial Statements

of Manufacturing Companies.

A Statement of Business Accounting Principles was composed of three

sections: (1) General Principles, (2) Income Statement Principles, and

(3) Balance Sheet Principles. Although A Statement of Business Account-

ing Principles identified a surplus statement, a surplus appropriation

statement, and a schedule supporting financial statements in addition

to an income statement and a balance sheet, the principles for these

three statements were included in the Income Statement Principles and

the Balance Sheet Principles. This composition of A Statement of Business

Accounting Principles was very similar to that of "A Statement of Account-

ing Principles" prepared in 1938 by Sanders, Hatfield, and Moore except

that the consolidated statements were excluded from the former. Despite

a negative statement by Kiyoshi Kurosawa, a chief drafter of the statement,
the author believes for several reasons that the preparation of A Statement of Business Accounting Principles was greatly influenced by the SHM
Statement of Accounting Principles.[14]

The first reason is that the political and legal background underlying the statement of accounting principles in Japan was nearly the same
as that of the SHM Statement of Accounting Principles in 1938. In addition to several regulations issued by Federal agencies and the stock
exchanges, the Federal Government of the United States enacted the
Securities Act of 1933 and the Securities Exchange Act of 1934. This
development was the direct cause for the undertaking by the Haskins &
Sells Foundation of the formulation of a code of accounting principles.[15]
In Japan, as mentioned earlier, the government enacted the Securities
Exchange Act in 1947 and the Certified Public Accountants Law in 1948.

---

[14]Concerning the relationship between the two statements, Kiyoshi
Kurosawa stated as follows:
A Statement of Business Accounting Principles is a
historical product of a series of movements toward the
improvement of financial statements in Japan. It is
not an import from the United States but a mixture of
the original accounting thoughts and practices developed
in Japan and those developed in Western countries such
as England, the United States, and Germany. It is superficial to consider that A Statement of Business Accounting Principles is merely a part of American systems
introduced after World War II.
(Kiyoshi Kurosawa, "Kaikei-Gensoku Sosetsu" [General Comments on Accounting Principles] in Kiyoshi Kurosawa, et al., Kigyo-Kaikei no Ippan-Gensoku
Shosetsu [Detailed Comments on the General Principles for Business Account-
ing][Tokyo, Japan: Dobunkan, 1955], p. 13.)

[15]Sanders, Hatfield, and Moore, op. cit., pp. xii-xiii.

As its foreward states, Business Accounting Principles are the standards which Certified Public Accountants should observe when they audit
financial statements based upon the Certified Public Accountants Law and
the Securities Exchange Act.[16] Both of these laws were modeled after
the American systems since no systems to protect the public investors
existed in Japan. A Statement of Business Accounting Principles was
the third cornerstone in the development of a democratic and sound
financial reporting system in Japan after World War II and it had to
be in harmony with the other two.

The second reason is that A Statement of Business Accounting Principles was prepared not by associations of professional accountants or
accounting educators but by a government-appointed committee. For the
first reason it was apparent that A Statement of Business Accounting
Principles had to be modeled after some American accounting principles.
There were, however, two alternatives from which an approach could be

---

[16]The Securities Exchange Act of Japan was enacted with a purpose
of permitting and facilitating the fair issuance and transfer procedures
as well as other transactions in securities, and providing for the ordering
circulation of securities in order to make possible a rational administration of the national economy in addition to protecting investors (Article
1). Concerning the audit of financial statements, the 1948 revised Act
states:

The balance sheet, income statement, and other financial
documents, which are prepared by the listed stock corporation and others prescribed by the ordinance and are
submitted by the Securities and Exchange Commission
based upon the Act, shall be accompanied with an audit
report by a certified public accountant independent
from the stock corporation involved (Article 193-2).

The Certified Public Accountants Law is a basic law governing all phases
of certified public accountant in Japan such as his business qualifica-
tion, examination, obligations, and responsibilities.

selected: (1) adopting the approach of the SHM Statement of Accounting
Principles, or (2) adopting the approach of the American Accounting
Association in their statements of accounting principles of 1936 and 1941.
The task assigned to the Committee was considerably restricted by
Article 193 of the Securities Exchange Act which read as follows:

> The balance sheet, income statement, and other financial
> documents., which are submitted to the Securities and
> Exchange Commission based upon the Act, shall be prepared
> in conformity with the wording, form, and preparation
> method prescribed in the SEC Regulation. The SEC Regula-
> tion will be prepared by the Commission based upon those
> generally accepted as fair and proper.

The task of the Investigation Committee on Business Accounting System
was. to identify those generally accepted as fair and proper and to provide a foundation of the SEC Regulation. To accomplish this task, the
Committee planned to take the following steps:

1. To establish four sets of accounting principles:
   (1) balance sheet principles, (2) income statement
   principles, (3) surplus statement principles, and
   (4) consolidated balance sheet principles.
2. To prepare standard forms of financial statements
   as a foundation of the SEC Regulation based upon
   the four sets of accounting principles.[17]

The Committee's plan and even the establishment of the government-
appointed Committee itself was greatly influenced by Kiyoshi Kurosawa's
basic view on the institutionalization of accounting principles or
accounting standards. He expressed his view in the following terms:

---

[17]Kigyo-Kaikei Seido Taisaku Chosakai (Investigation Committee on
Business Accounting System), "Kigyo-Kaikei Gensoku to Zaimushohyo tono
Kankei ni tsuite" (On a Relationship between A Statement of Business
Accounting Principles and Financial Statements), Kaikei (Accounting),
Vol. 56, No. 3, (July, 1949), p. 22.

> In countries with less modernized accounting systems
> such as Japan, "accounting" is extremely underestimated.
> If a volumtary association of professional accountants
> in Japan published such a statement of accounting
> standards as the American statements of accounting prin-
> ciples, it would be almost impossible for such standards
> to be accepted by the majority of business enterprise....
> Since the modern CPA system was established in Japan,
> accounting standards should systematically be codified
> and the codification should be undertaken by an authorita-
> tive organization supported by Law.[18]

This idea was crystalized in the Committee's plan to institutionalize

accounting standards by preparing the three statements: (1) A State-

ment of Business Accounting Principles, (2) the Working Rules for Pre-

paring Financial Statements, and (3) the SEC Regulation for Financial

Statements. Kiyoshi Kurosawa, a chief drafter of A Statement of Business

Accounting Principles, believed that the approach of the SHM Statement of

Accounting Principles was the best fit model upon which Japanese account-

ing principles should be established because of their practicability and

educational merits.[19]   The Investigation Committee on Business Accounting

System released in 1949, as interim reports, A Statement of Business

Accounting Principles and the Working Rules for Preparing Financial State-

ments. Based upon the latter, the Securities and Exchange Commission of

Japan released in 1950 "Regulation for Wording, Form, and Preparation

Method of Financial Statements" or, as it came to be known, the "SEC

---

[18]Kiyoshi Kurosawa, "Kaikei-Kijun no Kakuritsu to Iji ni tsuite" (Establishment and Maintenance of Accounting Standards), Sangyo-Keiri (Financial and Cost Accounting), Vol. 9, No. 5, (May, 1949), p. 8.

[19]The late Iwao Iwata, professor of accounting at Hitotsubashi University and a member of the Committee, emphasized theoretical merits of the approach of the American Accounting Associations at the Committee (Kigyo-Kaikei Seido Taisaku Chosakai, op. cit., pp. 23-24).

Regulation for Financial Statements."

    Theoretical Basis of Legitimation. According to the Committee's
original plan, A Statement of Business Accounting Principles was scheduled to be composed of four sets of accounting principles: (1) balance
sheet principles, (2) income statement principles, (3) surplus statement
principles and (4) consolidated balance sheet principles. The inclusion
of the consolidated balance sheet principles in the plan was suggested
by William G. Hessler, who prepared the GHQ Instructions.[20] The codifying of consolidated balance sheet principles, however, was excluded
from the Committee's task because the Anti-Monopoly Law of Japan prohibited a corporation from holding a large portion of the shares of
other corporations and the Corporation Income Tax Law did not accept the
joint tax return. As Committee's deliberation progressed, the Committee
decided to absorb the surplus statement principles into the balance sheet
and income statement principles. However, a chief drafter of the Committee proposed that a new set of principles be established which could be
applied to both the balance sheet and the income statement. He suggested
that this could be done by separating some principles of a common nature
from the balance sheet principles and the income statement principles.[21]
As a result, the Committee adopted the following format for A Statement of
Business Accounting Principles:

---

[20]Ibid., p. 42.

[21]Kigyo-Kaikei Seido Taisaku Chosakai, "Kigyo-Kaikei Gensoku"
"Business Accounting Principles), Kaikei (Accounting), Vol. 56, No. 5
(October, 1949), pp. 44-51. This idea was first suggested by Iwao
Iwata, but the content of the "general principles" was greatly influenced
by Kiyoshi Kurosawa's basic view.

I. General Principles
II. Income Statement Principles
III. Balance Sheet Principles.[22]

One of the most important characteristics of A Statement of Business

Accounting Principles was the identification of the following seven

principles under the heading of "general principles":

1. the principle of the true report
2. the principle of regular bookkeeping procedures
3. the principle of distinction between capital transactions and revenue transactions
4. the principle of fair disclosure
5. the principle of consistency
6. the principle of conservatism
7. the principle of unity of financial statements.

To know exactly what was meant by "principle" is difficult since neither

definition nor discussion of the concept of a "principle" or a "general

principle" was developed in A Statement of Business Accounting Principles.

Some of the "general principles" listed in it, such as the principles

of fiar disclosure, of consistency, and of convervatism, however, appar-

ently seem to be equivalent to "doctrines" in the American usage of the

term.[23] From a theoretical point of view, "doctrine" should be clearly

---

[22]A translated text of A Statement of Business Accounting Principles is shown at the end of Chapter IV.

[23]Some other "general principles," such as the principles of true report, regular bookkeeping procedures, and unity of financial statements, were nearly equivalent to the "Grundsätze der Bilanzwahrheit," Grundsätze der Ordnungsmässige Buchführung," and "Grundsätze der Bilanzeinheit" in the German Commercial Code. See Kiyoshi Kurosawa, "Kaikei Gensoku Sosetsu," pp. 5-7 and Iwao Iwata, "Kigyo-Kaikei no Ippan-Gensoku ni tsuite" (On General Principles of Business Accounting), Kigyokaikei (Accounting), Vol. 1, No. 9, (September, 1949), pp. 2-3.

distinguished from "principle."[24] If the principles are well developed,
the doctrines may be excluded from the body of accounting thought or a
set of accounting principles. It is interesting to speculate as to why
A Statement of Business Accounting Principles included the so-called
doctrines among the "general principles." It could mean that "doctrines"
and "principles" were not conceptually distinguished in A Statement of
Business Accounting Principles. From another point of view, the "general
principles" in A Statement of Business Accounting Principles could be
thought of as propositions which might be referred to as "imperatives."[25]
That A Statement of Business Accounting Principles included some
"doctrines" or "imperatives" as the "general principles" will be
explained for at least two reasons.

The first reason is concerned with the basic view of accounting
principles by the chief drafter of A Statement of Business Accounting
Principles. After having reviewed several searches for accounting
principles in the United States as reflected in discussions such as
Byrne's article, "To What Extent Can the Practice of Accounting be Re-

---

[24]William J. Vatter, for example, distinguishes "doctrines" from
"principles" as follows:
>...doctrines are normative standards which serve as bench
>marks for applying methods or procedures which give effect
>to certain principles. The best examples of doctrines in
>accounting are ideas like conservatism, consistency, and
>materiality.

>Given a set of conditions related to the conventions and
>doctrines of accounting, principles are generalizations
>as to the way in which certain objectives may be reached.

(William J. Vatter, "Postulates and Principles," Journal of Accounting
Research, Vol. 1, No. 2, (Autumn, 1963), p. 184.)

[25]Maurice Moonitz, The Basic Postulates of Accounting (New York:
AICPA, 1961), pp. 38-55.

duced to Rules and Standards?," A Statement of Accounting Principles by
Sanders, Hatfield, and Moore, and Gilman's Accounting Concepts of Profit,
Kiyoshi Kurosawa stated his basic view on the structure of accounting
principles in the following terms:

> Accounting principles are a dynamic structure consisting
> of a lower structure of conventions, a middle structure of
> doctrines, and an upper structure of rules or standards
> (principles in a narrow sense).
> This idea is nearly the same as Gilman's idea, but it is
> not necessarily the same. Unlike Gilman's idea, the author
> believes that conventions, doctrines, and standards are all
> factors of accounting principles in a broad sense. In-
> stitutions, such as accounting period and double-entry
> bookkeeping, have originally been developed as conventions,
> but they constitute the lower structure of accounting
> principles. General principles, such as the doctrine of
> consistency, the doctrine of disclosure, and the doctrine
> of conservatism, connect conventions at the lower structure
> with rules at the upper structure and constitute the middle
> structure of accounting principles. Accounting principles
> at the upper structure are composed of many, concrete rules
> or standards, such as the accrual basis, gross amount basis,
> realization basis, and cost basis, which directly guide
> accounting actions.[26]

This quotation indicates clearly that the reason why A Statement of
Business Accounting Principles included the "doctrines" was that, according to Kiyoshi Kurosawa's basic view on accounting principles, the
"doctrines" were the "general principles" themselves.

One can then ask if all seven "general principles" could be regarded
as "doctrines." The answer to this question is the second reason why A
Statement of Business Accounting Principles included some "doctrines" or
"imperatives" as "general principles." Of the seven general principles,

---

[26]Kiyoshi Kurosawa, Kindai Kaikei no Riron (A Theory of Modern Accounting) (Tokyo, Japan: Hakuto Shobo, 1955), pp. 116-17. This book is
composed of his nineteen articles published during five years from 1949
through 1953. The above quotation was originally included in his article,
"Kaikei Gensoku eno Tankyu" (A Search for Accounting Principles), which
was written while he was drafting A Statement of Business Accounting
Principles and published in Sangyo-Keiri (Financial and Cost Accounting),
Vol. 9, No. 6, (June, 1949).

the principles of fair disclosure, consistency, and conservatism are
doubtlessly doctrines. Kurosawa explains the other four general principles as follows:

> The principles of true report, of regular bookkeeping
> procedures, and of unity of financial statements are
> "mores" as well as "doctrines" and even institutions in a
> legal sense. The principle of distinguishing between
> capital transactions and revenue transactions is one of
> the accounting standards which should be developed from
> the foundation of the doctrines rather than being a doctrine
> itself....The principles of making a distinction between
> capital transactions and revenue transactions is not a
> doctrine but is a standard to guide certain accounting
> actions. It is, therefore, difficult to regard it as a
> general principle. Since it was urgent in Japan that this
> standard be institutionalized through law, it was included in
> the general principles. The general principles increase
> their effect as and when they are institutionalized.27

According to Kiyoshi Kurosawa, the principles of a true report, of regular
bookkeeping procedures, and of unity in financial statements are "mores"
as well as "doctrines." Unlike the generally accepted usage of the term
"mores" in the field of sociology, Kiyoshi Kurosawa considered "mores"
as a social requirement to change the nature of the existing custom,
for a new custom.28 In other words, he considered "mores" as a kind of
"doctrines" or "imperatives."

27Kiyoshi Kurosawa, "Kaikei Gensoku no Seidoteki Igi" (Significance
of Accounting Principles as an Institution) in Yasutaro Hirai (ed.),
Kigyo-Kaikei Gensoku Hihan (A Critique of A Statement of Business Accounting Principles) (Tokyo, Japan: Kunimoto Shobo, 1950), p. 10.

28Ibid., p. 8. The term "mores" is usually defined as "such of
folkways as are regarded as being of such social concern that their
violation produces shock, horror, moral revulsion or indignation, and
justifies the use of sanctions against violator." (Julius Gauld and
William L. Kolb [eds.] A Dictionary of the Social Science [New York:
The Free Press, 1964] , p. 273.)

Kurosawa's unique interpretation of the term "mores" seems to have
derived from his understanding of a special situation of accounting
practices which existed in Japan after World War II. Almost all political,
economic, and social systems or institutions in Japanese society had to
be changed after the conclusion of the war as mentioned in Chapter II.
The public Financial reporting system in Japan was no exception. Before
the establishment of A Statement of Business Accounting Principles in
1949, modern accounting conventions were not well enough developed to
provide a base upon which new modern accounting principles could be developed. This statement seems to contradict the first paragraph of the
foreward of A Statement of Business Accounting Principles which stated
that business accounting principles are summaries of those generally
accepted as fair and proper among accounting conventions developed
in practices of business accounting. Because this statement of the
situation of Japanese accounting practices had been accepted as true
by many Japanese accountants, Professor Kiyoshi Kurosawa held that
principles of true report, of regular bookkeeping procedures, and of
unity of financial statements were not the "mores" in the generally
accepted sense but the "mores" as "doctrines" or "imperative" and that
they should be included in the "general principles."[29]

From a theoretical point of view, the content or composition of the
"general principles" in A Statement of Business Accounting Principles in

[29]See, for example, Jiro Asaba, Kaikei Gensoku no Kiso Kozo (Basic
Structure of Accounting Principles) (Tokyo, Japan: Yuhikaku, 1959), p.
165 and the Japanese Accounting Association, "Kigyo-Kaikei Gensoku no
Toitsu o Chushin toshite" (Symposium on Unification of Business Accounting Principles), Kaikei (Accounting), Vol. 57, No. 1, (January, 1950),
p. 75.

A Statement of Business Accounting Principles is illogical in that they
are a mixture of different elements, such as "doctrines," "mores" or
"imperatives," and "rule." Concerning the basic nature of the "general
principles," Kiyoshi Kurosawa states as follows:

> The general principles are not only a set of doctrines
> controlling accounting standards such as the balance
> sheet principles and the income statement principles,
> but also include common principles supporting the audit-
> ing standards. One of the most important features of the
> "general principles" as general principles, is that they
> provided great leadership for general business accounting
> practices by serving as a base for a foundation for the
> auditing standards.[30]

The author admits that _A Statement of Business Accounting Principles_ was
established under special circumstances to develop a modern public,
financial reporting system, including the auditing system of the Certified
Public Accountant, in Japanese society and that its nature had to be
educational and practical rather than theoretical. It does not necessarily follow from this that the "general principles" are a mere list of
different elements which may constitute accounting principles as a social
institution. The principle of the true report, for example, is one of
the most important goals or objectives of business accounting and does
not constitute an accounting principles by itself. To accomplish such
an objective, accounting principles, as general guides to accounting
actions, should be developed.[31]

The second important characteristic of _A Statement of Business_

---

[30]The Japanese Accounting Association, _op. cit._, p. 74.

[31]A. C. Littleton, _Structure of Accounting Theory_ (Urbana, Illinois: American Accounting Association, 1953), p. 146 and p. 188. See also A Study Group at the University of Illinois, _A Statement of Basic Account- ing Postulates and Principles_ (Urbana, Illinois: The Center for Inter- national Education and Research in Accounting, 1964), p. 24.

Accounting Principles is that accounting principles were classified into
the "income statement principles" and the "balance sheet principles."
The institutional background of this composition of accounting principles
was discussed in the previous section. The "income statement principles"
were composed of the following eight principles:

1. the nature of income statement
2. the grouping of items in the income statement
3. operating income
4. non-operating income
5. net income for the period
6. surplus
7. the surplus statement
8. the surplus appropriation statement.

In the section of the "balance sheet principles," the following five
principles were listed:

1. the nature of the balance sheet
2. the grouping in the balance sheet
3. the arrangement of items in the balance sheet
4. the classificiation of balance sheet items
5. the valuation of assets in the balance sheet.

The accounting principles concerning surplus and the surplus statement were newly added and the principles concerning the inventory were
excluded for the purpose of modernizing the financial statement system
in Japan. The presentation of the "income statement principles" and the
"balance sheet principles," in A Statement of Business Accounting Principles, however, was very similar to that of a series of traditional
"working rules" developed in Japan and that of the SHM Statement of
Accounting Principles in the United States.[32] For an analytical purpose,

[32]According to Toshio Iino, some principles in A Statement of
Business Accounting Principles are the so-called "working rules" rather
than "principles." See Toshio Iino, "Kaikei-Koi to Kaikei-Gensoku"
(Accounting Actions and Accounting Principles), Kigyokaikei (Accounting), Vol. 4, No. 4, (April, 1952), p. 17.

the contents of these thirteen principles listed above will be reclassified

as follows:

I. Accounting Principles concerning   Corresponding principles
the developing process of account-   in A Statement of Business
ing information:[33]   Accounting Principles

    1. the principle of accrual basis ... II-1-(A)
    2. the principle of cost and
       periodic cost allocation   ... II-3-(G) and III-4-(1)-(B)
    3. the principle of realization ... II-1-(A), II-3-(B) and
                                   II-3-(F)
    4. the principle of matching
       cost with revenue   ... II-1, II-1-(C), II-3,
                                   II-3-(E), and II-3-(G)
    5. the principle of distinction
       between earned surplus and
       capital surplus   ... II-6 and III-4-(3)-(B)
    6. the principle of classifica-
       tion of accounts   ... II-1-(C), II-3-(A),
                                   II-3-(G), II-4, II-7-(A),
                                   II-7-(B), and III-4

II. Accounting principles concerning
the reporting of accounting
information:

    1. the principle of grouping
       for fair disclosure   ... II-2-(A), II-2-(B),
                                   II-3-(D), II-4, II-5,
                                   II-7, and III-2
    2. the principle of gross amount ... II-1-(B), II-3-(C) and
                                   III-1-(B)
    3. the principle of comprehensive
       presentation   ... II-1, III-1, and III-1-(A)

These principles are all established accounting principles in the

Western countries and they may be a set of minimum requirement for modern

accounting. In Japan, however, the identification of these principles was

---

[33]The developing process of accounting information includes the four
processes, such as (1) recording, (2) measurement, (3) classification,
and (4) modification, which were identified by A Study Group at the
University of Illinois. See A Study Group at the University of Illinois,
op. cit., pp. 24-31.

a revolutionary event rather than an evolutionary one. As analyzed in Chapter III, the 1934 Working Rules for Financial Statements by the Ministry of Commerce and Industry introduced Anglo-American accounting thought. It had to be placed then into the framework of the Japanese Commercial Code. The improvement in the financial reporting system at that time could not go far beyond the limits of the Commercial Code. A Statement of Business Accounting Principles was not necessarily related to the Japanese Commercial Code. Rather, it was supported by the 1947 Securities Exchange Act and the 1948 Certified Public Accountants Law both of which were modeled after American laws. The GHQ Instructions also opened the door for modern accounting. This means that A Statement of Business Accounting Principles could develop its logic based upon American accounting thought.

One of the most important influences of the American accounting thought was the introduction of the concept of "surplus" and also the distinction between "capital surplus" and "earned surplus." Although there existed some types of transactions which augmented capital surplus, such as paid-in surplus from issuance of per value stock in excess of par value, the term "legal reserve" was used for "capital surplus." When A Statement of Business Accounting Principles was released in 1949, the work of revising the Commercial Code was already underway by the Legal Institution Deliberation Council. Most members of the Investigation Committee on Business Accounting System knew that a no-par value stock system would be introduced into the Commercial Code. Because of the postwar inflation most fixed assets possessed by the Japanese stock corporations had to be revalued to current value to maintain real capital.

Until the concept of "capital surplus" was established by A Statement of Business Accounting Principles, however, the Japanese Corporation Income Tax Law had long taxed "capital surplus."[34] Under these circumstances, the Committee thought that the establishment of the concept of "capital surplus" was essential for the sound development of business enterprises and to the improvement of the financial reporting system. In other words, the distinction between capital and income was one of the basic objectives of A Statement of Business Accounting Principles.

In contrast with the so-called "comparison of net worth" method of the Commercial Code, A Statement of Business Accounting Principles employed the "matching concept" method of income determination which was based upon a dynamic view of accounting. From the viewpoint of clear disclosure of results of operations, the "comparison of net worth" method is no doubt inadequate since this method does show the process of income generation. According to the "matching concept," the periodic income determination depends upon the periodic determination of revenue and cost (revenue charge). A Statement of Business Accounting Principles listed the principle of realization for the periodic determination of revenue, the principle of accrual basis, and the principle of cost and periodic cost allocation for the periodic determination of revenue charge. A Statement of Business Accounting Principles also introduced a surplus statement to ensure the distinction between capital and income, and the distinction between "capital surplus" and "earned surplus." As a result

---

[34] Iwao Iwata, Kaikei-Gensoku to Kansa-Kijun (Accounting Principles and Auditing Standards) (Tokyo, Japan: Chuo-Keizai Sha, 1955), pp. 234-35.

of the introduction of the earned surplus statement, A Statement of Business Accounting Principles had to select one from (1) the "all inclusive" type of income statement, (2) the "current operating performance" type of income statement, and (3) the combined statement of income and earned surplus. A Statement of Business Accounting Principles required in principle the preparation of the "current operating performance" type of income statement although it also permitted the preparation of the combined statement of income and earned surplus. Even today there is still diversity of opinion as to whether extraordinary items and prior period adjustments should be entered into the determination of net income of the period in which they are recognized.[35] The reason why A Statement of Business Accounting Principles advocated the "current operating performance" income statement is not clear.

The asset valuation basis in A Statement of Business Accounting Principles was the cost basis except for temporarily held marketable securities and inventories. For the former, the market price (realizable value) basis was applied. For the latter the cost basis was a principle but the "cost or market, whichever is lower" rule could be applied. Thus, the balance sheet, which had long been subject to the inventory under the Commercial Code, became subject to the income statement under A Statement of Business Accounting Principles. This is evidence of the transformation of Japanese accounting principles from the static accounting to the dynamic accounting viewpoint.

---

[35]For the historical background of this problem, see The American Institute of Certified Public Accountants, Opinions of Accounting Principles Board 9 (New York: The American Institute of Certified Public Accountants, 1966), pp. 109-12.

Application. A Statement of Business Accounting Principles was the
first written pronouncement of "generally accepted accounting principles"
in Japan which could be comparable to those in Western countries. Compared with its predecessors, such as the Commercial Code, the 1934 Working Rules for Financial Statements, the contents of A Statement of
Business Accounting Principles represented modernized thinking by placing
a great emphasis on the income statement and providing a dynamic view of
accounting. From a practical or application point of view, the nature
of A Statement of Business Accunting Principles was also quite different
from those of its predecessors. As its foreward stated, A Statement of
Business Accunting Principles was a set of standards which should be
followed for all business enterprises on the one hand, and it was also a
set of standards which certified public accountants could follow when
they audited financial statements based upon the Securities Exchange Act.
That is, A Statement of Business Accounting Principles was expected to
perform a dual function just as is done by "generally accepted accounting principles" in the United States.

As mentioned earlier, the Investigation Committee on Business Accounting System released in 1949 A Statement of Business Accounting Principles
and the "Working Rules for Preparing Financial Statements." The Japanese
Securities and Exchange Commission released in 1950 the "SEC Regulation
for Financial Statements" based upon Article 193 of the 1948 Securities
Exchange Act.[36] Although the first motive for the establishment of A

---

[36]In August, 1952, the Securities and Exchange Commission was
abolished and its authorities and responsibilities were taken over by
the Financial Bureau, Ministry of Finance. Since 1952, the "SEC Regulation for Financial Statements" has been called the "Regulation for
Financial Statements by Ministry of Finance."

FIGURE 3   Relationships among A Statement of Business
Accounting Principles, the Working Rules for
Preparing Financial Statements, and the SEC
Regulation for Financial Statements

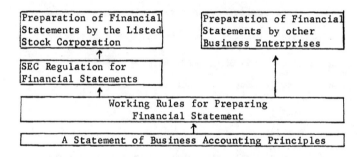

The financial statements which had to be prepared in accordance with
A Statement of Business Accounting Principles were: (1) an income statement, (2) a surplus statement, (3) a surplus appropriation statement,
(4) a balance sheet, and (5) schedules supporting financial statements.
The "Working Rules for Preparing Financial Statements" prescribed standard forms and preparation methods for financial statements based upon A
Statement of Business Accounting Principles. These working rules were a

practical guide for preparing financial statements in conformity with <u>A</u> <u>Statement</u> <u>of</u> <u>Business</u> <u>Accounting</u> <u>Principles.</u> Thus, general application of <u>A</u> <u>Statement</u> <u>of</u> <u>Business</u> <u>Accounting</u> <u>Principles</u> in financial statements became possible. In addition to the "Working Rules for Preparing Financial Statements," the Securities and Exchange Commission of Japan released in 1950 the "SEC Regulation for Financial Statements." For the accountants concerned with preparing financial statements to be filed with the Securities and Exchange Commission of Japan, the Regulation provided authoritative and final guidance. The basic idea and contents of the Regulation were in harmony with those of the Working Rules and <u>A</u> <u>Statement</u> <u>of</u> <u>Business</u> <u>Accounting</u> <u>Principles.</u>

The SEC Regulation for Financial Statements applied to corporations publicly offering shares of stock or debentures with a value of more than 50 million yen. The 1948 Securities Exchange Act required that financial statements submitted by those stock corporation be audited by independent certified public accountants. To judge the fairness of financial statement presentations, auditors must have certain standards.[37] The Auditing Standards of Japan required certified public accountants to check whether the accounting principles and procedures adopted by the company were in conformity with those of <u>A</u> <u>Statement</u> <u>of</u> <u>Business</u> <u>Accounting</u> <u>Principles</u>, and were applied on a basis consistent with that of the preceding business year. Most typical short-form auditor's reports, therefore, stated this fact in its "opinion" paragraph. This means that <u>A</u> <u>Statement</u> <u>of</u> <u>Business</u> <u>Accounting</u> <u>Principles</u> provided a set of standards by which

---

[37]R. K. Mautz and Hussein A. Sharaf, <u>The</u> <u>Philosophy</u> <u>of</u> <u>Auditing</u> (Iowa City, Iowa: American Accounting Association, 1961), p. 47.

certified public accountants measured the degree of fair presentation of financial conditions and results of operations of the company. Thus, A Statement of Business Accounting Principles was firmly institutionalized in the Japanese Society as "generally accepted accounting principles" when the legal audits by certified public accountants based upon the Securities Exchange Act began in 1951.

Sanctions and Administration. Under the Commercial Code, sanctions against the violator of its provisions were rendered by courts only when any person, who had an interest in a company, brought a suit against the company. This is because the Commercial Code was a private law. The number of such suits were few in Japanese society, however, primarily because of a lack of consciousness of right among the people. In this respect, A Statement of Business Accounting Principles was quite different from the Commercial Code. Although A Statement of Business Accounting Principles was an interim report of the Investigation Committee on Business Accounting System and not a law by itself, it was supported in effect by the Securities Exchange Act through the SEC Regulation for Financial Statements and by the legal audits of the certified public accountants. So far as corporations which were required to file their financial statements with the Securities and Exchange Commission or the Ministry of Finance since 1952 are concerned, the presentation of financial statements was examined by both the officers of the Securities and Exchange Commission and certified public accountants.

The Securities Exchange Act required corporations that publicly offering their shares of stock or debenture with a value of more than

50 million yen to submit a <u>Yukashoken</u> <u>Todokeidesho</u> (registration statement), a <u>Mokuromisho</u> (a prospectus), and a <u>Yukashoken</u> <u>Hokokusho</u> (periodic
report) (Articles 5, 13, and 24). The registration statement should
contain: (1) general information, (2) history, major lines of business,
and major facilities, (3) information on current operations, (4) financial
information, and (5) information on the new issues. The periodic report
(annual or semiannual) discloses: (1) general information, (2) major lines
of business and major facilities, (3) information on current operations,
and (4) financial information. In both statements, the financial information should include: (1) a balance sheet, (2) an income statement,
(3) a surplus statement, (4) a surplus appropriation statement, and (5)
schedules showing the details of major items in the balance sheet and
income statement.

The primary task of the officers of the Securities and Exchange
Commission (or Ministry of Finance) was to determine whether the financial
statements submitted to the Commission were prepared in conformity
with the SEC Regulation for Financial Statements and to order adjustments or resubmission of those statements not in conformity with the
SEC Regulation. The task of certified public accountants was to express
their opinions on the fairness of financial statement presentation on
the basis of an examination of the conformity of the financial state-
ments with <u>A</u> <u>Statement</u> <u>of</u> <u>Business</u> <u>Accounting</u> <u>Principles</u> based upon
Article 193-2 of the Securities Exchange Act. The number of Japanese
corporations which filed the periodic reports, including financial statements, with the Ministry of Finance and audited by certified public

accountants was as follows:[38]

	Number of stock Corporations which filed periodic report	Number of stock corporated which were audited
1959	1,415	1,187
1960	1,561	1,319
1961	1,882	1,729
1962	2,135	1,976

In addition to the administrative guidance by the officers of the Ministry of Finance, the expression of a qualified opinion or an adverse opinion and the disclaimer of opinion by a certified public accountant are sanctions which may be imposed on a violator of a set of accounting principles. Although comprehensive statistics on the pattern of opinions expressed by Japanese certified public accountants are not available, a survey of auditors' reports by Yoichi Kusakabe is very helpful in learning the extent to which corporation accountants complied with A Statement of Business Accounting Principles in the preparation of financial statements and the types of sanctions given by certified public accountants.[39] Yoichi Kusakabe selected 500 companies from those audited by certified public accountants during the five month period (March, 1961 through July, 1961). The pattern of auditors' reports revealed was as follows:

---

[38]Sources are statistics prepared by the Financial Bureau, Ministry of Finance and the Japanese Institute of Certified Public Accountants. (Quoted in Minoru Emura, Zaimushohyo Kansa -- Riron to Kozo (Financial Statements Audit -- Theory and Structure) (Tokyo, Japan: Kunimoto Shobo, 1963), p. 139) The differences in numbers between two columns indicate that Japanese banking, trust, and insurance companies were exempted from the legal audit by certified public accountants.

[39]Yoichi Kusakabe, "Wagakuni Kansa-Hokokusho no Jittai Chosa" (A Survey of Auditor's Reports in Japan), Kansa (Auditing Review) (May, 1962), pp. 26-40.

		number of companies
(1)	expression of unqualified opinions	280
(2)	expression of qualified opinions	200
(3)	expression of adverse opinions	7
(4)	disclaimer of opinions	13
		500

The reasons for the expression of qualified opinions by certified public accountants were divided into the following categories:

		number of cases
(1)	application of improper accounting procedures	150
(2)	change in consistent application of the procedure without good reasons	56
(3)	mispresentation of items in the financial statements	59
		265

The number of the stock corporations to be audited by certified accountants has considerably increased since the opening of the second section market in the Tokyo, Osaka, and Nagoya stock exchanges in October, 1961. At this present time, the following corporations are audited by certified public accountants:

1. Listed corporations on the stock exchanges in Japan
2. Corporations which plan to make registrations of offering of more than 50 million yen worth of securities in a year
3. Corporations which plan to register to sell more than 10 million yen worth of securities in a year
4. Corporations whose registrations on securities were approved
   (These four requirements are based on the Securities Exchange Act.)
5. Corporations which apply for listing on the stock exchanges in Japan
   (Based on the Listing Requirement of the Stock Exchanges in Japan.)
6. Corporations which have issued stock for over-the-counter sales on the Tokyo Stock Exchange
   (Based upon the Rule of Tokyo Securities Brokers

Association.[40]

As the number of stock corporations audited by certified public
accountants increased, the scope to which A Statement of Business
Accounting Principles was applied was enlarged and the effect of these
principles on the Japanese society became profound.

Revised Accounting Provisions of the Commercial Code

Legitimation. As mentioned in Chapter II, the important points of
the revision of the Japanese Commercial Code in 1950 were: (1) the
strengthening of shareholders' positions, (2) the rationalization of
managerial organization by the establishment of the board of directors,
and (3) the facilitation of corporation finance by the adoption of an
authorized capital system and by making possible the adoption of a
non-par value stock system. The revision of the accounting provisions
of the Commercial Code was mainly concerned with the strengthening of
the shareholders' positions. Then, to what extent did the revised
accounting provisions in 1950 facilitate the strengthining of the
shareholder's position? A Statement of Business Accounting Principles
requested the Commercial Code to respect the basic ideas developed in
the Statement as a sample of modernization of accounting provisions.
To what extent did the Commercial Code incorporate into it such accounting logic?

The composition of financial statements was not changed by the
revision in 1950. The financial statements in the Commercial Code were:
(1) an inventory, (2) a balance sheet, (3) a business report, (4) an

---

[40]Yoichi Kusakabe, Shintei Kaikei Kansa Shosetsu (A Comprehensive
Study on Auditing) (Tokyo, Japan: Chuokeizai Sha, 1965), pp. 49-50.

income statement, and (5) a statement of proposals pertaining to the legal reserve and to the distribution of profit or interest during construction (Article 281). The balance sheet remained the financial statement to which publicity was given. To strengthen the shareholders' position, the Commercial Code required the directors of corporation to prepare schedules supporting the five financial documents mentioned above within four months after the closing date of each accounting period and to keep them at the main and branch offices of the company (Article 293-5-1). The schedules were to state the business operations and financial condition of the company in detail, specifying

(1) the change in the stated capital and reserves,
(2) all transactions between the company and the directors, statutory auditors, and shareholders,
(3) the legal creation of security or pledge,
(4) the loan of money made if the company were non-financial,
(5) the aquisition of shares of other companies, and
(6) the disposition of any fixed assets (Article 293-5-2).

Whereas A Statement of Business Accounting Principles required the preparation of a capital surplus statement and an earned surplus statement, the Commercial Code required disclosure of information concerning transactions which affect capital surplus or earned surplus in the schedules. This is said to have been one point of reconciliation between the Commercial Code and A Statement of Business Accounting Principles.[41] Under the Commercial Code, however, the privilege to

---

[41]Tetsuzo Ota et al. "Shoho to Kaikei Gensoku tono Chosei-Mondai no Sai-Kento" (Symposium on Reconciliation of the Commercial Code and A Statement of Business Accounting Principles), Kigyokaikei (Accounting), Vol. 5, No. 10, (October, 1953), p. 19.

inspect or make copies from the schedules is limited to the shareholders of the company.

The revised Commercial Code of 1950 enlarged its concept of deferred assets to include commission and expenses for issuance of new capital shares (Article 286-2). This change in the concept of deferred assets was caused by the distinction between the legal capital reserve and the legal revenue reserve which constituted another feature of the revision in 1950. Under the old Commercial Code, the expenses for issuance of new cpital shares could be deducted from the paid-in capital from the issuance of par value stock in excess of par value. If the expenses for issuance of new shares were deducted from such a paid-in capital, the legal capital reserve would decrease by that amount and profit would increase by that amount. This would be, however, contraditory to the new idea of distinguishing the legal capital reserve from the legal revenue reserve. From the viewpoint of periodic income determination, any cost should be expensed in the period for which the service of cost is expired. The expense for issuance of new capital shares are cost of acquiring new capital and they should be allocated to a rather long period of time. From the Commercial Code point of view, they are fictitious assets which cannot be converted into cash. Thus, the Commercial Code required that the expense for issuance of new capital shares be amortized within three years (Article 286-2).

The distinction between capital and income is fundamental both in accounting and law. The implication of this statement, in law, however, seems to be different from that in accounting. In general, the account-

ing literature emphasizes the economic aspect of capital. That is,
capital is "a store of wealth from the use of which the owner hopes to
obtain additional wealth."[42] When the distinction between capital and
income is referred to in accounting, such distinction is usually considered as a prerequisite for an accurate measurement of income and
the efficiency of capital used for profit making purposes. From a
legal point of view, capital is a minimum amount of assets which should
be maintained in the company and indicates the margin of safety for the
creditors.[43] The distinction between capital and income is a prerequisite to an accurate measurement of the margin of safety for the
creditors. From this point of view, the distinction between the legal
capital reserve from the legal revenue reserve was necessary since the
latter was an accumulated retained income and originally available for
dividends.

To make the distinction between the legal capital reserve and the
legal revenue reserve effective, the Commercial Code required the following be set aside as legal capital reserves: (1) paid-in capital from
the issuance of par value stock in excess of par value, (2) paid-in
capital from the issuance of non-par value stock in excess of stated
value, (3) net amount resulting from a revaluation of assets, (4) paid-in

---

[42]Sanders, Hatfield, and Moore, op. cit., p. 11.

[43]Seiji Tanaka and Kinya Kubo, "Kabushiki-Kaisha no Kaikei-Ho"
(Accounting Law for the Stock Corporation) in Seiji Tanaka et al.,
Kaisha-Kaikei-Hoki Shokai (A Comprehensive Study on the Accounting Law
for the Corporations) (Tokyo, Japan: Shunju-Sha, 1959), pp. 94-95.

capital from reduction in value assigned to outstanding stock, and (5)
paid-in surplus from amalgamation (Article 288-2). Under the old Commercial Code, the legal reserve was composed of (1) retained income and
(2) paid-in capital from the issuance of par value stock in excess of
par value. The legal reserve was to be accumulated until it amounted
to one-fourth of the stated capital:

old legal reserve = accumulated retained income ≠ accumulated paid
in capital ≧ 1/4 x stated capital   ....(1)

The revised Commercial Code required each stock corporation to retain
at least one-twentieth of the income of each accounting period as legal
revenue until the accumulation amounted to one-fourth of the stated
capital (Article 288). Therefore, under the revised Code, the legal
reserve was shown as follows:

new legal reserve = legal capital reserve + legal revenue reserve
= accumulated paid-in capital prescribed in
Article 288-2 + accumulated retained income
(≧1/4 stated capital)   ....(2)

The amount of new legal reserve is obviously greater than that of old
legal reserve, if the amount of stated capital is equal. This means that
the degree of the protection of creditors was considerably strengthened.
Neither the asset valuation basis nor the method of income determination
was revised in 1950.

Application, Sanctions, and Administration. Despite several points
of revision, the accounting provisions of the Commercial Code were not
fundamentally refined. By 1950 a set of accounting principles, working
rules, and regulation was established along the line of 1948 Securities
Exchange Act. In 1951, the first legal audits by certified public
accountants began although they were preparatory accounting system audits

for the first six years until they were changed to the regular financial
statements audit in 1957. As mentioned earlier, the number of stock
corporations which were audited by certified public accountants numbered
approximately 2,000 by 1962. Since the total number of the corporations
in Japan amounted to more than 300,000, the application of the accounting
provisions of the Commercial Code covered a much broader scope than that
of Securities Exchange Act. The number of corporations with more than
one hundred million yen of capital stock was only 3,000. These 3,000
companies were in fact publicly held stock corporations and their impact
on the Japanese industrial society were great. Most of these companies
prepared their financial statements in conformity with either the SEC
Regulation or other accounting regulations specifically designed for
banks, electric power corporations, gas corporations, railroad and transportation corporations. From a social point of view, therefore, application of the accounting provisions of the Commercial Code was less significant.

Even if there were violators of the Commercial Code, no sanctions
could be assigned unless omeone brought a suit against the violators.
The number of such suits was quite small in Japan. Makoto Yazawa quoted
fifteen cases of suits concerning the accounting provisions of the Commercial Code since 1902.[44] According to Yazawa, these fifteen cases
cover almost all cases actually brought in this firld since the first
enforcement of the Japanese Commercial Code. Until the Regulation for
Corporate Balance sheets and Income Statements was released by the Ministry

---

[44]Makoto Yazawa, Kigyo-Kaikei-Ho Kogi (Lectures on Business Accounting Law)(Tokyo, Japan: Yuhikaku, 1958), pp. 34-121.

of Justice in 1963, the Commercial Code was virtually ineffective.

Summary

The improvement of the financial reporting after World War II began with the GHQ Instructions. The GHQ of SCAP released in 1947 a pamphlet entitled "Instructions for the Preparation of Financial Statements of Manufacturing and Trading Companies." To implement its own policies for democratizing the Japanese economy, the GHQ needed to gather information on the "Zaibatsu" companies. The primary purpose of the GHQ Instructions was to assist these companies in the preparation of clear, intelligible financial statements. Although the GHQ Instructions were a practical manual and did not necessarily develop accounting principles, they demonstrated American accounting practices. In other words, the GHQ Instructions were a pilot of the American accounting and introduced the surplus statement.

The movement toward the improvement of financial statements initiated by the GHQ, SCAP was taken over by the Investigation Committee of Business Accounting System. After about a year's deliberation, the Committee released in 1949 A Statement of Business Accounting Principles and the "Working Rules for Financial Statements." The release of these two statements of principles and working rules was directly related to the movement toward the democratization of investment in securities. The machinery of this movement was set by the enactment of the Securities Exchange Act in 1948 and the Certified Public Accountant Law in 1948. This machinery, however, needed lubricant. A Statement of Business Accounting Principles was a lubricant without which the machinery could not work effectively.

The above setting of modern financial reporting system was quite
similar to that in the United States. A Statement of Business Accounting
Principles was developed, however, not by the professional association of
accountants, such as AICPA or AAA in the United States, but th a government-
appointed committee. In this sense, A Statement of Business Accounting
Principles was a set of government-made accounting principles. Because
it was government-made, it emphasized practicability rather than theoretical reasoning. By supporting the SEC Regulation, A Statement of Business
Accounting Principles institutionalized itself firmly in the Japanese
society. In other words, A Statement of Business Accounting Principles
was developed and maintained by the support of the Securities Exchange
Act.

From a theoretical point of view, A Statement of Business Accounting
Principles represents the dynamic view of accounting and emphasized
periodic income determination by the "matching concept" method based
upon the cost principle. Although its composition was subject to
criticism, no one can deny that it has made a contribution to the
improvement of the financial reporting system in Japan.

The revision of the accounting provisions of the Commercial Code
was neither fundamental nor effective. The preparation of schedules
to support the financial documents was a favorable revision from a
financial reporting point of view. The Commercial Code, however, did
not change the composition of financial documents. Despite several
points of revision, the Commercial Code during this second state (1947
through 1962) seems to have disappeared behind A Statement of Business
Accounting Principles.

A <u>Statement</u> of <u>Business</u> <u>Accounting</u> <u>Principles</u>
(Released in July, 1949 and revised in July, 1954)

I. General Principles

    1. Any business accounting should furnish the true report on the
financial condition and results of operations of a given enterprise.

    2. Any business accounting should have a system of accounting
books in which all the transactions occurred in a given enterprise should be entered most accurately and systematically
through regular bookkeeping procedures.

    3. Capital transactions should clearly be distinguished from
revenue transactions and especially Capital Surplus should
not be confound with Earned Surplus.

    4. Any business accounting should show clearly to the interest
groups all necessary financial facts through the financial
statements of a given enterprise for the purpose of pre-
venting them from misunderstanding of its true business
conditions.

    5. Any business accounting should apply the established prin-
ciples and procedures of accounting consistently from period
to period and should not change them without good reasons.

        In case any considerable change is made in the principles
or procedures of accounting, the change should be disclosed
as a footnote to the financial statements.

    6. In case there is any foreseen possibility of some trans-
actions of adverse character affecting the financial
condition of a given enterprise, some proper, sound
accounting measures should be taken.

    7. The forms of financial statements may be varied accord-
ing to the purpose for which they are prepared. For
example, those prepared for the purpose of submitting
at the general meeting of shareholders, for credit
purpose, for tax purpose, etc., may necessitate several
variation in form. In any form, however, they should be
prepared from reliable accounting records and the presentation of true facts should not be distorted by the
policies of the management.

II. Income Statement Principles

(Nature of Income Statement)
    1. The income statement should show, for the period it covers, all
revenues, their corresponding expenses, and net income (or loss).

(A) The amount of expenses and revenues should be measured based upon receipts and disbursements and precisely allocated to the period in which they accrued. Unrealized revenue, as a rule, should not be included in the income for the current period.

The prepaid expenses and revenues received in advance should be excluded from the income calculation for the current period, while all the accrued expenses should be added to it.

The accrued revenues may be included in the income determination for the current period when they are listed on the asset side of the balance sheet.

(B) All revenue and expense items, as a rule, should be entered in the income statement at their full amounts. It is not permissible to exclude any item from the income statement by offsetting the whole or a part of expense item against those of revenue item.

(C) All the expenses and revenues should be classified according to their sources and the classified revenue items should be presented in the income statement in such manner as they are matched with the related expense items.

(Grouping of Items in the Income Statement)
2. The income statement should be divided at least into the two sections; the operating income and the net income section.

(A) In the operating income section all the revenues and expenses resulting from the main operations of the business should be presented in order to arrive at the operating income.

In an enterprise carrying on more than one line of business, expenses and revenues should be presented by each line of business.

(B) In the net income sections, all incomes and expenses resulting from sources other than main operations, such as interest income or expense, discount earned or paid, profit or loss from sale of securities, should be added to or subtracted from the operating income to arrive at the net income for the period.

(Operating Income)
3. In the operating income section, sales and cost of sales
   for a given period are first shown to calculate the gross
   income from sales and the operating income for the current
   period is presented by subtracting general and administrative expenses and selling expenses from the gross income
   from sales.

   (A) In an enterprise whose main operations consist of both
       selling merchandise and rendering services, the sales
       of merchandise and the operating revenue from rendering
       services are to be presented separately.

   (B) The amount of sales should, based upon the principle
       of realization, include only those realized by selling
       of goods and rendering of service. Unrealized revenues
       from goods on consignment out or on approval not yet
       sold, installment sales, and sales by subscription,
       should, as a rule, not be included in the revenue for
       the current period. For revenue from the contracted
       works, the completion of which will extend over a long
       period of time, a fairly estimated income for the completed
       portion of the work may be included in the revenue for
       the current period.

   (C) The amount of sales should, based upon the principle
       of gross amount, be presented in the form; total sales
       minus sales allowance and returned sales equal the net
       sales.

   (D) Cost of sales is that portion of cost of goods purchased
       or manufactured corresponding to that portion of goods
       sold. In the case of trading business, the cost of sales
       should be presented in the form; cost of merchandise pur-
       chased for the period plus the beginning balance of
       merchandise minus the ending balance of merchandise. In
       the case of manufacturing business, the cost of sales
       should be presented in the form; manufacturing cost of
       products for the current period plus the beginning
       balance of products minus the ending balance of products.

       The cost of merchandise purchased for the current period
       should be presented in the form; total amount of purchased
       goods minus purchase allowance and returned purchase equal
       the net amount of purchase.

   (E) The gross income from sales should be presented by sub-
       tracting the cost of sales from the net sales.

       In the case of service rendering business, the gross
       income should be presented by subtracting from the

service revenues the cost of services rendered.

(F) Any inter-departmental income arising from inter-
departmental transfers of merchandise, etc., within
a given enterprise should be eliminated from the
computation of the amount of sales and the cost of
sales.

(G) Operating income should be presented by deducting
from the gross income from sales selling expenses and
general and administrative expenses. The selling
expenses and the general and administrative expenses
should be presented in the operating income section
classified into subsections with appropriate captions
and, as a rule, they should not be included in the
cost of sales nor in the ending balance of inventory
except for the long-term contracted construction
work. A part of the selling expenses and of the
general and administrative expenses apportioned at
an appropriate rate may be included in the ending
inventory of work-in-process.

(Non-Operating Income)
4. Non-operating income section should be divided into non-operating
revenues section, listing interest income, discount earned,
income from sale of securities, and income from revaluation
of securities, and non-operation expenses section, listing
interest expense, discount paid, bad debt expense, loss on sale
of securities, and loss on revaluation of securities.

(Net Income for the Period)
5. Net income for the period should be presented by adding non-
operating income to and deducting non-operating expenses from
the operating income.

(Surplus)
6. Surplus should be classified into earned surplus arising from
retaining income and capital surplus consisting of the surplus
from the sources other than income.

Unless with good reason capital surplus should not be transferred directly or indirectly to earned surplus. In case
deficit cannot be covered with earned surplus, it may be
covered with capital surplus. In such a case the fact of
reduction of capital surplus should be disclosed in the
surplus statement and balance sheet.

(Surplus Statement)
7. The surplus statement should be divided into the earned surplus
section and the capital surplus section to show changes in each

type of surplus. The details of changes in earned surplus may be presented in the surplus section set up in the income statement and the details of changes in capital surplus may be shown in the balance sheet.

(A) In the first subsection of the earned surplus section of the surplus statement, the net amount of unappropriated earned surplus carried forward from the previous period is to be presented by deducting the appropriated amount of earned surplus from the beginning balance of unappropriated earned surplus carried forward from the previous period. In the second subsection, prior period adjustment and extraordinary items, such as profit or loss on sale of fixed assets, are to be added to or subtracted from the net amount of unappropriated earned surplus carried forward from the previous period to arrive at the ending balance of the earned surplus carried forward from the previous period. In the third section, the amount of unappropriated earned surplus for the current period should be computed by adding net income for the current period to the last figure shown in the previous section.

(B) The amount of capital surplus carried forward to the next period is to be presented in the following way by adding the increase in capital surplus during the current period to and deducting the decrease in capital surplus and the properly appropriated amount of capital surplus during the current period from the amount of capital surplus carried forward from the previous period. Capital surplus consists of (1) paid-in par value, (2) paid-in capital from the issuance of non-par stock in excess of stated value, (3) net amount resulting from a revaluation of fixed assets, (4) paid-in capital from reduction in value assigned to outstanding stock, and (5) paid-in surplus from amalgamation.

The computation of changes in capital surplus described above should, as a rule, be shown by each item of surplus.

(Surplus Appropriation Statement)

8. In the surplus appropriation statement, the amount of earned surplus carried forward to the next period should be presented by deducting the amount to be appropriated but not yet appropriated for the current period from the amount of unappropriated earned surplus for the current period.

(Since the amount of earned surplus to be appropriated for the current period should be decided at the general meeting of shareholders, which will be held in sixty days after the closing date of accounts, the surplus appropriation state-

ment is a statement of proposal pertaining to the disposition of profits.)

III. Balance Sheet Principles

(Nature of the Balance Sheet)
1. The balance sheet should present all the assets, liabilities,
and net worth possessed by a given enterprise at a certain
date in accordance with appropriate standards for grouping,
arrangement, classification, and valuation in order to disclose clearly the financial condition of the enterprise.

(A) The balance sheet should, as a rule, present truly
to the shareholders, creditors, and other interest
groups of a given enterprise all the assets it
possesses and all the liabilities it owes.

Any assets no longer recorded on books, resulting from
the application of the principle of regular bookkeeping
procedures, may not be listed in the balance sheet.

(B) All the assets, liabilities, and net worth should, as a
rule, be presented at their gross amounts. It is not
permissible to exclude from the balance sheet the whole
or a part of them by offsetting some items of assets
with those of liabilities or net worth.

(C) In the case some specific assets have been pledged for
the purpose of securing liabilities, these facts should
be disclosed in the balance sheet.

(D) Any operating expenses having effect on the future
periods and a large amount of extraordinary loss not
being covered with the net income for the current
period and/or with surplus may, so far as such treatment does not impair the sound financial foundation
of a given enterprise, be listed temporarily on the
asset side of the balance sheet in order to allocate
them to the subsequent periods.

(E) The total amount of the assets in the balance sheet
should always equal to the sum of the total amount of the
liabilities and that of net worth.

(Grouping in the Balance Sheet)
2. The balance sheet should be divided into an assets section, a
liabilities section, and a net worth section. The assets
section should be subdivided into current assets, fixed assets,
and deferred charges; the liabilities section into current
liabilities and fixed liabilities; the net worth section into
capital stock and surplus.

(Arrangement of Items in the Balance Sheet)

3. The items in the balance sheet representing assets and liabilities should be presented according to the current arrangement.

(Classification of Balance Sheet Items)

4. All the items to be listed in the balance sheet should be classified so as to satisfy the criteria such as clarity, consistency, and comparability.

   (1) Assets

All the assets should be classified into current assets and fixed assets. Even in the case such accounts as "Temporary Payments," "Suspense Account," etc., are used in the books, these titles of account should not be used in the balance sheet. They should be presented in the balance sheet under appropriate titles clearly showing their nature.

    (A) The following assets should be listed under the current assets section: cash on hand and in bank, marketable securities, merchandise, finished goods, partially finished goods, raw materials, work-in-process, notes receivable, accounts receivable and other short-term claims receivable within a year.

Notes receivable, accounts receivable, and short-term claims which are classified as current assets from the customers should be separated from other claims due from debtors other than customers. Of other claims, those claims due from the shareholders, officers, and employees of the company should also be shown separately from those due from affiliated companies under specific titles clarifying their true character.

Allowance for uncollectible amounts of notes receivable and accounts receivable should be shown as deductions from respective accounts.

    (B) Fixed assets should be divided into three sections: tangible fixed assets, intangible fixed assets, and investments.

Land, buildings, structures, machinery and equipment, vessels, delivery equipment, furniture and tools, construction in process etc., belong to tangible fixed assets.

Goodwill, patents, superficies, trademark, etc., belong to intangible fixed assets.

Share of investments in, and long-term loans to the affiliated companies belong to investments.

Depreciation on tangible fixed assets should be written off extending over the whole period of such assets' life by a certain method of depreciation and the accumulated amount of depreciation should be shown as deduction from the acquisition cost of fixed assets under the title of allowance for depreciation.

When any tangible fixed asset has been removed, its acquisition cost and allowance for depreciation should be excluded from the fixed asset section in the balance sheet.

All the intangible fixed assets should be written off by a certain method of amortization and they should be listed in the balance sheet with their acquisition costs less amortization.

(C) Deferred charges should be divided into prepaid expenses and deferred assets. The unexpired amounts of prepaid expenses should be deferred as assets and be allocated to the expenses for the subsequent periods. Deferred assets, such as organization expenses, expenses for issuance of new capital shares, development expenses, should be amortized by a certain method of amortization and they should be listed in the balance sheet with their unamortized amounts.

Prepaid expenses to be charged within a year from the balance sheet date are classified under the current assets section.

(2) Liabilities
All the liabilities should be classified into current liabilities and fixed liabilities based upon a certain criterion. Even in the case such assounts as "Temporary Receipts," "Suspense Account," etc., are used in the books of account, these titles should not be used in the balance sheet. They should be presented in the balance sheet under appropriate titles clearly showing their nature.

(A) The following liabilities should be presented under the current liabilities section: notes payable, accounts payables, accrued expenses payable, and other liabilities payable within a year.

Notes payable, accounts payable, and other
current liabilities due to trade creditors
should be separated from other liabilities
due to other creditors. Of other short-term
liabilities, those liabilities due to the
shareholders, officers, and employees should
also be shown separately from those due to
affiliated companies under specific titles
clarifying their true character. The liabilities
due to affiliated companies should be divided into
accounts payable and other liabilities

Allowance for taxes, allowance for repairs,
reserve for dearth of water for electric power
companies, etc., should be shown under the current
liabilities section.

Deferred revenues are to be shown under the current
liability section.

(B)   Fixed liabilities should be divided into debentures,
long-term liabilities and should be presented under
appropriate headings showing their true character.

Debentures should be listed at their face value and
the difference between the issuing price and face
value should be listed as bond discount or bond
premium in the balance sheet.

Reserve for employee's retirement and reserve for
special repairs are to be shown under the fixed
liabilities section.

A note on overdue long-term liabilities should be
added in the balance sheet.

(3)   Net Worth
Net Worth should be classified into capital stock and surplus.

(A)   Under the capital stock section, issued capital stock
should be shown classified by the kind of stock, such
as common stock, preferred stock, etc., and also should
be classified into par value stock and non-par stock.
A note on the total authorized number of shares, the
number of unissued shares, and the number of issued
shares should be added under the capital stock section.

(B)   Surplus should be classified into capital surplus
and earned surplus based upon a certain criterion.

Capital surplus should be shown classified into
paid-in capital from the issuance of stock in
excess of par value, paid-in capital from the
issuance of non-par stock in excess of stated
value, net amount resulting from a revaluation of
fixed assets, paid-in capital from reduction in
value assigned to outstanding stock, paid-in surplus from amalgamation, reserve for revaluation
based upon the Assets Revaluation Law, subsidies
from the government in aid of construction,
customer's contribution to the cost of construction
work, gains on insurance claims, etc.

Earned surplus is to be shown classified into
revenue reserve, voluntary reserve, and unappropriated surplus for the current period.

Unappropriated earned surplus for the current
period should be presented classified into ending
balance of unappropriated earned surplus carried
forward from the previous period and net income
for the current period.

(C) The deficit is to be shown as a deduction from
earned surplus in the balance sheet.

In case there exists no earned surplus or the
amount of deficit exceeds that of earned surplus,
the deficit is to be shown as a deduction from
the total of capital stock.

(Valuation of Assets in the Balance Sheet)
5. All the assets to be presented in the balance sheet should, in
principle, be recorded at their acquisition costs. In case any
assets are valued on a basis other than the cost basis, the
employed asset valuation basis is to be mentioned in the footnote to the balance sheet.

The acquisition costs of assets should be allocated to the
related accounting periods based upon the most adequate principle of cost allocation for each type of assets. The costs
of tangible fixed assets should be allocated to each period
during their life by a certain depreciation method. The costs
of intangible fixed assets, that is, the amount of consideration paid for their acquisition, and deferred assets should
be allocated to each relevant period by a certain amortization method.

(A) The acquisition costs of inventories, such as merchandise, finished goods, partially finished goods, raw
materials, work-in-process, supplies, etc., are to be

determined by their actual purchase prices or actual
production costs. In case application of FIFO, LIFO,
or average cost method is difficult to determine
their acquisition costs to be allocated, other
inventory valuation bases, such as base-stock
method, retail inventory method, etc., may be
applied.

Inventories, such as merchandise, finished goods,
and raw materials, may be valued at their market
prices if their market prices are lower than their
acquisition costs.

(B) Temporarily possessed marketable securities are, in
principle, to be valued at their market prices.
They may be valued at market prices less some
allowance for price fluctuations taking into consideration the market conditions.

(C) Accounts and notes receivable should be valued at
book value less reasonably estimated amounts for
bad debts.

(D) The acquisition cost of tangible fixed asset means
its purchase price or production price. In case a
fixed asset has been acquired by issuing shares or
debentures or in exchange for shares or debentures,
its cost means the face value or issuing price of
such securities.

In case some assets have been acquired by donation,
such assets should be valued at their fairly estimated
value.

Any tangible fixed assets totally depreciated should
be listed in the balance sheet at their scrap value
or memorandum value until they are actually removed.

(E) Only those intangible fixed assets which are actually
purchased should be listed in the balance sheet at
their acquisition costs, that is, the amounts of
consideration paid.

(F) Investments are, in principle, to be listed at their
acquisition costs or their invested value irrespective
of the fluctuation in their market prices.

CHAPTER V

AN ANALYSIS OF ACCOUNTING PRINCIPLES AT
THE THIRD STAGE OF THEIR DEVELOPMENT (1962 -   )

Legitimation Process

Regulation for Corporate Balance Sheets and Income Statements and the
1962 Commercial Code. The Ministry of Justice released in March, 1963,
"The Regulation for Corporate Balance Sheets and Income Statements." The
purpose of the Regulation was to make the accounting provisions od the
Japanese Commercial Code effective and then to improve the public financial
reporting system for general purpose. As analyzed in Chapter III, the
financial reporting practices in Japan at the first stage (1890 through
1947) were regulated primarily by the Commercial Code and supplemented by
the 1934 Working Rules for Financial Statements and by the 1941 Tentative
Standards for Financial Statements. The practical application of these
regulations in the financial statements, however, was not effective. At
the second stage (1947 through 1962), a modern financial reporting system
was established based upon the Securities Exchange Act, the Certified Public
Accountants Law, and A Statement of Business Accounting Principles. Although
the number of companies to which business accounting principles were applied
through the SEC Regulation was limited to approximately 2,000 of 300,000
corporations in Japan, these 2,000 corporations were all leading companies
representing all lines of Japanese industry and the public financial reporting practices in general were considerably improved.

The effectiveness of the financial reporting system based upon the
Securities Exchange Act was recognized even by professors of commercial
law. Professor Kitazawa, for example, states:

> The disclosure of business operations and financial information
> based upon the Securities Exchange Act is in detail and accurate
> since it is supported by the governmental agency and the certi-
> fied public accountants. This system does furnish much informa-
> tion necessary to the investment decisions by the shareholders,
> present and potential, supplementing the deficiencies in the
> accounting provisions of the Commercial Code. It also performs
> controlling functions over the directors of the company without
> any active actions by the shareholders. The system, therefore,
> is very effective in protecting the so-called non-controlling
> shareholders who do not actively participate in management and do
> not exert their rights in the shareholders' meeting.[1]

Most accountants of large corporations respected the SEC Regulation more
highly than the Commercial Code since they were required to file financial
statements prepared in conformity with the SEC Regulation with the Ministry
of Finance.[2] In other words, modern financial reporting practices supported
by the SEC Regulation and by A Statement of Business Accounting Principles
were gradually taking root in the Japanese society. Then, why did the
Ministry of Justice release a new regulation in 1963? From a practical

---

[1]Masahiro Kitazawa, "Kabushiki-Kaisha no Shoyu-Keiei-Shihai," (Owner-
ship, Management, and Control in the Stock Corporation) in Makoto Yazawa (ed.),
Gendai-Ho to Kigyo (Contemporary Laws and Business Enterprises) (Tokyo, Japan:
Iwanami Shoten, 1966), p. 92.

[2]Seiji Tanaka, "Shoho Kaisei-Yoko no Shoho-Gaku-Jo kara mita Mondaiten"
(Some Problems in a Tentative Statement of the Revision of the Commercial
Code Viewed from the Commercial Code Theory) in Seiji Tanaka et al., Shoho
Kaisei ni tomonau Shomondai (Some Problems Arising from the Revision of the
Commercial Code) (Tokyo, Japan: Ikkyo Shuppan, 1962), p. 112.
   Since the Securities and Exchange Commission was abolished in 1952, the
Ministry of Finance had jurisdiction over the "SEC Regulation." In 1963,
the regulation's title was changed to the "Regulation for Financial State-
ments by the Ministry of Finance."

point of view or from an accounting point of view, there seems to have been
no justification for the release of the new Regulation by the Ministry of
Justice.

From a legal point of view, however, there were several reasons why
the Ministry of Justice released the Regulation. The first legal justification
for the issuance of the Regulation was given by the "Law Pertaining to the
Operation of the Amendment to the Commercial Code" enacted in 1938. Article
49 of that law provided that the manner in which an inventory, a balance
sheet, and an income statement of a stock corporation are to be prepared
and other forms shall be prescribed by ordinance. The accounting provisions
of the Commercial Code were too few in number and too defective in substance
to be developed into a regulation for financial statements until the last
revision in 1962. As the financial reporting practices were established in the
Japanese society based upon A Statement of Business Accounting Principles and
the SEC Regulation, the differences between these practices and the accounting
provisions of the Commercial Code became serious. In 1962, as mentioned in
Chapter II, the accounting provisions of the Commercial Code were so well
revised that it became possible to develop a regulation to make an application
of these provisions to the practice effective.

As mentioned in Chapter IV, A Statement of Business Accounting Principles
was institutionalized through the SEC Regulation and had a great influence on
the financial reporting practices in Japan. If the revised accounting provisions of the 1962 Commercial Code had been completely in harmony with A
Statement of Business Accounting Principles and the SEC Regulation, the SEC
Regulation could have been applied to the area over which the Commercial Code
had its justification or the release of the new Regulation would not have

186

been essential. An officer of the Ministry of Justice, however, stated
that:

> Although the Commercial Code adopted most ideas developed in
> A Statement of Business Accounting Principles etc., the revised
> accounting provisions of the Commercial Code were not neces-
> sarily identical with those of A Statement of Business Account-
> ing Principles etc. This means that the revised Code judged A
> Statement of Business Accounting Principles etc. improper as a
> positive law at this present time. If A Statement of Business
> Accounting Principles etc. should be maintained as practical
> guides in the future, they need some revisions. It should be
> noted that accounting theories, techniques, and conventions should
> be respected in interpreting the provisions of the Commercial Code
> but we should not blindly follow them without critiques (in the
> past, this was the tendency).[3]

This statement implies that the Commercial Code was revised based upon its

own basic idea and logic and that it adopted the accounting ideas to the

extent that its underlying views could be effectively realized. The

officers of the Ministry of Justice considered that the issuance of the Re-

gulation was essential to an effective application of the Commercial Code

just as was the SEC Regulation.

The "Regulation for Corporate Balance Sheets and Income Statements,"

which consists of four chapters -- (1) general principles, (2) the balance

sheet, (3) the income statement, and (4) other principles -- specified the

preparation methods of balance sheets and income statements to be prepared

based upon Article 281 of the Commercial Code (Article 1). Although the 1962

[3]Akinobu Ueda, "Kaisha no Keisan no Kaisetsu" (Comments on the Accounting
Provisions for Corporations) in Akinobu Ueda, Takashi Yoshida, and Osamu
Mimura, Kabushiki-Kaisha no Keisan (Corporate Accounting Based upon the Com-
mercial Code) (Tokyo, Japan: Chuo-Keizai-Sha, 1963), p. 4.

Commercial Code still requires the directors to prepare an inventory, an
inventory is excluded from the financial documents to be submitted at the
ordinary general meeting of shareholders for approval.[4] Concerning the
general principles, Article 2 states:

> Every balance sheet and income statement shall be prepared in
> such a way as to furnish accurate judgment on the financial
> status and the operating results of the company.

Article 3 states:

> Any change in the valuation methods or in other accounting pro-
> cedures shall be disclosed as a footnote to the balance sheet
> or income statement. If the change is not material, no disclosure
> is needed.

Although Article 2 is usually interpreted as the principle of true and fair
disclosure or the principle of true report and the principle of fair disclosure, there is no unanimous interpretation on Article 3. Officers of
the Ministry of Justice interpret Article 3 as the principle of consistency.[5]
Most accountants, however, interpret that Article 3 is not the principles of
consistency comparable to that in A Statement of Business Accounting Principles.
Yasuichi Sakamoto, for example, states:

> The Regulation clearly permits the inconsistent application of
> valuation methods or other procedures. According to the Regula-
> tion valuation methods or other procedures may be changed from
> period to period without any good reasons. What is required by
> the Regulation is to disclose such changes as footnotes.[6]

---

[4]The 1962 Commercial Code, Article 283.

[5]Osamu Mimura, "Kabushiki-Kaisha no Taishaku Taishohyo oyobi Soneki
Keisansho ni kansuru Kisoku no Kaisetsu" (Comments on the Regulation for
Corporate Balance Sheets and Income Statements) in Ueda, Yoshida, Mimura,
op. cit., pp. 44-45.

[6]Yasuichi Sakamoto, "Kaisei Shoho to Zaimushohyo" (The Revised
Commercial Code and Financial Statements) in Katsuji Yamashita (ed.),
Keisan-Shorui Kisoku no Mondaiten (Some Problems in the Regulation for
Corporate Balance Sheets and Income Statements) (Tokyo, Japan: Chuo-
Keizai-Sha, 1965), p. 53.

Concerning the grouping in the balance sheet, Article 4 specifies:

A balance sheet shall be divided into an assets section, a liabilities section, and a net worth section with a total amount for each section.

The assets section shall be subdivided into current assets, fixed assets, and deferred assets, and the fixed assets shall be further divided into tangible fixed assets, intangible fixed assets, and investments (Article 5). As Professor Toshio Iino noted, the classification and treatment of long-term prepaid expenses by the Regulation are different from those of usual accounting.[7] According to the Regulation, prepaid expenses which are not expected to generate the receipt of services within one year shall be included in the intangible fixed assets subsection (Article 19). From an income determination point of view, the long-term prepaid expenses and deferred assets are homogeneous in nature because they are all costs which should be charged against revenue in the future periods.

From a legal point of view, however, the long-term prepaid expenses should be separated from the deferred assets. The 1962 revised Commercial Code permits the inclusion of four additional items in the category of deferred assets. They are: (1) preliminary (start-up) expenses, (2) development expenses, (3) experimental and research expenses, and (4) bond expenses.[8] The enlargement of the concept of deferred assets by the Commercial Code does not necessarily mean a change of its basic idea of assets. The prepaid

---

[7]Toshio Iino, "Accounting Principles and Contemporary Legal Thought in Japan," The International Journal of Accounting Education and Research, Vol. 2, No. 2, (Spring, 1967), p. 81.

[8]The 1962 Revised Commercial Code, Articles 286-2, 286-3, and 286-5.

expenses are viewed as the right of the company to claim the services from others to whom the company paid in advance for such services. Therefore, they shall be presented in the balance sheet as assets. The deferred assets are not assets but what is permitted by the Commercial Code to be listed on the assets side of the balance sheet.[9] According to the Commercial Code, assets are those which have a realizable value or those which represent a legal right and the assets shall be listed in the balance sheet. The deferred assets, which are fictitious assets, may be listed in the balance sheet, but the listing of such fictitious assets is voluntary. As will be discussed later, this basic idea of assets of the Commercial Code has an influence on the calculation of profits available for dividends.

Since the Regulation prescribed only the preparation method of the balance sheets and the income statements, it does not contain any substantial provisions for developing accounting information. The 1962 revised Commercial Code adopted several different valuation bases for different types of assets based upon a general principle of an historical cost basis. The following is a summary of the provisions concerning the asset valuation bases of the Commercial Code:

1. Current assets shall be valued at their acquisition or production cost. If market price is substantially lower than acquisition or production cost and if the recovery of the acquisition or production cost cannot reasonably be expected, the current assets shall be valued at market price.

---

[9]Mimura, op. cit., p. 53 and pp. 55-56.

If <u>market price</u> is lower than acquisition or production cost, even if it is not so substantial, the current assets <u>may</u> be valued at <u>market price</u> (Article 285-2).[10]

2. Fixed assets shall be valued at their acquisition or production cost less regular and reasonable depreciation or depletion charges.

   If an unpredictable diminution of value has occurred on fixed assets, a reasonable amount shall be deducted (Article 285-3).

3. Monetary claims shall be valued at the amount of the claims; but if such claims were purchased at the price below the amount of the claims or if there is any good reasons, they may be valued at a prudent lesser amount.

   If it is doubtful that the amount of claims is fully collectible, the estimated uncollectible amount shall be deducted (Article 285-4).

4. Debentures shall be valued at their acquisition cost; if the acquisition cost is other than the face value, they must be valued at an amount after a proper addition to or deduction from the acquisition cost.

---

[10]Concerning the interpretation of "market price" in the first paragraph of Article 285-2, there are two different opinions among lawyers. Some lawyers interpret "market price" as "realizable value" on the ground that the second sentence of the first paragraph was added for the purpose of maintaining corporate capital and of protecting creditors. Another group of lawyers interpret "market price" as "current replacement cost" on the ground that the first sentence of the first paragraph is a reflection of a dynamic accounting thought and that the intent of the second sentence should be the same as that of the first sentence: unexpired cost should be measured based upon the cash outlay basis.

Concerning the interpretation of "market price" in the second paragraph, no disagreement exists among lawyers, It is usually interpreted as "current replacement cost."

(Seiji Tanaka, Eisuke Yoshinaga, and Chuhei Yamamura, <u>Saizentei Konmentaru Kaisha-Ho</u> [Completely Revised Commentary on Corporation Law] [Tokyo, Japan: Keiso Shobo, 1968] , pp. 975-86)

The provisions of the second sentence of the first paragraph and the second paragraph of Article 285-2 shall be
applied to the debentures having stock exchange quotations,
and the provision of the second paragraph of the preceeding
Article to the debentures having no stock exchange quotations (Article 285-5).

5. Shares shall be valued at their acquisition cost.

The provisions of the second sentence of the first paragraph and the second paragraph of Article 285-2 shall be
applied to the shares having stock exchange quotations.

Shares having no stock exchange quotations shall be valued
at a reasonably reduced amount, if the financial condition
of the issuing company has been materially impaired (Article 285-6).

6. Goodwill may be listed in the assets section of the balance
sheet only in the case where it was purchased or arose in
a merger situation. It shall be valued at its acquisition
cost and shall be amortized by not less than the average
amount for a period in each period within five years after
the date of acquisition (Article 285-7).

In summary, the basic principle of asset valuation in the 1962 revised
Commercial Code is the historical cost basis. This is a result of reconciliation of the Commercial Code and A Statement of Business Accounting
Principles. The Commercial Code also adopted a lower-than-historical-cost
basis. The historical cost basis prohibits the recognition of unrealized gains
on the one hand and the lower-than-historical-cost basis permits the recognition of unrealized losses on the other hand. Thus, a combined application
of the historical cost basis and the lower-than-historical-cost basis is
much safer for the protection of creditors than the lower-than-market-price
basis in the old Commercial Code.

According to the Regulation, the liabilities section in the balance sheet
shall be subdivided into current liabilities, fixed liabilities, and "provisions" (Article 25). The concept of "provisions for specific future disbursements and/or expenses" was first recognized by the 1962 revised Com-

mercial Code.[11] This is also an example of the reconciliation of the
Commercial Code and A Statement of Business Accounting Principles. From
the legal point of view, they do not constitute real liabilities in a legal
sense since both the amount and person to whom they might be paid are uncertain. The concept of "provision" or "allowance" is not well established
even in accounting theory. For these reasons, the listing of "provisions"
were not necessarily enforced by the Commercial Code.

Concerning the grouping of net worth items in the balance sheet, Article
34 of the Regulation specifies that the net worth section shall be further
divided into stated capital, legal reserve, and surplus sections. When
the Commercial Code was revised in 1950, the concept of legal reserve was
divided into the legal capital reserve and legal revenue reserve. This is
said to have been a reflection of accounting thought on the Commercial Code.
The Commercial Code, however, did not abolish its traditional concept of
"legal reserve" regardless of the sources of such reserve. The provisions
concerning the legal capital reserve and the legal revenue reserve in the
1962 Code were not different from those in the 1950 Code except the following two points: (1) the base for the calculation of the amount of profits to
be retained for each period was changed and (2) the net amount resulting from
revaluation of assets was excluded from legal capital reserve because of
the adoption of a cost basis for asset valuation. To accountants the separation of capital from income and then the separation of capital surplus from

---

[11]Article 287-2 of the 1962 revised Commercial Code reads:
When the revisions for specific future disbursements
and/or expenses are listed in the liabilities section
of the balance sheet, the purpose thereof shall be
clearly disclosed in the balance sheet.

earned surplus are two of the most important concerns. To lawyers,

however, the separation of what is legally disposable from what is not

legally disposable is the most important concern. To them the separation

of capital surplus from earned surplus in the balance sheet is not necessary.[12]

The difference in the grouping of the net worth section of the Commercial

Code and of A Statement of Business Accounting Principles may be summarized

as follows:

(The grouping of the net worth based upon the Commercial Code)

(The grouping of the net worth based upon A Statement of Business Accounting Principles)

I. Stated capital
II. Legal reserve:
  A. Legal capital reserve:

    1. paid-in capital from par value stock
    2. paid-in capital from non-par stock
    3. paid in capital from capital reduction
    4. paid-in surplus from amalgamation

  B. Reserve for revaluation based upon the law
  C. Legal revenue reserve:
    legally retained income

III. Surplus
  A. Voluntary reserves:

I. Stated capital
II. Surplus:
  A. Capital surplus:
    1) legal capital reserve:
     1. paid-in capital from par value stock
     2. paid-in capital from non-par stock
     3. paid-in capital from capital reduction
     4. paid-in surplus from amalgamation
     5. net amount from revaluation of assets
    2) reserve for revaluation based upon the law
    3) other capital surplus
     1. subsidies from the government
     2. customer's contribution
     3. gains on insurance claims

[12]Mimura, op. cit., pp. 59-60. For the critical view on the Commercial Code concepts of legal reserve, see Kotaro Tanba, "Keisan Shorui Kisoku ni okeru 'Shihon no Bu' no Kubun Hyoji ni tsuite" (On the Grouping of 'Net Worth Section' in the Regulation for Corporate Balance Sheets and Income Statements) in Katsuji Yamashita (ed.), op. cit., pp. 225-34 and Iino, op. cit., pp. 83-84.

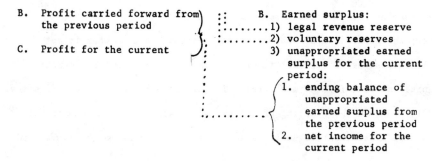

B. Profit carried forward from the previous period

C. Profit for the current

B. Earned surplus:
1) legal revenue reserve
2) voluntary reserves
3) unappropriated earned surplus for the current period:
   1. ending balance of unappropriated earned surplus from the previous period
   2. net income for the current period

The Regulation prescribed a special type of income statement in Articles 37, 38, 39, 41, 43, and 44. According to these Articles, the structure of the income statement based upon the Regulation is summarized as follows:

I. Regular Income Section:
  A. Operating Income Section:
    Operating revenue - Operating expenses = Operating income

  B. Non-operating Income Section:
    Operating income ≠ Non-operating revenue
            - Non-operating expenses ▪ Regular income

II. Special Income Section:
    Regular income ≠ Special profits
     - Special losses = Income for the current period

    Income for the current period

          ≠ Profits carried forward from the previous period = Unappropriated profits for the current period

The format of this statement is similar to a multiple-step, "all-inclusive" type of income statement prepared based upon the "matching concept" method of income determination.

How did the Regulation develop this type of income statement? By
which accounting profisions is this statement legally supported? Article
290 is the only provision concerning profits in the Commercial Code.[13]
Is there any logical relationship between Article 290 and the income statement presentation prescribed by the Regulation?

A Study group of Japanese accounting educators states as follows:

> The preparation method of the balance sheet prescribed in
> the Regulation is understandable in the light of accounting
> provisions of the Commercial Code. The accounting provision
> concerning income determination is Article 290. Since the
> Article 290 regards "income" as "an increase in net worth,"
> the Commercial Code seems to presume the so-called "comparison
> of net worth" method for income determination. Therefore, we
> cannot understand why the Regulation prescribed the preparation
> method of the income statement based upon the "matching concept"
> method.[14]

An income statement is one of the financial documents to be prepared based

upon Article 281 of the Commercial Code. Although there is no definition

of the income statement in the provisions of Commercial Code, the Regulation

---

[13]Article 290 of the 1962 Commercial Code reads:
Profits may be distributed as dividends to the extent of the
amount of the net worth in the balance sheet minus the following
amounts:
1. The amount of stated capital,
2. The total of the accumulated legal capital reserve and
accumulated legal revenue reserve,
3. The amount of the legal revenue reserve required to be
retained for the current period,
4. If the total amount of deferred assets listed in the
balance sheet based upon Articles 286-2 and 286-3 exceeds
the total amount of the legal capital reserve and the legal
revenue reserve prescribed in the preceding sections 2 and 3,
such excess.

[14]Kanri-Kaikei Iinkai (A Study Group on Management Accounting), "Shoho
Keisan Kitei narabini Kabushiki-Kaisha no Taishaku-Taishohyo oyobi Soneki-
Keisansho ni kansuru Kisoku no Jisshi ni saishite no Kaikei-Shori Mondai ni
tsuite no Ikensho" (Comments on the Application of Accounting Provisions of
the Commercial Code and the Regulation for Corporate Balance Sheets and
Income Statements), Kaikei (Accounting), Vol. 84, No. 5, (November, 1963),
p. 143.

states that the income statement shall be prepared in such a way as to
furnish accurate judgment on the "operating results of the company"
(Article 2). As far as this statement is concerned, the Commercial Code
and the Regulation seem to presume the preparation of an usual income statement in accounting usage. The regular income section of the income statement represents the "current operating performance" type of income statement. It presents the "operating results of the company" for a given
period of time.

The special income section, however, is quite different from the
second half of the regular "all-inclusive" type of income statement.
According to Article 42 of the Regulation, the following special profits
and losses shall be included:

1. the amount of the liquidation of the voluntarily retained
   earnings which were applied for the original purposes;
2. the amount of the provisions (prescribed in Article 287-2
   of the Commercial Code) which were applied for the purpose
   other than original; and
3. prior period adjustments and extraordinary items.

Item (3) may be included in the non-operating income section as non-operating revenue or non-operating expenses. Whether item (3) is presented in the
separate section or included in the non-operating income section does not
change the nature of the income statement. The inclusion of item (1) and
item (2) mentioned above in the income statement does change its nature
since they were related to the appropriated income of the prior period
but not relevant to the income determination for the current period. The
inclusion of these items in the income statement is justified for the purpose
of income determination specified by the Commercial Code to calculate the
amounts of profits available for distribusion. All factors which affect

the amounts of profits available for dividends should be presented in the income statement for approval by shareholders.[15]

The last figure in the income statement, that is, unappropriated profits for the current period is not necessarily equal to the amount of profits available for dividends. As mentioned earlier, the 1962 Commercial Code enlarged the concept of "deferred asset" to include (1) preliminary (start-up) expenses, (2) development expenses, and (3) experimental and research expenses (Article 286-2 and 286-3). These deferred assets, however, are fictitious assets which do not have realizable value. That is, these items are recognized as assets from a periodic income determination point of view, but are not from a creditors' protection point of view. If the total amount of these deferred assets exceeds the total amount of accumulated legal reserves, the amount of true assets having realizable value becomes smaller than the amount of the stated capital. From the viewpoint of creditors' protection, the amount of stated capital indicates the minimum amount of true assets to be maintained. Thus, Article 290 of the Commercial Code requires that the excess of the deferred assets, prescribed in Articles 286-2 and 286-3, over the total amount of legal reserves be deducted from the amount of profits available for dividends. In this case, the amount of profits available for dividends is calculated by the following formula:

---

[15]Mimura, op. cit., p. 63.

> The amount of profits available for dividends = unappropriated
> profits for the current period - the amount of the legal revenue
> reserve required to be retained for the current period (= 1/10 x
> cash dividends for the current period) - the excess of the defer-
> red assets over the legal reserve.

This calculation is not presented either in the income statement or in the
balance sheet, but in the statement of proposals pertaining to the disposal of profits.

Article 290 of the Commercial Code is a provision which prescribed
the maximum amounts of profits avaialble for dividends. It is not a
provision concerning the income determination. In other words, the
income statement prescribed by the Regulation is not supported by any
substantial provision of the Commercial Code. This income statement is
a special type of income statement which is rearranged to meet the special
purpose of the Japanese Commercial Code. It could more accurately be
designated as a "statement of profits available for distribution."[16]

Revised Statement of Business Accounting Principles. When it was
revised in 1962, the Commercial Code adopted the basic ideas of A Statement of Business Accounting Principles to the extent that the adoption of a
dynamic view of accounting satisfied the original purpose of the Commercial
Code . Several significant discrepancies, however, still remained unbridged between the Commercial Code and A Statement of Business Accounting
Principles. From a theoretical point of view, these discrepancies cannot
or need not be bridged since the purposes of the Commercial Code and A
Statement of Business Accounting Principles are not necessarily identical.

---

[16]Iino, op. cit., p. 85.

From a legal point of view, however, these discrepancies should be bridged since the Securities Exchange Act is a special law of the Commercial Code and the Securities Exchange Act and all related regulations should be in conformity with the Commercial Code.[17] The relationships among the Commercial Code, the Securities Exchange Act, A Statement of Business Accounting Principles, and other related regulations are shown in Figure 4.

FIGURE 4   The Relationships among the Commercial Code, the Securities Exchange Act, A Statement of Business Accounting Principles, and other related regulations.

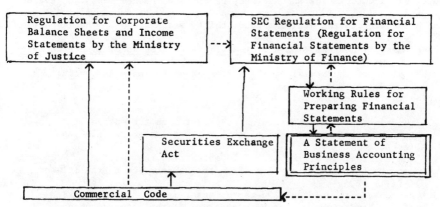

- - - - - - -> the flow of theoretical impact
——————→ the flow of legal impact

---

[17]Takeo Suzuki, "Shoken-Torihiki-Ho to Kabushiki-Kaisha-Ho" (The Securities Exchange Act and the Stock Corporation Law) in Kotaro Tanaka (ed.), Kabushiki-Kaisha-Ho Koza, I (Stock Corporation Law Handbook, I) (Tokyo, Japan: Yuhikaku, 1955), pp. 354-55 and p. 361.

Professor Kurosawa, who was a chief drafter of A Statement of
Business Accounting Principles in 1949 and was also in charge of the
revision in 1963, states these relationships in the following terms:

> The adoption of the basic ideas of A Statement of Business
> Accounting Principles by the 1962 Commercial Code created
> a new legal relationship between them. A new impact was
> given that the Commercial Code requested the revision of A
> Statement of Business Accounting Principles. Thus, A State-
> ment of Business Accounting Principles was partially revised.
> We would not regard this revision as an internal or theoretical
> improvement of A Statement of Business Accounting Principles.[18]

He also states that "the accounting provisions of the Commercial Code,
including the Regulation of the Ministry of Justice, pushed back the development of accounting to the stage at about thirty years ago."[19] What impacts
did the Commercial Code have on A Statement of Business Accounting Principles?
The major points of the revision of A Statement of Business Accounting
Principles in 1963 were as follows.

1. the separation of the surplus statement into the earned
   surplus statement and the capital surplus statement (II-6 and
   II-7).
2. the elimination of the principle concerning the large
   amount of extraordinary loss from the Balance Sheet Principles
   (III-1- [D]).
3. the change in wording of deferred asset items and the addition
   of the bond discount and bond expenses to the deferred assets
   (III-4-[1]-[C]).
4. the change in valuation basis for inventories (III-5-[A]).
5. the change in valuation basis for temporarily held marketable
   securities (III-5-[B]).

As mentioned earlier, the 1962 Commercial Code did not accept the
concepts of capital surplus and earned surplus. Under the Commercial Code,

---

[18]Kiyoshi Kurosawa, "Kaikei Gensoku Shusei no Shoten" (A Focus of the
Revision of A Statement of Business Accounting Principles), Sangyo-Keiri
(Financial and Cost Accounting), Vol. 23, No. 12, (December, 1963), p. 50.

[19]Ibid.

the net worth of the stock corporation is composed of (1) the stated capital, (2) legal reserve, and (3) surplus, although the legal reserve is divided into the legal capital reserve and the legal revenue reserve. From the viewpoint of the Commercial Code the grouping of the net worth into two groups is important: (1) what should legally be maintained in the company and (2) what may legally be disposed. Even those which are classified as capital surplus from an accounting point of view may legally be disposed unless they are classified as legal capital reserve prescribed in Article 288-2 of the Commercial Code. On the other hand, a part of retained earnings, which could be disposed from an accounting viewpoint, must be maintained as legal revenue reserve from the viewpoint of the Commercial Code. In the Commercial Code, only one concept of "surplus" is sufficient which represents what may legally be disposed. The income statement prescribed by the Regulation contained the earned surplus statement in its "special income section."

Influenced by the Commercial Code, A Statement of Business Account-ing Principles revised its Income Statement Principles 6 and 7 as follows:

(Earned Surplus)
6. Earned surplus is a surplus consisting of retained income and it should be distinguished from capital surplus arising from sources other than income.

   Unless there is good reason, capital surplus should not be transferred directly or indirectly to earned surplus.

   In case a deficit cannot be covered with earned surplus, it may be covered with capital surplus.

(Earned Surplus Statement)
7. The earned surplus statement should show changes in earned surplus for an accounting period with unappropriated earned surplus for the current period. If these items of earned surplus are shown in the earned surplus accounting section

set up in the income statement, the preparation of the
independent earned surplus statement may be omitted....

Under the old Statement of Business Accounting Principles, one prepara-

tion method was suggested for the earned surplus section of the surplus

statement. Since the income statement of income and earned surplus,

however, the revised Statement permitted the preparation of such a

combined statement and the choice between method A and method B to

facilitate the reconciliation with the Regulation.[20]

(Method A)

Beginning balance of unappropriated earned surplus
carried forward from the previous period ....(A)
- Appropriated amount of earned surplus   ....(B)
_____

Net amount of unappropriated earned surplus
carried forward from the previous period ....(C)
$\neq$ Prior period adjustments and extraordinary items.(D)
_____

Ending balance of earned surplus carried
forward from the previous period   ....(E)
$\neq$ New income for the current period   ....(F)
_____

Unappropriated earned surplus for the
current period   ....(G)

_____

[20]Minoru Emura, "Joyokin ni kansuru Kaisei no Mondaiten" (Some
Problems in the Revision of the Treatment of Surplus), **Kaikei** (Accounting),
Vol. 84, No. 6, (December, 1963), p. 20.

(Method B)

Net amount of unappropriated earned surplus
carried forward from the previous period ....(C)
$\neq$ Prior period adjustments and extraordinary items.(D)

Ending balance of earned surplus carried
forward from the previous period   ....(E)
$\neq$ Net income for the current period   ....(F)

Unappropriated earned surplus for the
current period   ....(G)

Notes:
  Beginning balance of unappropriated earned
  surplus carried forward from the previous
  period   ....(A)
  - Appropriated amount of earned surplus ....(B)

Net amount of unappropriated earned surplus
carried forward from the previous period ....(C)

By the revision of Income Statement Principles 6 and 7, A Statement of Business Accounting Principles replaced the term, "surplus" and "surplus statement" for "earned surplus" and "earned surplus statement," and eliminated the "capital surplus statement" from a set of financial statements. The capital surplus statement was included in a set of schedules supporting financial statements. The separation of the earned surplus statement from the capital statement itself would be considered as an improvement since the earned surplus and the capital surplus differ from each other in nature.[21] Although the Revised Statement of Business Accounting Principles did not abolish the concept of "capital surplus," the

[21]Kaichiro Banba, "Kigyo-Kaikei Gensoku Shusei no Tohi" (An Evaluation of the Revision of A Statement of Business Accounting Principles), Kaikei (Accounting), Vol. 84, No. 6, (December, 1963), p. 1 and Shigeo Aoki, "Kigyo-Kaikei Gensoku no Ichibu Shusei eno Kenkai" (A Comment on the Partial Revision of A Statement of Business Accounting Principles), Sangyo-Keiri (Financial and Cost Accounting), Vol. 24, No. 1, (January, 1964), p. 74.

changes in Income Statement Principles 6 and 7, coupled with a change
in Balance Sheet Principle 4-(3)-(B), created the impression that the
importance of the "capital surplus" or "capital surplus statement" was
disparaged by the Revised Statement.[22]

The distinction between capital surplus and earned surplus has been
and is one of the most basic principles in A Statement of Business
Accounting Principles. The importance of the surplus statement was
repeatedly emphasized by the Business Accounting Deliberation Council in
"A Statement of Opinions on Reconciliation of the Commercial Code and A
Statement of Business Accounting Principles" (1951) and the Series of
Opinion No. 1, "On Composition of Financial Statements" (1960). Then,
what does this change in A Statement of Business Accounting Principles
mean? The author believes that an accounting theory of "capital surplus"
was not so well established as to be convincing to the lawyers in Japan.[23]

---

[22]Emura, op. cit., p. 15 and p. 18. Balance Sheet Principle 4-(3)-(B)
was revised as follows:

. . . .

> Capital surplus should be shown classified into paid-in
> capital from the issuance of stock in excess of par value,
> paid-in capital from the issuance of non-par stock in
> excess of stated value, paid-in capital from reduction in
> value assigned to outstanding stock, paid-in surplus from
> amalgamation, and reserve for revaluation based upon the
> Asset Revaluation Law.

. . . .

Compared with the old Balance Sheet Principle 4-(3)-(B), the following items
were excluded from the revised principle:
  (1) net amount resulting from a revaluation of fixed assets,
  (2) subsidies from the government in aid of construction,
  (3) customer's contribution to the cost of construction work, and
  (4) gains on insurance claims.

[23]Some Japanese accountants insist that those items which are traditionally regarded as "capital surplus" in accounting literature but are excluded
from the legal capital reserve in the Commercial Code are not capital surplus

The second point of revision was the elimination of the principle
concerning the large amount of extraordinary losses from the Balance
Sheet Principles 1-(D). Thus, the Balance Sheet Principle 1-(D) was
changed to:

> Special expenses having effect on the future periods may
> be listed temporarily on the asset side of the balance
> sheet in order to allocate them to the subsequent periods.

The main reason for the elimination of this principle from the text of A
Statement of Business Accounting Principles is that the Commercial Code
did not accept deferred assets other than those prescribed in the Code.
The following comment on this revision by a member of the Council indi-
cates how ambiguous the basic view of A Statement of Business Accounting
Principles was:

> The sound development of accounting practices will be promoted
> not by laws but by the establishment of ethical norms of account-
> ing. To do this is the function of accounting principles. The
> principle of deferring the large amount of extraordinary losses
> accepted by A Statement of Business Accounting Principles does
> not positively support the deferring of such losses but suggest
> a method to disclose such extraordinary losses otherwise it
> might be hidden among other items so that companies can follow a
> proper accounting procedure.[24]

If the principle of deferring the large amount of extraordinary losses had
been an ethical norm, no revision would have been needed. If the deferring
of such losses had been a proper accounting procedure supported by a sound
accounting theory, no revision would have been needed. The revision seems
to be a compromise with or a surrender to the Commercial Code.

---

but profits or earned surplus. See for example, Toshiyoshi Okabe, "Kensetsu
Joseikin wa hatashite Shihon-Joyokin de aruka" (Are Governmental Subsidies
Really Capital Surplus?), Kaikei (Accounting), Vol. 86, No. 2, (August, 1964),
pp. 24-54.

[24]Kiyoshi Kurosawa, "Shusei Kigyo-Kaikei Gensoku Kaisetsu" (Comments
on the Revised Statement of Business Accounting Principles), Kigyokaikei
(Accounting), Vol. 15, No. 13, (December, 1963), p. 119.

The change in the description of deferred asset items and the addition of the bond discound and bond expenses to the deferred assets are additional examples of the influences of the 1962 revised Commercial Code on A Statement of Business Accounting Principles. The Revised Statement of Business Accounting Principles adopted the "cost or market, whichever is lower" rule for the valuation of inventories and temporarily held marketable securities in addition to the historical cost basis. Although the application of the "cost or market, whichever is lower" rule was allowed even under the old Statement of Business Accounting Principles (III-5- A), the application was not necessarily enforced. This change in the valuation basis was not made based upon the logic of A Statement of Business Accounting Principles but made to be in conformity with the revised Commercial Code. Since the revised Statement does not explain the meaning of the term "market price," used in the Commercial Code may well be interpreted as "realizable value." If the revision of A Statement of Business Accounting Principles was made to be in conformity with the revised Commercial Code, the term "market price" used in the revised Statement should also be interpreted as "realizable value." The application of such a "cost or market, whichever is lower" rule apparently contradicts the basic principle of cost allocation in A Statement of Business Accounting Principles.

In Chapter II, the author noted that A Statement of Business Accounting Principles is a compound of two things, differing in their nature -- general and special. This may be rephrased by a theoretical guide to the accounting actions and a practical guide to the accounting actions. From the beginning,

however, <u>A</u> <u>Statement</u> <u>of</u> <u>Business</u> <u>Accounting</u> <u>Principles</u> has been function-
ing in the Japanese economic environment as a practical guide to accounting
actions rather than a theoretical guide, being supported by the Securities
Exchange Act.

The Securities Exchange Act had no substantial accounting provisions.
The financial statements to be filed with the Securities and Exchange Commission were prepared in conformity with the SEC Regulation. The SEC Reg-
ulation was theoretically supported by <u>A</u> <u>Statement</u> <u>of</u> <u>Business</u> <u>Accounting</u>
<u>Principles</u> and there was no conflict between them. In other words, <u>A</u> <u>State-
ment</u> <u>of</u> <u>Business</u> <u>Accounting</u> <u>Principles</u> has been institutionalized as a
practical guide to the accounting practices through the SEC Regulation. The
revision of the Commercial Code in 1962 posed a serious problem to <u>A</u> <u>State-
ment</u> <u>of</u> <u>Business</u> <u>Accounting</u> <u>Principles</u>. <u>A</u> <u>Statement</u> <u>of</u> <u>Business</u> <u>Accounting</u>
<u>Principles</u> was required to choose between the two: a general and theoretical
guide or a special and practical guide to the accounting actions. If it had
chosen the first one by severing itself from the SEC Regulation, the revision
of the Statement would not have been necessary or it would have been revised
based upon its own theory. <u>A</u> <u>Statement</u> <u>of</u> <u>Business</u> <u>Accounting</u> <u>Principles</u> was
in a sense "government-made" and it could not sever the relationship with
the SEC Regulation. So far as <u>A</u> <u>Statement</u> <u>of</u> <u>Business</u> <u>Accounting</u> <u>Principles</u>
is a guide to the accounting practices related to the SEC Regulation, it
cannot be free from the influence of the Commercial Code since the Code is a
basic law which has a priority over the Securities Exchange Act.

In the process of the revision of the Commercial Code, A Statement of Business Accounting Principles had an influence in the Commercial Code. After the revision of the Commercial Code it, in turn, was obliged to invite criticism from the Commercial Code, Until 1962, many statements issued by the Business Accounting Deliberation Council, including A Statement of Business Accounting Principles, were agreements among the Council's members, mainly among accounting educators.[25] It was the first time for A Statement of Business Accounting Principles to invite such criticism from areas other than accounting.

As analyzed above, the revision of A Statement of Business Accounting Principles resulted in a compromise with or a surrender to the Commercial Code. The author believes that the one-sided revision of A Statement of Business Accounting Principles based upon the logic of the Commercial Code gave us a valuable lesson for the future development of accounting principles in the Japanese society.

Application Process

Regulation for Corporate Balance Sheets and Income Statements. Although the Regulation became effective on April 1, 1963, it was not applied to the first accounting period ending after April 1, 1963 of the stock corporation existing at the time of the enforcement of the Regulation.[26]

---

[25] Rintaro Aoki, "Kigyo-Kaikei Gensoku no Seikaku" (A Character of A Statement of Business Accounting Principles), Kigyokaikei (Accounting), Vol. 16, No. 1, (January, 1964), p. 20.

[26] Supplementary Provisions to the Commercial Code (Law No. 82), Article 8.

Since most of the Japanese stock corporations use six months for the accounting period, the Regulation was scheduled to be applied to those stock corporations whose accounting period ended during October, 1963. Immediately after the application of the Regulation, a Japanese accounting professor undertook a field survey on "Financial Reporting at the General Meetings of Shareholders of the Japanese Stock Corporations." This survey was initially scheduled to cover about four thousand stock corporations. The final report of the survey is not available. A part of the survey was reported by Minoru Emura in the January, 1964 issue of the Kigyokaikei (Accounting).[27]

After reviewing the financial statements -- balance sheets and income statements -- prepared by about fifty corporations, Minoru Emura states his general impression in the following terms:

> In summary, about fifty companies prepared their financial statements in conformity with the standard forms which were published by the Financial Department of the Federation of Economic Organizations in October, 1963...The income statements prepared in conformity with the revised Commercial Code and the Regulation provided the detailed information. In general, the non-operating income sections were elaborated....
> Since the balance sheets were considerably detailed in the past, great changes in presentation were not found.[28]

---

[27]Minoru Emura, "Jugatsu-Ki Kessan Go Sha no Kessan Hokokusho o miru" (A Look at the Financial Statements Prepared by Five Stock Corporations during October, 1963), Kigyokaikei (Accounting), Vol. 16, No. 1, (January, 1964), pp. 173-84.

[28]Ibid., pp. 175 and 178.

When the Regulation for Corporate Balance Sheets and Income Statements was enacted, there was no unanimous opinion concerning the nature
of the Regulation among lawyers and accountants. Most Japanese lawyers
considered the Regulation by the Ministry of Justice as "compulsory" prescriptions which should be followed by all stock corporations. Some
accountants considered seriously that a traditional system of accounting
might be destroyed by the Regulation.[29] Some accountants considered the
Regulation as "instructive" prescription which is not applicable or enforceable for all corporations.[30]

In practice, however, nearly all Japanese stock corporations, except
very small sized corporations, have been preparing their balance sheets
and income statements in conformity with the Regulation since 1963. No
one can deny that the Regulation made a contribution to the improvement of
financial statements to be submitted at the general meeting of shareholders.
The analysis in Chapter III indicated that the accounting provisions of the
Commercial Code were virtually ineffective. By the enactment of the Regulation for Corporate Balance Sheets and Income Statements the accounting provisions of the revised Commercial Code began to take firm root in the financial reporting practices in Japan.

---

[29] Atsunori Kitagawa, "Kigyo-Kaikei Gensoku towa Ittai Nani Ka" (What
Is A Statement of Business Accounting Principles?), Kigyokaikei (Accounting),
Vol. 16, No. 1, (January, 1964), p. 26.

[30] Kiyoshi Kurosawa, "Kigyo-Kaikei Gensoku to Zaimu-Shohyo Kisoku"
(A Statement of Business Accounting Principles and the Regulation for
Financial Statements) in Katsuji Yamashita (ed.), Keisan-Shorui Kisoku
no Mondaiten (Some Problems on the Regulation for Corporate Balance Sheets
and Income Statements) (Tokyo, Japan: Chuo-Keizai-Sha, 1965), p. 21.

Revised Statement of Business Accounting Principles. The revision of
A Statement of Business Accounting Principles in conformity with the revised
Commercial Code changed the nature of the Statement and destined its
future course of development. When the Statement was revised in 1963, a
member of the Business Accounting Deliberation Council proposed to establish
two sets of accounting principles: (1) an ideal set of accounting principles
as a theoretical guide and (2) a practical set of accounting principles in
conformity with the related regulations.[31] This proposal was rejected by
the Council. Thus, the relationship of A Statement of Business Accounting
Principles to the legal system became closer. Before the revision in 1963,
A Statement of Business Accounting Principles was an element of a set of
financial reporting systems based upon the Securities Exchange Act. After
the revision, A Statement of Business Accounting Principles also became an
element of the financial reporting system based upon the Commercial Code
since the Securities Exchange Act was subject to the Commercial Code. This
means that the statement expressed in the third paragraph of the foreword
(see page 75) became ineffective.

By changing its character or by subordinating itself to the Commercial
Code, A Statement of Business Accounting Principles could remain as a
practical guide to the accounting practices for the Securities Exchange Act
prupose. Following the revision of A Statement of Business Accounting Principles, the SEC Regulation for Financial Statement was also revised in conformity with the Commercial Code and the title of the Regulation was changed

[31]Tatsuo Osumi, "Kaikei Shori no Datosei to Tekihosei" (Appropriateness
and Legitimacy of Accounting Treatments), Kigyokaikei (Accounting), Vol. 16,
No. 1, (January, 1964), p. 26.

to "The Regulation for Financial Statements by the Ministry of Finance." The effective application of accounting principles in a broad sense also depends upon the attitudes of accountants toward the principles. Especially the task of the certified public accountants as independent auditors is quite important. Without proper recognition of the social responsibility of certified public accountants by the public and by themselves, the public financial reporting service cannot be effectively performed.

Until the end of 1964, the public financial reporting system in Japan encountered no serious trouble. The rush of bankruptcies and financial trouble cases of Japanese stock corporations at the end of 1964 and during the early months of 1965 raised a number of serious doubts and questions about the credence to be placed in the public financial reporting system. Several fairly large listed corporations, such as Nippon Special Steel Works, Sun Wave Industry, and Sanyo Special Steel Works, were among these bankrupt companies. These companies had published their incorrect financial state-ments for several accounting periods and in some cases the certified public accountants who audited these financial statements tolerated the existing window-dressing. In the cases of the Sun Wave Industry and the Nippon Special Steel Works, the certified public accountants expressed the adverse opinions in their audit reports. Sanyo Special Steel Works initiated the practice of "window-dressing" during the accounting period ended March 31, 1958 and the concealed deficit amounted to about twelve billion yen at the time the firm entered bankruptcy in December, 1964. Ukichi Ueda, the certified public accountant for Sanyo Special Steel Works, admitted that for as long as seven years he knew of the "window-dressing," and that he did not disclose the actual situation because of the persuasive urging of the president of the company.[32]

Window-dressing by these companies was discovered only when they entered bankruptcy. Window-dressing or the disregard of proper accounting procedures supported by the "generally accepted accounting principles," however, was not necessarily monopolized by those companies that suffered bankruptcy. Without the ultimate step of bankruptcy, the presentation of inaccurate financial statements may not critically harm the shareholders and creditors. From the management point of view, to show constant and relatively high earning power and good financial condition in the financial statements might be even a virtue. The continued payment of a stable level of dividends might be a wise managerial policy. None of these considerations, however, justifies the disregard of or serious departure from "generally accepted accounting principles" for developing reliable accounting information.

Many Japanese corporations have attempted to publish inaccurate financial statements to offset the unfavorable results on their earning power of the depression which began in 1961. The awareness of the presentation of misleading financial statements by some Japanese corporations remained unknown to the public until December, 1966. In December, 1966, the Ministry of Finance required thirteen listed corporations to refile their financial statements for several accounting periods because of the false presentation of results of operations and financial conditions. At the same time, the

---

[32]Koichi Sato, "Funshoku-Tosan Kaisha no Jizen-Boshi Hosaku" (Preclusive Measures for Window-dressing of Bankrupt Companies), Waseda-Shogaku (Waseda Commercial Review), No. 180, (June, 1965), p. 9.

Ministry of Finance announced the punishment of sixteen certified public
accountants who presented false audit reports for these thirteen corporations. Although the Ministry of Finance did not announce the name of
these corporations, The Nihon Keizai Shinbun (The Japan Economic Journal),
a Japanese daily newspaper, reported a summary of the "window-dressing"
practiced by these corporations.[33] The income data before and after
corrections of eight corporations are shown in Table 3 (page 221).

Sanctions and Administration Process

Regulation for Corporate Balance Sheets and Income Statements. Although the Regulation for Corporate Balance Sheets and Income Statements
contained no penal provisions, any substantive violation of the Regulation
did constitute a Commercial Code violation. The Japanese Commercial Code
does contain the following provisions dealing with the liabilities of
directors and statutory auditors to encourage the effective application
of the Code:

1. (General obligation of directors)
   The directors shall be obliged to obey any law or ordinance
   and the article of incorporation as well as resolutions adopted
   at a general meeting of shareholders and to perform their
   duties faithfully on behalf of the company (Article 254-2).
2. (Liabilities of directors to the company)
   In the following cases, directors who have done any one of
   the acts mentioned below shall be jointly liable for damages
   to the company, in the case of item (1) for the amount which
   has been distributed illegally, in the case of item (2) for
   the amount of loans not yet repaid, or in the cases of items
   (3) to (5) inclusive for the amount of any damage caused to
   the company:
   (1) Where they have submitted to a general meeting of
       shareholders a statement of proposal for the distri-
       bution of profits in contravention of the provision
       of Article 290, paragraph 1;

---

[33]The Nihon Keizai Shinbun (The Japan Economic Journal), January 15,
1967, p. 5, January 17, 1967, p. 7, and January 25, 1967, p. 7.

(2)   Where they have loaned money to another director;
(3)   Where they have carried on any transaction in contra-
      vention of Article 264, paragraph 1;
(4)   Where they have carried on any transaction mentioned
      in Article 265;
(5)   Where they have done any act which violates any law or
      ordinance or the articles of incorproations (Article 266).

3. (Liabilities of directors to a third party)
    If directors have been guilty of wrongful intent or of serious
    negligence in conducting their duties, they shall be jointly
    liable for damages to a third party. The same shall also apply
    in cases where a false statement has been made in respect of any
    material items in application forms for shares of debentures,
    prospectus, documents prescribed in Article 281 (financial
    documents) or schedules mentioned in Article 293-5 (schedules
    to support financial documents), or where a false registration
    or public notice has been made (Article 266-3).

4. (Liabilities of statutory auditors to the company)
    If statutory auditors neglected any of their duties, such
    auditors shall be jointly liable for damages to the company
    (Article 277).

5. (Joint liabilities of directors and statutory auditors)
    In any case in which statutory auditors are liable for damages
    to the company or to a third party, and directors are likewise
    liable therefor, the statutory auditors and directors shall be
    jointly liable (Article 278).

Of these provisions, Article 266 (1) is directly concerned with the

discussion here. The penal provisions for the liabilities of directors

mentioned in Article 266 (1) is as follows:

The persons mentioned in Article 486 paragraph 1 (promoters,
directors, statutory auditors, etc.) and examiners shall be
liable to imprisonment with hard labor for a term not exceeding
five years or to a fine not exceeding three hundred thousand
yen in any case of the following cases:
(1)   (omitted)
(2)   (omitted)
(3)   Where they have distributed profits or interest in
      contravention of the provisions of any law or ordinance
      or of the articles of incorporations;
(4)   (omitted)

The penalty for the violation of Article 266-3 (preparation, registration,

or public notice of false documents) is a payment of a fine not exceeding

three hundred thousand yen (Article 490 and 498).

Since the Commercial Code is a private law, these provisions for
liabilities of directors and statutory auditors and the penal provisions
are not applied unless the facts of violation by directors and statutory
auditors of the provisions are proved at the court. In January, 1965,
Sadao Hattori, a Japanese certified public accountant and a lawyer,
brought a suit against sixteen directors of Sun Wave Industry Company
for one hundred million yen damage to the company due to the payment of
dividends in contravention of the provision of Article 290 and the "generally accepted accounting principles" prescribed in A Statement of Business
Accounting Principles.[34] This was the first suit case concerning the violation of the provision of Article 290 of the 1962 Commercial Code. Hattori
tried to establish a judicial precedent for this type of the Commercial
Code violation but eventually lost the suit. In a legal sense, therefore,
no violation of the Commercial Code has occurred to date.

Revised Statement of Business Accounting Principles. From a legal
point of view, the Revised Statement of Business Accounting Principles is
under the jurisdiction of the Ministry of Finance. The administrative guid-
ances by the officers of the Ministry of Finance, called "corporation report
examiners," may be considered as legal sanctions which are imposed on a violator of a set of accounting principles. As mentioned in the previous section,
in 1966 thirteen Japanese corporations were required to refile their periodic
reports with the Ministry of Finance. Two types of refiling are legally distinguished by the Securities Exchange Act. The first one is to refile the

[34]The Nihon Keizai Shinbun (The Japan Economic Journal), January 22, 1965,
p. 15.

revised registration statement and/or the revised periodic report with the
Ministry of Finance whenever the corporation believes it necessary to revise
the previously filed reports.[35] This may be called a "voluntary" refiling.
The second type of refiling is based upon the order of the Minister of
Finance. The Minister of Finance may order a corporation to refile the
revised reports by giving it the reason for revision of the previously
filed reports. This is done after he makes the "corporation report
examiners" review these reports and when he finds any false statement or
omission of any material items in the report.[36] This may be called an
"ordered" refiling.

In the cases of the thirteen corporations in 1966, the Minister of
Finance did not order these corporations to refile their reports but
the "corporation report examiners" suggested the "voluntary refiling.
Following the suggestions by the Ministry of Finance, these corporations
refiled the revised reports "voluntarily." In the case of the "ordered"
refiling, the penal provision is applied to the company which filed the
false report.[37] Thus, none of these thirteen corporations was subject to
the penal provision. On the other hand, sixteen certified public accountants,
who audited the previously filed financial statements by these thirteen
corporations were subject to the penal provision. On the other hand,
sixteen certified public accountants, who audited the previously filed
financial statements by these thirteen corporations did not disclose the

---

[35]The Japanese Securities Exchange Act, Articles 7 and 24.

[36]Ibid., Articles 10, and 24.

[37]Ibid., Article 205. In this case, the company is liable to a fine
not exceeding thirty thousand yen.

false statements contained in these financial statements, were punished
by the Minister of Finance according to Article 30 of the Certified Public
Accountants Law. Twelve certified public accountants were suspended from
their practices for three months, two certified public accountants for
two months, and two certified public accountants for one month.

As mentioned in Chapter IV, the expression of a qualified opinion
or an adverse opinion and the disclaimer of opinion by a certified public
accountant are other sanctions which may be imposed on a violator of a
set of accounting principles. Table 4 (page 222) presents statistics
on the pattern of opinions expressed by Japanese certified public accountants on the financial statements prepared by the corporations listed on both
the First Section Market and the Second Section Market of the Tokyo Stock
Exchange. These statistics were prepared by the Research Department of the
Tokyo Stock Exchange based upon the published auditors' reports. Table 4
indicates that more than half of the corporations listed on the Tokyo Stock
Exchange did not apply proper accounting procedures to some items although
the number of corporate financial statements to which certified public
accountants expressed adverse opinions or disclaimed the expression of
their opinions was decreasing. Table 5 (page 222) notes the reasons why
certified public accountants expressed qualified opinions. They were classified under three major categories. Table 5 indicates that Japanese
certified public accountants qualified an average of two or three items per
corporation.

Summary

The development of accounting principles at the third stage (1962-   )
in Japan presented a strong contrast with that of the second stage
(1947-1962). During the second stage, A Statement of Business Accounting
Principles played a most important role in developing a modern financial
reporting system in Japanese industrial society by theoretically supporting
the SEC Regulation. The revision of the Commercial Code in 1962 marked a
turning-point in the history of the development of accounting principles
in Japan. In 1962, the Japanese Commercial Code, which represented a
static view of accounting for the purpose of protecting creditors, introduced a dynamic view of accounting, which was represented by A Statement
of Business Accounting Principles, to the extent that the original purpose
of the Code could be achieved. By this revision the wide gap existing
between the old Commercial Code and A Statement of Business Accounting
Principles was considerably narrowed. In 1963, the Ministry of Justice
enacted the Regulation for Corporate Balance Sheets and Income Statements
to ensure the effective application of the accounting provisions of the
Commercial Code. As was expected, the Regulation was honestly followed by
most Japanese corporations when they prepared the financial statements
submitted at the general meeting of shareholders. No one can deny that
the revision of the Commercial Code and the.enactment of the Regulation has
made a contribution to the standardization of public financial reporting
in Japan.

Until 1962 A Statement of Business Accounting Principles was considered
as a general guide to accounting actions both theoretically and practically.

Individual principles developed in A Statement of Business Accounting Principles were theoretically supported by a dynamic view of accounting which assumed that a central purpose of accounting was to determine business income periodically based upon the "matching concept." Some of the principles developed from a dynamic accounting point of view apparently contradict the principles of the static view of accounting. The revision of the Japanese Commercial Code in 1962 was a challenge in a sense to the Japanese accounting represented by A Statement of Business Accounting Principles. The Commercial Code asked A Statment of Business Accounting Principles to modify some of the principles in accordance with the revised provisions of the Code. The request of the Commercial Code might be an ordeal to A Statement of Business Accounting Principles. In 1963, A Statement of Business Accounting Principles accepted the request of the Commercial Code and revised itself partially to keep a harmony with the 1962 Commercial Code. By the partial revision in 1963 A Statement of Business Accounting Principles became increasingly a practical guide to accounting practice rather than a theoretical guide.

TABLE 3   Income Data of Eight Corporations
Which Refiled Financial Statements
with the Ministry of Finance

(Money Amounts in Millions of Yen)

Accounting Period Ended	Net Income (Sekisui Chemical Co.)		Net Income (Daishowa Paper Mfg. Co.)		New Income (Topy Industry Co.)	
	Before Correction	After Correction	Before Correction	After Correction	Before Correction	After Correction
March 31, 1962	442	252	393	-71	200	150
Sept. 30, 1962	510	-153	463	-333	151	52
March 31, 1963	558	19	520	-19	150	77
Sept. 30, 1963	600	260	755	810	177	77
March 31, 1964	489	253	495	495	175	69
Sept. 30, 1964	616	126	507	507	281	-528
March 31, 1965	379	-348	399	399	224	-794
Sept. 30, 1965	-808	-545	248	285	---	---

Accounting Period Ended	Net Income (Toyo Bearing Mfg. Co.)		Net Income (Toa Oil Co.)		New Income (Ricoh Co.)	
	Before Correction	After Correction	Before Correction	After Correction	Before Correction	After Correction
March 31, 1962	848	710	---	---	566	290
Sept. 30, 1962	783	619	-10	-194	653	105
March 31, 1963	580	205	235	235	412	-181
Sept. 30, 1963	932	715	210	210	567	-285
March 31, 1964	625	591	144	-505	587	308
Sept. 30, 1964	636	153	-276	-756	492	60
March 31, 1965	540	50	-9	-9	-221	-267
Sept. 30, 1965	21	383	85	185	11	60

Accounting Period Ended	Net Income (Nichimen Jitsugyo Co.)		Net Income (Furukawa Electric Co.)	
	Before Correction	After Correction	Before Correction	After Correction
March 31, 1962	426	176	1,048	748
Sept. 30, 1962	410	236	747	224
March 31, 1963	510	543	441	-629
Sept. 30, 1963	712	764	581	229
March 31, 1964	572	517	756	756
Sept. 30, 1964	807	707	819	819
March 41, 1965	469	469	733	933
Sept. 30, 1965	53	123	1,075	1,075

Source: The Nihon Keizai Shinbun (The Japan Economic Journal), January 15, 1967, p. 5, January 17, 1967, p. 7, and January 25, 1967, p. 7.

TABLE 4   Pattern of Auditors' Report

	Number of Corporations					
	Jan. - June 1963	July - Dec. 1963	Jan. - June 1964	July - Dec. 1964	Jan. - June 1965	July - Dec. 1965
(1) Expression of unqualified opinions	464	462	574	500	535	559
(2) Experssion of qualified opinions	560	534	480	512	511	463
(3) Expression of adverse opinions	25	30	20	28	29	13
(4) Disclaimer of opinions	45	26	24	14	16	5
	1,094	1,052	1,098	1,054	1,091	1,040

TABLE 5   Reasons for the Expression of Qualified Opinions

	Number of Cases					
	Jan. - June 1963	July - Dec. 1963	Jan. - June 1964	July - Dec. 1964	Jan. - June 1965	July - Dec. 1965
(1) Application of improper accounting procedures	1,018	943	825	904	848	734
(2) Change in consistent application of the procedure	296	251	104	145	90	61
(3) Misrepresentation of items in the financial statements	613	434	408	396	389	360
	1,927	1,628	1,337	1,445	1,327	1,155

Source: Research Department, Tokyo Stock Exchange. Quoted in Japanese Institute of Certified Public Accountants, JICPA News, Nos. 49 (March, 1964), pp. 6-8, 54 (July, 1964), pp. 5-6, 62 (January, 1965), pp. 5-6, 71 (August, 1965), pp. 9-10, 79 (February, 1966), pp. 9-10, and 85 (July, 1966), pp. 10-12.

CHAPTER VI

SUMMARY AND CONCLUSION

Summary of the Analytical Method of the Study

This study has attempted to analyze historically the social function of accounting principles in Japan to determine the nature of
Japanese accounting principles which have been developed in a unique
social climate. The reasons for selecting "Japanese accounting principles" as an object of study are: (1) no study of "Japanese accounting
principles" has been undertaken in the new area of international accounting, and (2) the author believed, based upon preliminary observation,
that a historical study of the Japanese accounting principles would
contribute to the establishment of international accounting principles
because Japanese accounting principles were developed under the influence
of both Franco-German legal thought and Anglo-American accounting thought.

This study has emphasized the social function of accounting principles based upon the assumption that a set of accounting principles
exists and serves as a rule for social control. In a highly industrialized society, the business enterprise, for which accounting information is developed and communicated, constitutes a social institution.
It is a social institution which is composed of several interest groups,
such as management, shareholders, creditors, suppliers of goods and
services, labor, customers, and government. Without co-operation among
all interest groups, who control the factors of production, the business
enterprise could not achieve its particular goal. The interests of these

groups, however, are not necessarily the same. They are often in conflict
with each other. These groups need specific accounting information, as
well as certain nonquantitative information, to optimize their decisions
concerning their relationships with the business enterprise. It locically
follows from this recognition of the informational needs of industrialized society that developing accounting information for the business
enterprise and communicating it to its interest groups constitute a
social system of actions, and that accounting information should be
developed and communicated so that any conflict among interest groups
can be reduced or eliminated. Thus, it becomes necessary to establish
a set of accounting principles, to be called "generally accepted accounting principles," as a rule for social control which guides the development and communication of appropriate accounting information. If a set
of accounting principles did not serve as a rule for social control, such
a set of accounting principles would lose its significance in our highly
industrialized society.

The functional approach to the study of accounting principles is
especially important and useful in the field of international accounting.
One of the most central problems in the field of international accounting
is the attempt to establish a set of international accounting principles
because without these principles the development and communication of
internationally understandable accounting information could not be
achieved satisfactorily. This attempt is not easy and it will undoubtedly
require a long time to develop such a set of principles. Every effort,
however, should be directed toward this objective. The first step in

developing international accounting principles is to ascertain the possibility of the formulation of such a set of principles. The mere identification and comparison of currently accepted accounting principles and practices in each country are not sufficient for this purpose. The author believes that a basic analysis of how a set of accounting principles has been developed, applied, supported, and maintained in each country can offer a meaningful starting point for the identification and acceptance of international accounting principles.

If the assumption that a set of accounting principles exists and serves as a rule for social control is accepted and if the significance of the functional approach to the study of accounting principles in the field of international accounting is properly recognized, the best conceptual framework as an element for systematic analysis of the social function of accounting principles should be selected.[1] The author selected Talcott Parsons' framework which was originally designed for the functional analysis of a system of actions after reviewing his application of the same framework to a system of law. The Talcott Parsons' framework was composed of (1) adaptation, (2) goal gratification, (3) integration, and (4) latent-pattern maintenance and tension management. To apply these concepts as a framework for analysis to this study, the author rephrased them as (1) legitimation, (2) application, (3) sanctions, and (4) administration. These four concepts represent four independent functional imperatives or "problems" which must be met satisfactorily

---

[1]For the details of "conceptual frameworks for research," see Maurice Duverger, An Introduction to the Social Sciences, trans. by Malcolm Anderson (New York: Frederick A. Praeger, Publisher, 1941), pp. 225-48.

if equilibrium and/or continuing existence of the system is to be maintained.

The study analyzed historically, for two reasons, all sets of accounting principles, including laws and regulations, each of which was developed under a special circumstance of the Japanese industrial society. The first reason was concerned with a general view of history which was best expressed by Littleton and Zimmerman in the following terms:

> One of the major lessons from history is that the present grew out of the past and grows into the future. This is the significance of Aristotle's thought: "If you would understand anything, observe its beginning and its development."[2]

This view is also expressed as: "History-as-Event generates History-as-Narrative, which in turn produces History-as-Maker-of-Future-History."[3] The second reason was rather special and was related to a unique pattern of the development of accounting principles in Japan. A Statement of Business Accounting Principles was the first written pronouncement of accounting principles in Japan comparable in their functions to American accounting principles which were developed by the American Institute of Certified Public Accountants. The Japanese Commercial Code and other related regulations as guides to accounting actions performed nearly the same functions as A Statement of Business Accounting Principles although it might not be appropriate to call them accounting principles. A separate study of A Statement of Business Accounting Principles, there-

---

[2]A. C. Littleton and V. K. Zimmerman, Accounting Theory: Continuity and Change (Englewood, New Jersey: Prentice-Hall, Inc., 1962), p. 11.

[3]Jaques Barzun and Henry F. Graff, The Modern Researcher (New York: Harcourt, Brace & World, Inc., 1957), p. 50.

fore, would be incomplete from the viewpoint of a functional approach.

Summary of the Results of the Analysis

The Development and Nature of Accounting Principles at the First

Stage. This study analyzed the Commercial Code, the Working Rules for

Financial Statements by the Ministry of Commerce and Industry, and the

Tentative Standards of Financial Statements of Manufacturing Companies by

the Planning Board as a first group of accounting principles in Japan.

One of the most basic characteristics of the development of accounting

principles during the first stage (1890-1947) was that the Commercial Code

was a basic and general guide to accounting practices in Japan. The

general purpose of the Japanese Commercial Code was to promote sound

business activities by protecting the property rights of persons engaged

in commercial transactions in Japan. Concerning the stock corporation,

the Commercial Code identified the management group, (including the

statutory auditors), the shareholders group, and the creditors group as

interest groups. Despite the tendency toward separation of the manage-

ment group from the shareholders group, the relationship of the corpora-

tion to its management and shareholders group was considered as an

internal relationship from the legal point of view. The relationship

between the corporation and its creditors was an external one. Thus,

the protection of the creditors was the primary concern of the Com-

mercial Code and the protection of the shareholders was secondary. This

basic idea of the Commercial Code was not changed by its revisions in

1911 and 1938.

The accounting provisions in the Japanese Commercial Code were pre-

scribed in accordance with this basic idea of the Commercial Code.
Although the Commercial Code required every corporation to prepare: (1)
an inventory, (2) a balance sheet, (3) a business report (4) an income
statement, and (5) a statement of proposals pertaining to the disposal
of profits, it emphasized the inventory and the balance sheet rather than
the income statement. All assets to be listed in the inventory and in
the balance sheet were initially limited to those which had a realizable
value and they were required to be valued at their market prices in the
sense of "realizable value." The Code's assets valuation basis was
changed to a lower-than market-price basis in 1911 and further changed in
1938 to include a partial cost basis. In 1938, the Commercial Code
adopted a cost-less-depreciation basis for fixed assets and introduced
the concept of deferred assets by recognizing (1) organization expense,
(2) bond discount, and (3) interest during construction as deferred
assets. These changes in the accounting provisions were made to enable
a corporation to pay dividends in the early years of its life.

The Japanese Commercial Code contained no provision for periodic
income determination. It prescribed the calculation of the amount of
profits available for dividends by the "comparison of net worth method."
According to this method, the amount of profits available for dividends
was calculated by the following formula:

> The amount of profits available for dividends = (assets -
> liabilities) - stated capital - legal reserve - capital
> impairment, if any.

The concept of profit developed in the Commercial Code represented the
maximum amount of assets left in the company at a certain date which could

be available for distribution without menacing the safety of the creditors position. This was a static concept and presents a sharp contrast to a modern concept of operational business income. The Commercial Code's concept of profit was concerned not about the process of income-generating activities but the result of all business activities.

Although the Japanese Commercial Code was a single basic law governing business traders, including business corporations, the accounting provisions of the Code did not serve satisfacotily as a sound guide for financial reporting practices. The first reason for this unfavorable result was the lack of supporting working rules for the preparation of financial statements. The second reason was the attitude of corporate executives toward disclosure of financial information for the use by the various interest groups. It was quite evident that most Japanese corporate directors were extremely reluctant to disclose financial data even to company shareholders. This attitude of corporate directors stemmed mostly from the unique structure of Japan's industrial society in that almost all leading business corporations were controlled directly or indirectly by ten big Zaibatsu families. The executivies of these Zaibatsu companies were composed of the member of the Zaibatsu families or of their faithful managers and they did not believe that full disclosure of financial information was necessary. The third reason was the attitude of the "absentee" or "non-controlling" shareholders to the financial information of their corporations. Their decisions to purchase stock were not based upon the financial information but upon the reputation of the management group of those corporations.

The system of sanctions against the violators of the Commercial Code was remedical rather than preventive in nature. Although the Commercial Code was under the jurisdiction of Japanese courts, the courts could not exert any direct power to encourage the enforcement of the prescribed accounting provisions. Only when a law suit was brought by a victim of misapplication of those provisions, could the court apply some legal sanctions against the violator of the Code. The statutory auditors prescribed in the Commercial Code were initially expected to perform a role as protectors of shareholders by examining the fairness of the financial statements prepared by the directors of the company. The statutory auditors of Japan did not perform such a role.

The need for more informative financial statements was first recognized by the Japanese government in relation to the industrial rationalization movement in approximately 1930. The Ministry of Commerce and Industry issued the Working Rules for Financial Statements to promote a national movement of industrial rationalization by the improvement of financial statements. The Working Rules for Financial Statement were administrative in nature although they were not promulgated as an ordinance. The direct purpose of the Working Rules for Financial Statements was to supplement the accounting provisions of the Commercial Code since the latter were few in number and defective in substance. The Working Rules prescribed the standard methods of preparing a balance sheet, an inventory, and an income statement which were then to be submitted at the general meeting of shareholders.

One of the most important features of the Working Rules for Financial Statements was the introduction of Anglo-American accounting thought into the framework of traditional Japanese law. The Working Rules for Financial Statements recognized the following five types of deferred assets: (1) bond discount, (2) bond expenses, (3) interest during construction, (4) development expenses, and (5) organization expenses. This idea of deferred assets was partially recognized in the 1938 Commercial Code. This was an evidence that the Working Rules supplemented the accounting provisions of the Commercial Code. In addition, the Working Rules partially introduced the cost basis for asset valuation.

The income statement prescribed in the Working Rules for Financial Statements was a comprehensive type of income statement based upon the "matching concept." The income statement designed for a manufacturing company contained the following sections for: (1) manufacturing cost accounting, (2) sales income accounting, (3) operating income accounting, and (4) net income accounting. In addition, the illustrated standard form of income statement contained the section for "accounting for the appropriation of net income." The income statement illustrated in the Working Rules was a dynamic statement showing an entire picture of income from its production to its disposition.

In summary, the content of the Working Rules for Financial Statements was educational and theoretical rather than practical on the one hand, and was more accounting-oriented than law-oriented on the other hand. If the Working Rules had been promulgated as a regulation supporting the Japanese Commercial Code as originally scheduled, the public financial reporting in Japan would have been significantly improved. The Working

Rules for Financial Statement of 1934 was no doubt a cornerstone in the development of modern, public financial reporting in Japan.

The nature of the 1941 Tentative Standards for Financial Statements of Manufacturing Company by the Planning Board represented a great contrast to the 1934 Working Rules for Financial Statements. The Tentative Standards were issued by the Planning Board, a central government agency for control of the national economy during wartime. The primary purpose of the Tentative Standards was not to supplement the Commercial Code but to implement the policies of the Corporate Accounting Control Ordinance of 1940. Under the emergency circumstance of wartime, the government needed financial information on all manufacturing companies in order to exert control over them. This was necessary because all manufacturing companies represented more or less the war potential of Japan.

From a theoretical point of view, the basic accounting ideas underlying the Tentative Standards for Financial Statements were not materially different from those of the Working Rules for Financial Statements of 1934. The Tentative Standards, however, did not express such basic ideas as "standards." They represented minimum requirements for financial information by the manufacturing companies and were, in fact, a statement of "standardized accounting" for the exclusive use by the government.

The Development and Nature of Accounting Principles at the Second Stage. The study analyzed in Chapter IV the Instructions for the Preparation of Financial Statements of Manufacturing and Trading Companies issued by the General Headquarters of Supreme Commander for the Allied Powers (GHQ Instructions), A Statement of Business Accounting Principles, and the Revised Commercial Code of 1950 as a second group of accounting principles in their history of development in Japan.

The improvement of the financial reporting practices after World War II began with the GHQ Instructions. The Japanese industry before and during the war was mostly controlled by the "Zaibatsu." The democratic and sound development of the Japanese industrial society needed the prompt dissolution of the "Zaibatsu" system. This was also necessary from a political point of view reflected in the basic documents of the occupation powers because the "Zaibatsu" companies represented the war potential of Japan. The GHQ of SCAP felt the necessity to gather financial information on the "Zaibatsu" companies to implement its own policies to democratize the Japanese economy. The primary purpose of the GHQ Instructions was to assist those companies in the preparation of clear, intelligible financial statements.

One of the most important features of the GHQ Instructions was the introduction and demonstration of a complete set of the American accounting practices. The surplus statement was first introduced into Japan by the GHQ Instructions. None of the five financial documents prescribed by the Japanese Commercial Code disclosed the historical record concerning the disposition of profits. In other words, the directors' responsibility for the disposition of profits was not disclosed by these financial documents. This was apparently a deficiency in Japanese accounting practice from the viewpoint of full disclosure of the directors' responsibility. Under these circumstances, the introduction of the surplus statement was quite significant.

Just as the Tentative Standards for Financial Statements of 1941, the GHQ Instructions did not necessarily develop accounting principles by themselves. The GHQ Instructions were a practical manual prescribed in accordance with the generally accepted accounting principles of the United States. As mentioned earlier, American accounting thought was incorporated partically into the 1934 Working Rules for Financial Statements, but they were not wholly accepted by practicing Japanese accountants. Although the application of the GHQ Instructions was limited to the financial statements submitted by approximately one thousand "restricted" companies to SCAP, the GHQ Instructions greatly influenced the improvement of Japanese accounting practices after World War II for two reasons: (1) these companies were all leading companies representing all lines of industry in Japan, and (2) SCAP authorities had jurisdiction over the effective administration of the GHQ Instructions.

The movement for the improvement of financial statements initiated by the GHQ of SCAP was assumed by the Investigation Committee on Business Accounting System in 1948. In 1949, the Investigation Committee released A Statement of Business Accounting Principles and the "Working Rules for Financial Statements." The release of these two statements by the Investigation Committee was directly related to the movement toward the democratization of investment in securities which constituted the second step in the development of a democratic and sound Japanese economy. The enactment of the Securities Exchange Act and the Certified Public Accountant Law in 1948 was a preliminary step of a modern financial reporting system in Japan.

This setting was quite similar to that in the United States. A Statement of Business Accounting Principles was developed, however, in a quite different way from that in the United States. Neither the Japanese Institute of Certified Public Accountants nor the Japanese Accounting Association, both of which are professional societies of accountants equivalent to the AICPA and AAA respectively, made serious efforts to establish accounting principles. Although many noted men from the rank of accounting professors and businessmen, in addition to several top-ranking governmental officials, joined in the Committee, the Investigation Committee was sponsored by the government and was placed under the Control of the Economic Stabilization Board and later of the Ministry of Finance.

The primary purpose of A Statement of Business Accounting Principles was to support the Securities Exchange Act and the Certified Public Accountants Law. To be institutionalized by supporting the Japanese SEC Regulation, which was enacted pursuant to Article 193 of the Securities Exchange Act. A Statement of Business Accounting Principles needed to emphasize practical rather than theoretical reasoning. A chief drafter of A Statement of Business Accounting Principles was aware that accounting principles could not be effectively applied to accounting practice unless they were institutionalized through law or regulation in view of the past experience in financial reporting practices in Japan. The format of A Statement of Business Accounting Principles was apparently modeled after A Statement of Accounting Principles prepared by Sanders, Hatfield, and Moore although the identification of "general principles" was mostly dependent upon Kurosawa's unique idea.

From a theoretical point of view, A Statement of Business Accounting Principles contrasted with the Japanese Commercial Code in that the former represented the synamic view of accounting and emphasized the periodic income determination by the "matching concept" method based upon the cost principle. The introduction of the concept of "surplus" was another important feature of A Statement of Business Accounting Principles. Although it was not a "autogenous" type of accounting principles, A Statement of Business Accounting Principles performed almost the same function as the American accounting principles as a guide to the accounting actions. Since all listed corporations on the Japanese stock exchanges were required to be audited by independent certified public accountants, the extent to which these corporations applied accounting principles was examined by these professional accountants.

The revision of the accounting provisions of the Commercial Code in 1950 was neither fundamental nor effective.. The addition of a new Article to require the preparation of schedules to support the financial documents was only a favorable revision from a financial reporting point of view. During the second stage, the Commercial Code seems to have disappeared behind A Statement of Business Accounting Principles.

The Development and Nature of Accounting Principles at the Third Stage. The development of accounting principles at the third stage may be best characterized as a revival of law-oriented accounting principles. During the second stage, the public financial reporting practices in Japan were greatly improved and supported theoretically by A Statement

of Business Accounting Principles and also supported legally by the
Securities Exchange Act and Certified Public Accountants Law. Because
A Statement of Business Accounting Principles represented the dynamic
view of accounting, financial reporting practices during the second stage
emphasized the significance of the income and surplus statements rather
than the inventory and balance sheet.

The revision of the Commercial Code in 1962 marked a turning-point
in the history of the development of accounting principles in Japan.
Since 1890 the Commercial Code has been a single basic law governing
business enterprises although its accounting provisions were not properly applied to the practices for many years. Several laws and regulations were promulgated to carry out varying policies established under
the changing political and economic conditions. In 1962, the Commercial
Code restated its legitimacy by materially revising the several accounting provisions. In view of the currently prevailing accounting practices
supported by A Statement of Business Accounting Principles, the Commercial
Code adopted the basic accounting ideas developed in A Statement of
Business Accounting Principles to the extent that its own purposes could
be effectively accomplished.

In 1963, the Ministry of Justice enacted the Regulation for Corporate
Balance Sheets and Income Statements to ensure the proper of application of the accounting provisions of the Commercial Code. The regulation specified the methods to prepare balance sheets and income statements
to be submitted at the general meeting of shareholders. One of the most
important features of the 1962 Commercial Code was the joint use of two

asset valuation bases: (1) the historical cost basis and (2) the lower-than-historical cost basis. The Commercial Code enlarged the concept of asset to include many items as deferred assets and adopted the historical cost basis in principle for asset valuation. The Commercial Code, however, did not permit the direct application of the historical cost basis to all asset items but it required the application of a much safer basis for the protection of creditors.

The income statement prescribed by the Regulation was quite unique from an accounting point of view. The format of the income statement was similar to the multiple-step, "all-inclusive" type of income statement prepared by the "matching concept" method. The content of the income statement prescribed by the Regulation was quite different from the regular "all-inclusive" type of income statement in that it included several items which were not relevant to the income determination for the current period, such as the amount of the liquidation of the voluntary retained earnings and the amount of the provisions which were applied for purposes other than originally reported. The purpose of the income statement prescribed by the Regulation was to calculate the amount of profits available for dividends.

Despite conflicting opinions among lawyers and accountants concerning its legal power, the Regulation was honestly followed by most Japanese corporations when they prepared financial statements. Although the accounting provisions of the Commercial Code are still vulnerable to criticism from an accounting point of view, no one can deny that the 1962 Commercial Code, coupled with the enactment of the 1963 Regulation, have contributed to the improvement and unification of public financial reporting in Japan.

During the second stage of the development of accounting principles,
A Statement of Business Accounting Principles played a very important
role in the improvement of financial reporting to the shareholders, both
present and potential. Most principles developed in A Statement of
Business Accounting Principles were theoretically supported by the
dynamic view of accounting which assumes that a central concern of
accounting is to determine business income periodically based upon the
"matching concept." After the revision in 1962, the Commercial Code
requested A Statement of Business Accounting Principles to modify some
of the principles to harmonize with the revised provisions of the code.

This request of the Commercial Code was a challenge to the domain
of the accountant from the domain of the lawyer. When it was established
in 1949, A Statement of Business Accounting Principles proclaimed its
theoretical priority to laws and regulations. A Statement of Business
Accounting Principles was "government-made" and was institutionalized
by the Japanese SEC Regulation. Despite its proclamation, therefore,
A Statement of Business Accounting Principles could not be free from the
revision of the Commercial Code. In 1963, A Statement of Business
Accounting Principles lost its autonomy.

Conclusion

Several sets of accounting principles were developed to serve for
different purposes under the changing political and economic conditions
which characterized each stage of the development of the industrialized

economy in Japan since the Meiji Restoration in 1868. The history of
the development of accounting principles in Japan was in parallel with
the development of the Japanese economy. As with the development of
economy guided by the government, the initiative for developing accounting principles was taken by the government and each set of accounting
principles was developed by the government itself or the government-
appointed committees.

In the United States, "accounting principles" or "accounting standards" have been developed by the efforts of the professional societies
of accountants and they have been clearly distinguished from "laws" or
"regulations." These accounting principles may be called "autogenous"
type of accounting principles because they are neither laws themselves
nor a part of law. In Japan, however, the distinction between "accounting principles" and "regulations" has not been clear. Since the accounting provisions of the Commercial Code and other related regulations have
performed the function equivalent to accounting principles as a guide
for accounting practices, they may also be called accounting principles.
They are referred to as "compulsory" type of accounting principles because
of their legal compulsion.

A Statement of Business Accounting Principles has performed the
same function as that of the "autogenous" type of accounting principles,
such as AICPA's accounting principles. Because it was not a law or
regulation by itself, A Statement of Business Accounting Principles was
not a "compulsory" type of accounting principles. Although it was not
an "autogenous" type of accounting principles either in a strict sense,
the establishment of A Statement of Business Accounting Principles

indicated a partial transformation from the "compulsory" to the "autogenous" type of accounting principles.

The development of accounting principles at the third stage which began in 1962 may be characterized as a challenge of law to accounting or a revival of the "compulsory" type of accounting principles. The revision of the Commercial Code in 1962 and the enactment of the Regulation for Corporate Balance Sheets and Income Statements in 1963 pushed back A Statement of Business Accounting Principles behind the Commercial Code. In other words, most parts of the domain of accounting were invaded by the Commercial Code. The revision of A Statement of Business Accounting Principles in accordance with the revised accounting provisions of the Commercial Code implied that A Statement of Business Accounting Principles can no longer be an "autogenous" type of accounting principles.

From a legal point of view, the revision of A Statement of Business Accounting Principles was quite logical since any convention or a statement of conventions could not be legitimate if it were in contravention of law. The revision of A Statement of Business Accounting Principles, not for theoretical improvement but for harmony with the Commercial Code, furnished a valuable lesson. The lesson is that a set of accounting principles other than a law or a regulation cannot maintain its autonomy in Japan unless its theory satisfied the basic idea of the law. This also implies that a set of accounting principles should be supported by a well established general theory of accounting.

From a viewpoint of international accounting, the history of development of accounting principles in Japan reveals that the transplantation of the "autogenous" type of accounting principles into a country, where the "compulsory" type of accounting principles is dominant, is not always successful. In Japan, the "autogenous" type of accounting principles was absorbed into the "compulsory" type of accounting principles.

BIBLIOGRAPHY

BOOKS

American Accounting Association. Accounting and Reporting Standards for Corporate Financial Statements and Preceeding Statements and Supplements. Iowa City, Iowa: American Accounting Association, 1957.

_____. The Committee to Prepare A Statement of Basic Accounting Theory. A Statement of Business Accounting Theory. Evanston, Illinois: AAA, 1966.

American Institute of Certified Public Accountants. Accounting Research and Terminology Bulletins. Final Edition. New York: American Institute of Certified Public Accountants, 1961.

_____. Opinions of Accounting Principles Board 9. New York: The American Institute of Certified Public Accountants, 1966.

_____. Committee on Auditing Procedure. Auditing Standards and Procedures. New York: American Institute of Certified Public Accountants, 1963.

_____. Committee on International Relations. Professional Accounting in 25 Countries. New York: AICPA, 1964.

Ando, Yoshio. Showa Keizai-Shi eno Shogen -Jo- (A Witness to the Economic History of Showa Era, I). Tokyo, Japan: Mainichi-Shinbun-Sha, 1965.

Asaba, Jiro. Kaikei Gensoku no Kiso Kozo (Basic Structure of Accounting Principles). Tokyo, Japan: Yuhikaku, 1959.

Bales, Robert F. Interaction Process Analysis: A Method for the Study of Small Group. Cambridge, Massachusetts: Addison-Wesley Press, 1950.

Barzun, Jaques, and Graff, Henry F. The Modern Researcher. New York: Harcourt, Brace & World, Inc., 1957.

Bedford, Norton M. Income Determination Theory -- An Accounting Framework. Reading, Massachusetts: Addison-Wesley, 1965.

Bevis, Herman W. Corporate Financial Reporting in a Competitive Economy. New York: The Macmillan Company, 1965.

Bisson, T. A. _Zaibatsu Dissolution in Japan_. Berkeley and Los Angeles: University of California Press, 1954.

Butow, J. C. _Japan's Decision to Surrender_. Stanford, California: Stanford University Press, 1954.

Code Translation Committee of the League of Nations Association of Japan. _The Commercial Code of Japan, annotated_, I. Tokyo, Japan: The League of Nations Association of Japan, 1931.

Cohen, Jerome B. _Japan's Economy in War and Reconstruction_. Minneapolis, Minnesota: University of Minnesota Press, 1949.

Dahrendorf, Ralf. _Class and Class Conflict in Industrial Society_. Stanford, California: Stanford University Press, 1959.

Duverger, Maurice. _An Introduction to the Social Sciences_. Translated by Malcolm Anderson. New York: Fredrick A. Praeger, Publisher, 1941.

Emura, Minoru. _Zaimushohyo Kansa -- Riron to Kozo_ (Financial Statements Audit -- Theory and Structure). Tokyo, Japan: Kunimoto Shobo, 1963.

Etzioni, Amitai. _Modern Organizations_. Englewood Cliffs, New Jersey: Prentice-Hall, Inc., 1964.

Fukuda, Sumio. _The New Commercial Code of Japan_. Tokyo, Japan: The Tokyo News Service, Ltd., 1948.

Fukushima, Masao. "Zaisan-Ho -- Ho-Taisei Junbiki" (Property Law in the Preparatory Period of the Legal System). _Nihon Kindai-Ho Hattatsushi_, I (Historical Development of Japanese Modern Laws, 1). Edited by Nobushige Ukai, _et al._ Tokyo, Japan: Keiso-Shobo, 1958, pp. 3-101.

Gauld, Julius, and Kolb, William L., eds. _A Dictionary of the Social Science_. New York: The Free Press, 1964.

Gilman, Stephen. _Accounting Concepts of Profit_. New York: The Ronald Press Company, 1939.

Gordon, Robert Aaron. _Business Leadership in the Large Corporation_. Berkeley and Los Angeles: University of California Press, 1966.

Grady, Paul. _Inventory of Generally Accepted Accounting Principles for Business Enterprises_. New York: American Institute of Certified Public Accountants, 1965.

Hatfield, Henry Rand. _Modern Accounting_. New York: D. Appleton and Company, 1909.

Hendriksen, Eldon S. Accounting Theory. Homewood, Illinois: Richard D. Irwin, Inc., 1965.

Holding Company Liquidation Commission. Nihon Zaibatsu to sono Kaitai Shiryo (Data on the Dissolution of Japanese Zaibatsu). Tokyo, Japan: Holding Company Liquidation Commission, 1950.

_____. Nihon Zaibatsu to sono Kaitai (Japanese Zaibatsu and Their Dissolution). Tokyo, Japan: Holding Company Liquidation Commission, 1951.

Iwata, Iwao. Kaikei-Gensoku to Kansa Kijun (Accounting Principles and Auditing Standards). Tokyo, Japan: Chuo-Keizai-Sha, 1955.

Kajinishi, Mitsuhaya, et al. Nihon ni okeru Shihonshugi no Hattatsu (The Development of Capitalism in Japan). Tokyo, Japan: Tokyo University Press, 1958.

_____. Nihon Shihonshugi no Botsuraku, III (The Decline of Japanese Capitalism, III). Tokyo, Japan: Tokyo University Press, 1963.

_____. Nihon Shihonshugi no Botsuraku, IV (The Decline of Japanese Capitalism, IV). Tokyo, Japan: Tokyo University Press, 1964.

Kanazawa, Yoshio. "Sangyo-Ho -- Ho-Taisei Saihenki" (Industrial Law in the Rearrangement Period of the Legal System). Nihon Kindai-Ho Hattatsushi, IV (Historical Development of Japanese Modern Laws, IV). Edited by Nobushige Ukai, et al. Tokyo, Japan: Keiso-Shobo, 1958, pp. 137-172.

Kato, Toshihiko. "Ginko Seido -- Ho-Taisei Junbiki" (Bank System in the Preparatory Period of the Legal System). Nihon Kindai-Ho Hattatsushi, V (Historical Development of Japanese Modern Laws, V). Edited by Nobushige Ukai, et al. Tokyo, Japan: Keiso-Shobo, 1958, pp. 137-172.

Kawashima, Takeyoshi. Nihonjin no Ho-Ishiki (Legal Consciousness of the Japanese People). Tokyo, Japan: Iwanami-Shoten, 1967.

Kaizai-Dantai-Rengokai. Keizai-Dantai-Rengokai Jyunen-Shi -Jo- (The First Ten Years of the Federation of Economic Organizations, I). Tokyo, Japan: Keizai-Dantai-Rengokai, 1962.

_____. Keizai-Dantai-Rengokai Jyunen-Shi -Ge- (The First Ten Years of the Federation of Economic Organizations, II). Tokyo, Japan: Keizai-Dantai-Rengokai, 1963.

Kimura, Wasaburo. Nihon ni okeru Boki Kaikeigaku no Hatten (Development of Bookkeeping and Accounting in Japan). Tokyo, Japan: Choryusha, 1950.

246

Kitazawa, Masahiro. "Kabushiki-Kaisha no Shoyu-Keiei-Shihai" (Owner-
    ship, Management, and Control in the Stock Corporation).
    Gendai-Ho to Kigyo (Contemporary Laws and Business Enterprises).
    Edited by Makoto Yazawa. Tokyo, Japan: Iwanami Shoten, 1966,
    pp. 58-106.

Kuroki, Masanori. Shin-Shoho ni motozuku Kaisha Kessan Jitsumu
    (Corporate Accounting Practices based upon the New Commercial
    Code). Tokyo, Japan: Chuo-Keizai-Sha, 1963.

Kurosawa, Kiyoshi. Kaikeigaku (Accounting). Tokyo, Japan: Chikura
    Shobo, 1947.

_____. "Kaikei Gensoku no Seidoteki Igi" (Significance of Accounting
    Principles as an Institution). Kigyo-Kaikei Gensoku Hihan (A
    Critique of A Statement of Business Accounting Principles). Edited
    by Yasutaro Hirai. Tokyo, Japan: Kunimoto Shobo, 1950, pp. 3-13.

_____. "Kaikei-Gensoku Sosetsu" (General Comments on Accounting
    Principles). In Kiyoshi Kurosawa, et al. Kigyo-Kaikei no Ippan-
    Gensoku Shosetsu (Detailed Comments on the General Principles for
    Business Accounting). Tokyo, Japan: Dobunkan, 1955, pp. 3-25.

_____. "Kigyo-Kaikei-Gensoku to Zaimu-Shohyo-Kisoku" (A Statement
    of Business Accounting Principles and the Regulation for Financial
    Statements). Keisan-Shorui-Kisoku no Mondaiten (Some Problems on
    the Regulation for Corporate Balance Sheets and Income Statements).
    Edited by Katsuji Yamashita. Tokyo, Japan: Chuo-Keizai-Sha, 1965,
    pp. 17-44.

_____. Kindai Kaikei no Riron (A Theory of Modern Accounting).
    Tokyo, Japan: Hakuto Shobo, 1955.

Kusakabe, Yoichi. Shintei Kaikei Kansa Shosetsu (A Comprehensive Study
    on Auditing). Tokyo, Japan: Chuo-Keizai-Sha, 1965.

Ladd, Dwight R. Contemporary Corporate Accounting and the Public.
    Homewood, Illinois: Richard D. Irwin, Inc., 1963.

Littleton, A. C. Accounting Evolution to 1900. New York: Russell &
    Russell, 1966.

_____. Structure of Accounting Theory. Urbana, Illinois: American
    Accounting Association, 1953.

_____, and Zimmerman, V. K. Accounting Theory: Continuity and
    Change. Englewood Cliffs, New Jersey: Prentice-Hall, Inc., 1962.

Mattessich, Richard. <u>Accounting and Analytical Methods</u>. Homewood,
Illinois: Richard D. Irwin, Inc., 1964.

Mautz, R. K., and Sharaf, Hussein A. <u>The Philosophy of Auditing</u>.
Iowa City, Iowa: American Accounting Association, 1961.

Mimura, Osamu. "Kabushiki-Kaisha no Taishaku Taishohyo oyobi Soneki
Keisansho ni kansuru Kisoku no Kaisetsu" (Comments on the
Regulation for Corporate Balance Sheets and Income Statements).
In Akinobu Ueda, Takashi Yoshida, and Osamu Mimura. <u>Kabushiki-
Kaisha no Keisan</u> (Corporate Accounting based upon the Commercial
Code). Tokyo, Japan: Chuo-Keizai-Sha, 1963, pp. 41-78.

Moonitz, Maurice. <u>The Basic Postulates of Accounting</u>. New York:
American Institute of Certified Public Accountants, 1961.

Mueller, Gerhard G. <u>International Accounting</u>. New York: The Macmillan
Company, 1967.

Nakamura, Kikuo. <u>Kindai Nihon no Hoteki-Keisei - Shinpan</u> (Legal
Formation of Modern Japan, new ed.). Tokyo, Japan: Yushindo, 1963.

Nihon Ginko, Chosa Kyoku (Research Bureau, the Bank of Japan). <u>Nihon
Kinyu-Shi Shiryo -- Showa-Hen</u>, VII (The Data on the Financial
History of Japan -- Showa Era Section, VII). Tokyo, Japan:
Ministry of Finance, Printing Bureau, 1963.

_____, Tokei Kyoku (Statistics Department, the Bank of Japan).
<u>Honpo Keizai Tokei -- 1964</u> (Economic Statistics of Japan -- 1964).
(Economic Statistics of Japan -- 1964). Tokyo, Japan: Statistics
Department, the Bank of Japan, 1965.

Nishikawa, Kojiro. "The Early History of Double-entry Bookkeeping in
Japan." <u>Studies in the History of Accounting</u>. Edited by A. C.
Littleton and B. S. Yamey. Homewood, Illinois: Richard D. Irwin,
Inc., 1956, pp. 380-87.

Noguchi, Yu. <u>Nihon Shihonshugi Keiei-Shi -- Senzen-Hen</u> (The Development
of Japanese Capitalism from the Viewpoint of Business History --
Pre-war Section). Tokyo, Japan: Ochanomizu-Shobo, 1960.

Ota, Tetsuzo. "Shoken-Shihon Sei no Fukki to sono Joken" (Conditions for
the Resumption of Security Capital Market). <u>Keiei-Keiri to Konin-
KaikeiShi</u> (Business Accounting and Certified Public Accountants).
Edited by Yasutaro Hirai. Tokyo, Japan: Kunimoto Shobo, 1949,
pp. 3-16.

Parsons, Talcott. "The Law and Social Control." <u>Law and Sociology</u>.
Edited by William M. Evan. New York: The Free Press of Glencoe,
1962.

_____. The Social System. New York: The Free Press, 1951.

_____, and Shils, Edward A. "Values, Motives, and Systems of Action." Toward A General Theory of Action. Edited by Talcott Parsons and Edward A. Shils. New York: Harper & Row, 1962.

_____, and Smelser, Neil J. Economy and Society. New York: The Free Press, 1956.

_____, Bales, Robert F.; and Shils, Edward A. Working Papers in The Theory of Action. Glencoe, Illinois: The Free Press, 1933.

Paton, W. A., and Littleton, A. C. An Introduction to Corporate Account- ing Standards. Iowa City, Iowa: American Accounting Association, 1964

Pattilo, James W. The Foundation of Financial Accounting. Baton Rouge, Louisiana: Louisiana State University Press, 1965.

Reischauer, Edwin O. Japan -- Past and Present. 3rd ed., rev. Tokyo, Japan: Charles E. Tuttle Company, Inc., 1964.

Sakamoto, Yasuichi. "Kaisei Shoho to Zaimushohyo" (The Revised Commercial Code and Financial Statements). Keisan-Shorui Kisoku no Mondaiten (Some Problems in the Regulation for Corporate Balance Sheets and Income Statements). Edited by Katsuji Yamashita. Tokyo, Japan: Chuo-Keizai-Sha, 1965, pp. 45-60.

Sanders, Thomas Henry; Hatfield, Henry Rand; and Moore, Underhill. A Statement of Accounting Principles. New York: American Insti- tute of Accountants, 1938.

Schumpeter, E. B. "Industrial Development and Government Policy." The Industrialization of Japan and Manchukuo 1930-40. Edited by E. B. Schumpeter. New York: The MacMillan Company, 1940, pp. 789-861.

Scott, DR. The Cultural Significance of Accounts, Reprint. Columbia, Missouri: Lucas Brothers Publishers, n.d.

Shiho-Sho Minji-Kyoku (Civil Affairs Bureau, the Ministry of Justice). Shoho Kaisei Horitsu-An Riyusho (A Commentary on the Draft of the Revised Commercial Code). Tokyo, Japan: Shimizu-Shoten, 1937.

Smelser, Neil J. The Sociology of Economic Life. Englewood Cliffs, New Jersey: Prentice-Hall, Inc., 1963.

Smith, Thomas C. Political Change and Industrial Development in Japan: Government Enterprise, 1868-1880. Stanford, California: Stanford University Press, 1965.

Sprouse, Robert T., and Moonitz, Maurice. A Tentative Set of Broad Accounting Principles for Business Enterprises. New York: American Institute of Certified Public Accountants, 1962.

Storey, Read K. The Search for Accounting Principles -- Today's Problems in Perspective. New York: American Institute of Certified Public Accountants, 1964.

Study Group at the University of Illinois. A Statement of Basic Accounting Postulates and Principles. Urbana, Illinois: The Center for International Education and Research in Accounting, 1964.

Suekawa, Hiroshi, ed. Shiryo Sengo Nijyunen-Shi -- Horitsu (Data on the Twenty-Year History After the War -- Laws). Tokyo, Japan: Nihon Hyoronsha, 1966.

Suzuki, Takeo. "Shoken-Torihiki-Ho to Kabushiki-Kaisha-Ho" (The Securities Exchange Act and the Stock Corporation Law). Kabushiki-Kaisha-Ho Koza, I (Stock Corporation Law Handbook, I). Edited by Kotaro Tanaka. Tokyo, Japan: Yuhikaku, 1955. pp. 351-68.

_____, and Ishii, Teruhisa. Kaisei Kabushiki-Kaisha-Ho Kaisetsu (Comments on the Revised Stock Corporation Law). Tokyo, Japan: Nihon Hyoronsha, 1950.

Takahashi, Kamekichi. Meiji Taisho Sangyo Hattatsushi (Historical Development of the Japanese Industries in Meiji and Taisho Eras). Tokyo, Japan: Kashiwa Shobo, 1966.

_____. Taisho Showa Zaikai Hendo-Shi -Jo- (The Changing Japanese Business World in Taisho and Showa Eras, I). Tokyo, Japan: Toyo Keizai Shinpo-Sha, 1954.

Tanaka, Kotaro. "Kabushiki-Kaisha-Ho Jyosetsu" (An Introduction to the Stock Corporation Law). Kabushiki-Kaisha-Ho Koza, I (Stock Corporation Law Handbook, I). Edited by Kotaro Tanaka. Tokyo, Japan: Yuhikaku, 1955, pp. 1-32.

Tanaka, Seiji. "Shoho Kaisei-Yoko no Shoho-Gaku-Jo kara mita Mondaiten" (Some Problems in a Tentative Statement of the Revision of the Commercial Code Viewed from the Commercial Code Theory). In Seiji Tanaka, et al. Shoho Kaisei ni tomonau Shomondai (Some Problems Arising from the Revision of the Commercial Code). Tokyo, Japan: Ikkyo Shuppan, 1962. pp. 109-39.

_____, and Kubo, Kinya. "Kabushiki-Kaisha no Kaikei-Ho" (Account-
ing Law for the Stock Corporation). In Seiji Tanaka, et al.
Kaisha-Kaikei-Hoki Shokai (A Comprehensive Study on the Accounting
Law for the Corporations). Tokyo, Japan: Shunjusha, 1959.
pp. 61-206.

_____; Yoshinaga, Eisuke; and Yamamura, Chuhei. Saizentei
Konmentaru Kaisha-Ho (Completely Revised Commentary on Corporation Law). Tokyo, Japan: Keiso Shobo, 1968.

Tanba, Kotaro. "Keisan-Shorui-Kisoku ni okeru 'Shihon no Bu' no Kubun
Hyoji ni tsuite" (On the Grouping of 'New Worth Section' in the
Regulation forCorporate Balance Sheets and Income Statements).
Keisan-Shorui-Kisoku no Mondaiten (Some Problems on the Regulation
for Corporate Balance Sheets and Income Statements). Edited by
Katsuji Yamashita. Tokyo, Japan: Chuo-Keizai-Sha, 1965, pp. 225-
34.

Uchiyama, Shigeru. "Nihon Konin-Kaikeishi Seido" (Certified Public
Accountants System in Japan). Kaikei-Kansa (Auditing). Edited
by Shunjusha. Tokyo, Japan: Shunjusha, 1951, pp. 165-96.

Ueda, Akinobu. "Kaisha no Keisan no Kaisetsu" (Comments on the Accounting Provisions for Corporations). In Akinobu Ueda, Takashi Yoshida,
and Osamu Mimura. Kabushiki-Kaisha no Keisan (Corporate Accounting
Based upon the Commercial Code). Tokyo, Japan: Chuo-Keizai-Sha,
1963, pp. 3-6, pp. 10-13, pp. 20-21 and pp. 32-37.

_____. "Shoho no Kaisei ni tsuite" (On the Revision of the Commercial
Code). In Seiji Tanaka, et al. Shoho Kaisei ni tomonau Shomondai
(Some Problems Arising From the Revision of the Commercial Code).
Tokyo, Japan: Ikkyo Shuppan, 1962, pp. 17-38.

Vatter, William J. "Obstacles to the Specification of Accounting
Principles." Research in Accounting Measurement. Edited by
Robert K. Jaedicke; Yuji Ijiri; Oswald Neilsen. Evanston, Illinois:
American Accounting Association, 1966, pp. 71-87.

Votaw, Dow. Modern Corporations. Englewood Cliffs, New Jersey: Prentice-
Hall, Inc., 1965.

Yamamura, Chuhei. "Kansa-Yaku Seido" (The Statutory Auditors System).
Kabushiki-Kaisha-Ho Koza, III (Stock Corporation Law Handbook, III).
Edited by Kotaro Tanaka. Tokyo, Japan: Yuhikaku, 1956, pp. 1177-1200.

Yazawa, Makoto. Kigyo-Kaikei-Ho Kogi (Lectures on Business Accounting Law).
Tokyo, Japan: Yuhikaku, 1958.

Yoshinaga, Eisuke. "Keisan Shorui" (Accounting Documents). Kabushiki-
Kaisha-Ho Koza, IV (Stock Corporation Law Handbook, IV). Edited
by Kotaro Tanaka. Tokyo, Japan: Yuhikaku, 1956, pp. 1475-1512.

PUBLIC DOCUMENTS

Economic and scientific Section, GHQ, SCAP. Mission and Accomplishments
of the Occupation in the Economic and Scientific Fields. Tokyo,
Japan: Economic and Scientific Section, GHQ, SCAP, 1949.

Research and Statistics Division, Economic and Scientific Section,GHQ, SCAP.
Instructions for the Preparation of Financial Statements of
Manufacturing and Trading Companies. Tokyo, Japan: Research and
Statistics Division, Economic and Scientific Section, GHQ, SCAP, 1947.

Supreme Commander for the Allied Powers. SCAPINS-- from 4 September 1945
to March 1952. Tokyo, Japan: General Headquarters, Supreme
Commander for the Allied Powers, 1952.

U.S. Department of State. Occupation of Japan-- Policy and Progress.
Publication 2671, Far Eastern Series 17. Washington, D.C., n.d.

_____. Report of the Mission on Japenese Combines-- Part I: Analytical
and Technical Data. Publication 2628, Far Eastern Series 14.
Washington, D.C. March, 1946.

PROCEEDINGS AND REPORT

American Accounting Association, Committee on International Accounting,
International Dimensions of Accounting in the Curriculum, A Recommenda-
tion by the Committee on the International Accounting (Leaflet).
Americal Accounting Association, Spring, 1966.

Center for International Education and Research in Accounting. Proceedings--
International Conference on Accounting Education. Urbana, Illinois:
The Center for International Education and Research in Accounting, 1962.

Ninth International Congress of Accountants. Proceedings-- The New Horizons
of Accounting. Paris, France: Ninth International Congress of
Accountants, 1967.

ARTICLES

American Accounting Association, Executive Committee. " A Tentative Statement of Accounting Principles Affecting Corporate Reports." The
Accounting Review, Vol. XI, No. 2 (June, 1936), pp. 187-91.

_____. "Accounting Principles Underlying Corporate Financial Statements."
The Accounting Review, Vol. XVI, No. 2 (June, 1941), pp. 133-39.

Aoki, Rintaro. "Kigyo-Kaikei Gensoku no Seikaku" (A Character of A
Statement of Business Accounting Statement). Kigyokaikei, Vol. 16,
No. 1 (January, 1964). pp. 16-20.

Aoki, Shigeo. "Kigyo-Kaikei Gensoku no Ichibu Shusei eno Kenkai"
(A Comment on the Partial Revision of A Statement of Business
Accounting Principles). Sangyo-Keiri, Vol.24, No. 1 (January,
1964), pp. 73-77

Banba, Kaichiro. "Kigyo-Kaikei Gensoku Shusei no Tohi" (An Evaluation
of the Revision of A Statement of Business Accounting Principles).
Kaikei, Vol. 84, No. 6 (December, 1963), pp.1-13

Bedford, Norton M. "The International Flow of Accounting Thought." The
International Journal of Accounting Education and Research, Vol. 1, No.
2 (Spring, 1966), pp. 1-7.

Byrne, Gilbert R. "To What Extent Can the Practice of Accounting Be Reduced
to Rules and Standards?" The Journal of Accountancy. Vol. 64, No. 5
(November, 1937), pp. 364-79.

Catlett, George R. "Factors That Influence Accoounting Principles." The
Journal of Accountancy. Vol. 110, No. 4 (October, 1960), pp. 44-50.

_____. "Relation of Acceptance to Accounting Principles." The Journal of
Accountancy, Vol. 109, No. 3 (March, 1960), pp.33-38

Chu, Saichi. "Kigyo-Kaikei Gensoku no Za" (The Position of A Statement of
Business Accounting Principles). Kaikei, Vol. 87, No. 1 (January,
1965), pp. 78-92.

Eaton, Marquis G. "Financial Reporting in a Changing Society." The Journal
of Accountancy, Vol. 104, No. 2 (August, 1957), pp. 25-31

Emura, Minoru. "Joyokin ni kansuru Kaiseo no Mondaiten" (Some Problems in
the Revision of the Treatment of Surplus). Kaikei, Vol. 84, No. 6
(December, 1963), pp. 15-30

_____. "Jugatsu-Ki Kessan Go Sha no Kessan Hokokusho o miru" (A Look at
the Financial Statements Prepared by Five Corporations during October,
1963). Kigyokaikei, Vol. 16, No. 1 (January, 1964), pp.173-84

Fantl, Irbing L. "Letters to the Journal." The Journal of Accountancy,
Vol. 120, No.3 (September, 1965), p. 29.

Hasegawa, Yasubei. "Keiri Tosei no Zenbo" (An Entire Picture of Accounting
Control). Waseda Shogaku, Vol. 16, No. 4 (January, 1941), pp. 1-42

_____. "Shoho Kaisei ni tomonau Kaisha-Keisan no Shomondai" (Some Problems
on the Corporate Accounting Arising from the Revision of the Commercial
Code). Kaikei, Vol. 42, No. 3 (March, 1938), pp.1-35

Iino, Toshio. "Accounting Principles and Contemporary Legal Thought in Japan."
The International Journal of Accounting Education and Research, Vol.2,
No. 2 (Spring, 1967), pp. 65-87.

_____. "Kaikei-Koi to Kaikei-Gensoku" (Accounting Actions and Accounting Principles). Kigyokaikei, Vol. 4, No. 4 (April, 1952), pp. 9-17

Iwata, Iwao. "Kigyo-Kaikei no Ippan-Gensoku ni tsuite" (On General Principles of Business Accounting). Kigyokaikei, Vol. 1, No. 9 (September, 1949), pp. 2-6

_____. "Shoho ni okeru Keiri Taikei" (Accounting System in the Commercial Code). Kaikei, Vol. 56, No. 1 (February, 1949), pp. 26-47.

Japanese Accounting Association. "Kigyo-Kaikei Gensoku no Toitsu o Chushin toshite" (Symposium on Unification of Business Accounting Principles). Kaikei, Vol. 57, No. 1 (January, 1950), pp. 67-106.

_____. "Taishaku-Taisho-Hyo Junsoku Tokyu" (Symposium on the Working Rules of the Balance Sheet). Kaikei, Vol. 46, No. 5 (May, 1940), pp. 77-120.

Jennings, Alvin R. "International Standards of Accounting and Auditing." The Journal of Accountancy, Vol. 114, No. 3 (September, 1962), pp. 36-42.

Kanri-Kaikei Iinkai. "Shoho Keisan Kitei narabini Kabushiki-Kaisha no Taishaku-Taishohyo oyobi Soneki-Keisansho ni kansuru Kisoku no Jissi ni saishite no Kaikei-Shori Mondai ni tsuite no Ikensho" (Comments on the Application of Accounting Provisions of the Commercial Code and the Regulation for corporate Balance Sheets and Income Statements). Kaikei, Vol. 84, No. 5 (November, 1963), pp. 141-53.

Katano, Ichiro. "Nihon Zaimushohyo Seido no Tenkai to Kadai" (Development of Corporate Financial Reporting in Japan and Its Problems). Kigyokaikei, Vol. 18, No. 2 (February, 1966), pp. 10-23.

_____. "Nihon Zaimushohyo Seido no Tenkai to Kadai -3-" (Development of Corporate Financial Reporting in Japan and Its Problems -3-). Kigyokaikei, Vol. 18, No. 5 (May,1966), pp.10-27.

_____. "Nihon Zaimushohyo Seido no Tenkai to Kadai -5-" (Development of Corporate Financial Reporting in Japan and Its Problems -5-). Kigyokaikei, Vol. 18, No. 9 (September, 1966), pp. 27-43.

Kato, Ryohei. "Gorikyoku Zaimu-Junsoku to Jitsumu-Kanshu tono Kosaku-II-" (The Working Rules for Financial Statements by the Ministry of Commerce and Industry and the Accounting Practices-II-). Kaikei, Vol. 38, No. 5 (May, 1936), pp. 69-92.

Kester, Roy B. "Sources of Accounting Principles." The Journal of Accountancy, Vol. 74, No. 6 (December, 1942), pp. 531-35.

Kigyo-Kaikei Seido Taisaku Chosakai (Investigation Committee on Business Accounting System). "Kigyo-Kaikei Gensoku to Zaimushohyo tono Kankei ni tsuite" (On a Relationship between A Statement of Business Accounting Principles and Financial Statements). Kaikei, Vol. 56, No. 3 (July, 1949), pp. 21-44

_____. "Kigyo-Kaikei Gensoku" (Business Accounting Principles). <u>Kaikei</u>, Vol. 56, No. 5 (October, 1949), pp. 43-70.

Kitagawa, Atsunori. "Kigyo-Kaikei Gensoku towa Ittai Nanika" (What is A Statement of Business Accounting Principles?). <u>Kigyokaikei</u>, Vol. 16, No. 1 (January, 1964), pp. 61-65.

Kraayenhof, Jacob. "International Challenge for Accounting." <u>The Journal of Accountancy</u>, Vol. 109, No. 1 (January, 1960), pp. 34-38.

Kurosawa, Kiyoshi. "Kaikei Gensoku eno Tankyu" (A Search for Accounting Principles). <u>Sangyo-Keiri</u>, Vol. 9, No. 6 (June, 1949), pp. 4-6.

_____. " Kaikei Gensoku no Kaisei Mondai" (Some Problems on the Amendment to the Business Accounting Principles). <u>Kaikei</u>, Vol. 66, No. 1 (July, 1954), pp. 1-18.

_____. "Kaikei-Kijun no Kakuristsu to Iji ni tsuite" (Establishment and Maintenance of Accounting Standards). <u>Sangyo-Keiri</u>,Vol. 9, No. 5 (May, 1949), pp. 7-9.

_____. "Kaikei Gensoku Shusei no Shoten" (A Focus of the Revision of A Statement of Business Accounting Principles). <u>Sangyo-Keiri</u>, Vol. 23, No. 12, (December, 1963), pp. 48-52.

_____. "Keidanren no Kaikei Gensoku no Kaisei ni kansuru Iken ni tsuite" (Comments on "An Opinion on the Revision of A Statement of Business Accounting Principles" by the Federation of Economic Organizations). <u>Kaikei</u>, Vol. 58, No. 3 (September, 1950), pp. 131-35

_____. "Shusei Kigyo-Kaikei Gensoku Kaisetsu" (Comments on the Revised Statement of Business Accounting Principles). <u>Kigyokaikei</u>, Vol. 15, No. 13 (December, 1963), pp. 114-19.

_____. "Shusei Kaikei Gensoku soron" (General Comments on the Revised Statement of Business Accounting Principles). <u>Sangyo-Keiri</u>, Vol. 14, No. 8 (August, 1954), pp. 42-50

Kusakabe, Yoichi. "Wagakuni Kansa-Hokokusho no Jittai Chosa" (A Surbey of Auditor's Reports in Japan). <u>Kansa,</u> (May, 1962), pp.26-40.

May, George O. "Principles of Accounting." <u>The Journal of Accountancy</u>, Vol.64, No. 6 (December, 1937), pp. 423-25

Mueller, Gerhard G. "Some Thoughts about the International Congresses of Accountants." <u>The Accounting Review</u>, Vol. XXXVI, No. 4 (October, 1961), pp. 548-54.

_____. "Whys and Hows of International Accounting." <u>The Accounting Review</u>, Vol. XL. No. 2 (April, 1965), pp. 386-94.

Murase, Gen. 'Nichi, Ei, Bei Sangoku ni okeru Kaikei Gensoku Seitei no Yurai" (A Brief History of the Establishment of Accounting Principles in Japan, England, and the United States). Kigyokaikei, Vol. 6, No. 1 (January, 1954), pp. 111-13.

Nakagawa, Shuho. 'Kikakuin Zaimushohyo Junsoku no Seikaku" (The Nature of the Tentative Standards for Financial Statements by the Planning Board). Kaikei, Vol. 50, No. 5 (May, 1942), pp. 52-68.

Okabe, Toshiyoshi. "Kensetsu Joseikin wa hatashite Shihon-Joyokin de aruka" (Are Governmental Subsidies Really Capital Surplus?). Kaikei, Vol. 86, No. 2 (August, 1964), pp. 24-54.

Osumi, Tatsuo. "Kaikei Shori no Datosei to Tekihosei" (Appropriateness and Legitimacy of Accounting Treatments). Kigyokaikei, Vol. 16, No. 1 (January, 1964), pp. 21-26.

Ota, Tetsuzo, et al. "Shoho to Kaikei Gensoku tono Chosei-Mondai no Sai-Kento" (Symposium on Reconciliation of the Commercial Code and A Statement of Business Accounting Principles). Kigyokaikei, Vol. 5, No. 10 (October, 1953), pp. 16-32.

Sato, Koichi. "Funshoku-Tosan Kaisha no Jizen-Boshi Hosaku" (Preclusive Measures for Window-dressing or Bankrupt Companies). Waseda-Shogaku, No. 180 (June, 1965), pp. 1-18.

_____. "Shoken Torihiki Iinkai Kisoku Dai-Juhachi-Go no Hihanteki Kaisetsu" (Critical Comments on the SEC Regulation). Waseda-Shogaku, No. 91 (March, 1951), pp. 21-41.

Scott, DR. "Accounting Principles and Cost Accounting." The Journal of Accountancy, Vol. 67, No. 2 (February, 1939), pp. 70-76.

_____. "Tentative Statement of Principles." The Accounting Review, Vol. XII, No. 3 (September, 1937), pp. 296-303.

Someya, Kyojiro. "Roshi-Kankei ni Yakudatsu Zaimu-Shiryo" (Financial Data for the Improvement of Labor Relations). Waseda-Shogaku, No. 200 (December, 1967), pp. 37-61.

_____. "The Use of Fund Statements in Japan." The Accounting Review, Vol. XXXIX, No. 4 (October, 1964), pp. 983-89.

Stead, Gordon W. "Toward A Synthesis of Accounting Doctrine." The Accounting Review, Vol. XXIII, No. 4 (October, 1948), pp. 355-59.

Stewart, Andrew. "Accountancy and Regulatory Bodies in the United States." The Journal of Accountancy, Vol. 65, No. 1 (January, 1938), pp. 33-60.

Suzuki, Takeo. "Seigen-Kaisha Ichiranhyo Settei ni kansuru Oboegaki" (Memorandum Concerning the Establishment of a Schedule of Restricted Concerns). Nihon Kanri Horei Kenkyu, Vol. 1, No. 6 (September 1, 1946), pp. 46-47.

_____. "Shoken no Minshuka" (Security Democratization). Nihon Kanri Horei Kenkyu, No. 20 (June 1, 1948), pp. 106-8.

Ueno, Michisuke. "Waga Kuni Keizai Saiken ni okeru Kaikeigaku no Igi" (The Significance of Accounting for the Reconstruction of the Japanese Economy). Kaikei, Vol. 56, No. 1 (February, 1949), pp. 179-97.

Wilkinson, Theodore L. "Can Accounting be an International Language?" The Price Waterhouse Review, Vol. VIII, No. 2 (Summer, 1963), pp. 15-21.

_____. "United States Accounting as Viewed by Accountants of Other Countries." The International Journal of Accounting Education and Research, Vol. 1, No. 1 (Fall, 1965), pp. 3-14.

Yazawa, Makoto. "Kosei Torihiki Iinkai to Shoken Torihiki Iinkai" (The Fair Trade Commission and the Securities and Exchange Commission). Nihon Kanri Horei Kenkyu, No. 25 (March 1, 1949), pp. 28-49.

_____, and Ootori Tsuneo. "Kaisha-Ho no Sengo no Tenkai to Kadai -I-" (The Development of the Corporation Act after World War II and Its Problems -I-). Hogaku Seminar, No. 142 (January, 1968), pp. 2-11.

_____. "Kaisha-Ho no Sengo no Tenkai to Kadai -II-" (The Development of the Corporation Act after World War II and Its Problems -II-). Hogaku Seminar, No. 143 (February, 1968), pp. 46-57.

Yoshida, Takashi. "Kigyo-Kaikei Gensoku no Zaimushohyo-Taikei to Shoho" IFinancial Statements Listed in A Statement of Business Accounting Principles and the Commercial Code). Kansa, (February, 1951), pp. 23-32.

Zimmerman, Vernon K., and Wyatt, Arthur R. "Recognizing a New Dimension." The Illinois CPA, Vol. XXV, No. 2 (Winter, 1962), pp. 44-47.

MISCELLANEOUS

JICPA News, Nos. 49 (March, 1964), 54 (July, 1964), 62 (January, 1965), 71 (August, 1965), 79 (February, 1966), 85 (July, 1966).

Mueller, Gerhard G. "Curriculum Aspects of International Accounting Matters." Mimeographed copy of the paper presented at the Second International Conference on Accounting Education in London, August 31, 1967.

The Nihon Keizai Shinbun (The Japan Economic Journal), January 22, 1965, January 15, 17, and 25, 1967.